STUDIES IN GDR CULTURE AND SOCIETY

Proceedings of the Sixth International Symposium on the German Democratic Republic

Editorial Board:
Margy Gerber, Chief Editor
Volker Gransow
Nancy A. Lauckner
W. Christoph Schmauch
Duncan Smith
Alexander Stephan

UNIVERSITY
PRESS OF
AMERICA

Library of Congress Catalog Card Number: 80-6255

TABLE OF CONTENTS

Part Two: Literature

Part Three: Fine Arts

Preface

The articles collected in this volume were presented as papers at the Sixth Symposium on the German Democratic Republic, which was held on the grounds of the World Fellowship Center near Conway, New Hampshire from June 13-20, 1980. The broad scope of the topics, varying from economic and social themes to literature and the fine arts, reflects the interdisciplinary nature of this annual symposium. The reader will also encounter a variety of approaches to the study of the GDR and to the GDR itself; this is in keeping with the pluralistic intention of the Symposium, which has no particular ideological or political basis. The contributions include works by lesser known specialists as well as by established scholars in the area of GDR studies. This, too, is an indication of the openness and informality of the Symposium.

Two of the papers have appeared previously, in somewhat different form. The editors wish to thank the GDR Monitor and Lang Verlag in Bern for permission to use the article of Alexander Stephan, and Germanic Notes for permission to print the article of Christine Cosentino. The editors are also indebted to the GDR artists Harald Kretzschmar, Elizabeth Shaw, and Harri Parschau, and the publishing house Volk und Wissen for permission to include the caricatures treated in the article by Gail Hueting.

Margy Gerber (Bowling Green St. Univ.)
   Chief Editor

Volker Gransow (FU Berlin/U. Bielefeld)
Nancy A. Lauckner (Univ. of Tenn./Knox.)
W. Christoph Schmauch (World Fellowship)
Duncan Smith (Brown University)
Alexander Stephan (Univ. of Calif.)

The International Symposium on the
German Democratic Republic

The German Democratic Republic is an historical fact. Those of us who have followed its development from Soviet Zone of Occupation to German
Democratic Republic to, by its own definition, developed socialist society have been fascinated by
the various aspects of change--in GDR society itself and in the attitudes of its 17 million citizens. And parallel to the development of the GDR
has been the evolution of the western view of the
GDR: from "Russian Zone" or simply "the Zone" to
"East Germany" to "GDR"--in quotation marks--to
general acceptance of the existence of a second
German state.

Since 1966 our summer programs at World Fellowship have included the GDR, and in 1975 the
first week-long Symposium on the GDR was organized,
primarily by Germanists from various universities
across the country. The subsequent growth of the
Symposium into an interdisciplinary, international
forum, attended each year by some fifty scholars
from the United States, Canada, the FRG, and--in
the last years--the GDR, is an indication both of
the lively interest in the GDR and the need that
is being felt by GDR specialists in this country
and abroad to exchange expertise and views on the
various aspects of GDR culture and society and to
regard the GDR in its entirety, rather than divided along the lines of the traditional disciplines.
New categories for comparison and analysis have to
be found if the GDR is to be properly understood--
just as the citizens of the GDR are trying to find
a new self-understanding within the complex reality of GDR society itself.

Given the fragility of peace in today's world and the precariousness of the human condition on our planet in general, these endeavors take on great importance--the study of the GDR is not only an interesting undertaking but an existential necessity. All who have worked so hard to make the Symposia and now this volume possible are rewarded by this opportunity to share with you, the reader.

Conway, New Hampshire
May 1, 1981

W. Christoph Schmauch
Executive Director
World Fellowship

Political Culture in the GDR:
Propositions for Empirical Research

Volker Gransow

Up to the mid-seventies the usage of the term
"political culture" by western social scientists
was more or less restricted to analyses of either
capitalist or developing societies. Today there
is a tendency to adapt the concept to various self-
styled socialist countries as well. Especially in
regard to the GDR, however, these endeavors appear
to be less productive than they could be. The purpose of this essay is to give a preliminary answer
to the question of whether it is possible to extend the concept of political culture to make it
more useful for GDR research.

I would like to proceed in five steps: 1) a
short discussion of the concept in general; 2) a
few remarks about existing analyses of East German
political culture; 3) an indication of what mass
cultural activities can tell us about the political culture of the GDR; 4) a discussion of leisure
activities in the GDR; 5) a few reflections on
literary developments in the seventies.

The Concept and its Scope

The word "culture" has a long tradition. Its
meanings as an improvement of soil and soul can be
traced back to Cicero and even earlier in history.
"Political culture" is much more modern. As far
as I know, the term was first used in the twenties.
However, it was neither exactly defined nor empir-
ically utilized at that time. The "breakthrough"
of "political culture" came in the late fifties

when American political scientists like Gabriel
Almond, Lucian Pye, and Sidney Verba--in short,
the Committee on Comparative Politics--introduced
the term to the international forum. In their
view such a term was necessary for three reasons:
1) a complex phenomenon like politics cannot be
understood by concentrating on the analysis of
institutions, as was the case with the traditional
representatives of governmental law; 2) political
science should become more open towards the problems of the third world; 3) in order to analyze
democracy it is necessary to analyze the experi-
ince of democratic behavior. The members of the
Committee on Comparative Politics reflected both
the theoretical and the political sources they
were drawing on: theoretically, their thoughts
were mainly based on the theory of functional social systems and the psychocultural or "behaviorist" approaches; politically, the American "fa-
thers" of "political culture" bore in mind that
the widening of U.S. foreign policy after World
War II demanded a widening of the instrumentation
of political science. Their reflections led to
the following definition by Gabriel Almond and
Sidney Verba: "The term 'political culture' . . .
refers to the specifically political orientations
- attitudes towards the political system and its
various parts, and attitudes towards the role of
the self in the system."[1]

Defined in this way, political culture may
be further structured. The orientation towards
a "basic belief system," i.e., the study of behav-
iors, feelings, and opinions, forces the analyst
to rely heavily on "data" mostly gained from opinion polls. Thus it is not surprising that the
eastern countries were left out in the first empirical studies employing the term. It is equally
unsurprising that the members of the Committee on
Comparative Politics stated as an "output" that
democratic attitudes are most developed in the
Anglo-Saxon world, since precisely this was the
"input." Books on political culture published
more recently show that it is possible to make
basic assumptions about democratic behavior, etc.

2

In the early seventies the notion of political culture was slowly integrated into communist studies. Responding to the uncertainty of communist studies after détente as well as to the use of the term in the Soviet Union by the highest authorities, students of communism tried political culture as a tool of analysis. Frederick C. Barghoorn understood Soviet political culture as "ideological-partisan, elitist, subject-participatory."[2] Other scholars published books on the political cultures of China, Cuba, Yugoslavia, and Poland. Archie Brown made an important contribution by stating that "political culture on its own, of course, explains nothing."[3] He pleaded especially for the consideration of historical factors, thus severely criticizing both behaviorism and the structural-functional theory.

In 1977 Archie Brown and Jack Gray published a collection of essays by various British authors entitled Political Culture and Political Change in Communist States. Political culture was understood here as "the subjective perception of history and politics, the fundamental beliefs and values, the foci of identification and loyalty, and the political knowledge and expectations which are the product of the specific historical experience of nations and groups."[4]

Another aspect was added by Robert C. Tucker, who argued for the inclusion of political culture in communist studies, especially the study of "political ethnography," "cultural processes," and "communist movements not in power" as counter-cultures in noncommunist social settings.[5] Equally important was an essay by Frederic Fleron, Jr. presenting the idea of analyzing not only conflicts between "communist goal culture" and "national traditional culture" but the elements of imported foreign culture as well. One dimension of imported foreign culture could be the advanced technology of capitalist countries.[6]

I think the contributions of Brown, Fleron, and Tucker show the usefulness of the concept in general. The interpretation of communist culture as influenced by "goal culture," "traditional culture," and "imported foreign culture" is a means of combining the analysis of phenomena observable in all industrial societies with the study of phenomena which are specific to communist-governed societies. The integration of historical aspects overcomes the behaviorist shortcomings of the original concept. The well-known objection "not enough data" is simply not true. The empirical projects of UNESCO alone provide enough reasonable data on "actually existing socialism" in general, and the GDR in particular.

Other factors seem to be much more valid targets of criticism. First, the concentration on the "basic belief system" neglects the fact that the extent to which values are legitimized in society may be a function of institutional power. Further, it is necessary to add the hypothesis that normative concensus is nothing in itself and may be understood in terms of the socialization of one class by another. Secondly, a restriction of "culture" to "intellectual culture" can be refuted by pointing to the fact that there can be no "material culture" without "intellectual culture." Therefore it seems more reasonable to speak of objective and subjective culture. Objective culture can be defined as the totality of all creative possibilities given to a society as a result of the activities of past generations. Subjective culture is the ability of individuals to appropriate and develop the objective culture.

Bearing these criticisms in mind, I think it is possible to propose the following understanding of the concept "political culture" as a tool for analysis of the GDR: it may be useful to assume that in a country like the GDR political culture is characterized by communist goal culture, traditional culture, and imported foreign culture. In order to analyze these relationships one must consider the subjective perceptions of society and politics, the foci of identification and political knowledge, which are understandable only by ex-

4

plaining their historical, political, sociological, and economic preconditions.

Actually Existing Analyses.

As far as I know, relatively few attempts have been made to deal with the political culture of the GDR. The well-known books by Sontheimer/ Bleek and Rüdiger Thomas, for example, don't have chapters on political culture. One reason for this may be that the German social sciences still have to catch up with the United States, where the term was invented. Among the small number of studies I will discuss here two are from the U.S. and only one from each of the Germanies.

The first is a textbook on the GDR sponsored by the Bavarian Office for Political Education.[7] It includes a chapter on political culture written by Irma Hanke, who points out that East German political culture is mainly a permanent process of education to imbue the people with the ideological goals of the party. This process is, as she maintains, especially observable in factory life, mass communication, education, and the divergent positions towards religion. Her conclusions are sceptical: "Ob die stets neue Einbindung in die Zwänge der Produktion allerdings eine befreiende, eine emanzipatorische Wirkung zeitigt, ob sie die Situation der Entfremdung aufhebt, mag füglich bezweifelt werden" (p. 113).

A different interpretation of East German political culture is given by Christa Ziermann of East Berlin in her contribution to a book on the intellectual culture of socialist society.[8] Christa Ziermann states: "Politische Kultur umfaßt in der entwickelten sozialistischen Gesellschaft sowohl ein Höchstmaß an politisch-ideologischer Bewußtheit und marxistisch-leninistischen Kenntnissen als auch die Fähigkeit, alle Erscheinungen des gesellschaftlichen Lebens politisch zu beurteilen, politisch zu erfassen, ein Gefühl für politische Entscheidungen herauszubilden" (p. 14). Unfortunately she does not go into details about the actual improvement of political consciousness. Instead she presents some figures about the number of party members (nearly 2 million), the number of trade unionists (nearly 8 million), the number of members of the Association of German-Soviet Friendship (4 million), and the number of people serving on several committees (nearly two million). She does not give further information about the remnants of apolitical behavior or the poison of anti-communism against which the citizens of the GDR are to be guarded.

More details are to be found in the American text <u>Politics in the German Democratic Republic</u> by John M. Starrels and Anita M. Mallinckrodt.[9] The authors of this book focus their attention on the issues surrounding GDR political culture by: 1) examining those aspects of its basic philosophy which touch upon the concept; 2) looking at the historical evolution of the phenomenon; 3) describing some of its doctrines and values; 4) focusing upon selected aspects of political socialization. Similar to Barghoorn's study on the USSR, they conclude that the political culture of the GDR is an ideological, elitist, and subject-participatory system.

Two other American scholars, Arthur M. Hanhardt and Gregory P. Swin, analyzed GDR political culture in respect to the Writing Workers' Movement and GDR literature since Bitterfeld.[10] They came to the conclusion that the political culture of the GDR is gaining a vitality that in the gray years of the past would have sent its cultural representatives fleeing either abroad or into silence. However, as they go on to say: "This may change. The mentality and venality of the functionaries have by no means disappeared. But for now, the political culture of the GDR is more interesting, more integrated and more challenging than ever before" (pp. 176-77).

Summarizing, one can say that the four studies discussed here have the following characteristics in common: 1) they focus on political at-

titudes; 2) they stress the importance of education; 3) they differ from traditional research on
political culture by giving some attention to
factory work and no attention to voting behavior.

Regarding the third point, I might comment
that voting behavior is not totally uninterest-
ing:

Table 1. Local Elections (May 1979)

Place	Votes against the official list (%)
Berlin-Prenzlauer Berg	0.52
Berlin-Marzahn	0.25
Grevesmühlen (District Rostock)	0.02
Strasburg (District Neubrandenburg)	0.01
Dresden	0.19
Leipzig	0.51

Source: Neues Deutschland, May 23, 1979

Table 1 may indicate that much more communist consciousness is to be found in small rural towns
than in the traditional strongholds of the working class. However, I think it is more reasonable to suggest that the extent of social control
is much greater in the villages than in the big
cities. But this is only meant to be a marginal
note.

Commenting generally on the four studies
just mentioned, I would point out that their
scope is not broad enough to answer the questions
raised in the first part of this paper about the
contents of political culture. They rightly deal
with political attitudes, political socialization,
and factory life. But there should be further
investigation of the historical and economic background, of the process of political and economic

decision making (on all levels--the Politburo of
the SED decides, for example, whether a hospital
is to be constructed, and how greenhouses are established),11 and of the relationship between
Party, class, and masses--there is a certain tendency in the GDR to speak of the leading role of
the working class and its vanguard party without
explaining the ways in which the working class is
supposed to try and catch up with its vanguard.
I have to admit that I won't meet these demands
in this paper either, but I think they should
still be mentioned. And even the little information I will give in this limited paper partly
goes beyond the scope of the existing analyses
of East German political culture.

Mass Cultural Activities

There are indications that the cultural policies of the SED and the trade unions have had
some effect on the East German working class.
More than 3 million workers (about 40%) take part
in programs which further culture and education,
including continuing education, appreciation of
art and literature, and development of the workers' own creative abilities. Workers' festivals
draw millions of visitors. There are specific
programs for continuing education. Combined with
the efforts of the comprehensive schools and job
training, mass cultural activities have led to a
rapid change in the structure of job qualifica-
tions; as illustrated in Table 2 below.

Reading these figures one should keep in
mind that this achievement could be attained only
by devoting public funds to the various educational problems, to the disadvantage of other cultural
activities. Equally important is the fact that
as late as 1977 33.9% of all female workers didn't
have a specialized worker certificate.12 And one
should not forget that mass cultural activities
face severe problems arising from the bad physical working conditions which 30% of all working
people in the GDR have to endure. "Auch der
schönste Gummibaum ändert nichts an wirklicher
Kulturlosigkeit - an Lärm, an schwerer körperli-

cher Arbeit oder an anderen Mißständen."[13]

Table 2. Structure of Job Qualification (%)

Year	Univ. Degree	Skilled Workers' Certificate	No Certificate
1955	4.4	25.6	70.0
1965	7.4	45.6	47.0
1975	13.6	62.2	24.2
1980 (Plan)	18.0	66.0	16.0

Source: Berufliche Bildung für heute und morgen
(E. Berlin: Panorama, 1978), p. 61

In regard to the political side of mass cultural activities the following data produced by new sociological investigations may be of interest:

Table 3. Attitudes towards the Discussion of the Plan in Industrial Enterprises

Figures given in order to take part in the discussion of the plan are:	Manager (Leiter)	Worker (%)
important	64.3	31.8
in part important	30.9	54.9
unimportant	4.8	13.3

Source: Helmut Schönfeld/Joachim Donath, Sprache
im sozialistischen Industriebetrieb
(E. Berlin: Akademie, 1978), p. 174

Opinion polls like these, information about the problems caused by shift work, and a certain self-criticism of the more or less schematic mass cultural activities throw a different light on the successes indicated in Table 2. According to official statements, the basic goal of the culture of labor is to create better working conditions. Equally officially, its aim is to make work an "instrument of liberation."[14] On the one hand, the program of the SED proclaims the gradual transition to communist society; on the other, a leading GDR sociologist has stated that it would be impossible to create "alle Voraussetzungen für die sozialistische Lebensweise in wenigen Jahrzehnten."[15] These statements point to the importance of the East German philosophical debate about "contradictions" and underline its practical relevance. The few data presented so far indicate that it might be more sensible to pursue these discussions than to paint a black-and-white picture of one kind or the other.

Leisure Time

To gain an impression of the use of leisure time in the GDR it may be helpful to take a look at the preconditions for leisure:

Table 4. Equipment of Households with Consumer Durables (1979)

Rate of Occurrence (per 100 Households)

Refrigerators	Washing Machines	TV Sets	Private Cars
102.2	79.9	103.5	36.3

Source: Statistisches Taschenbuch der Deutschen Demokratischen Republik (E. Berlin: Staatsverlag, 1980), p. 104

It is clear that the GDR citizen has a good starting point in regard to both housework and consumption. Important aspects of leisure activities are presented in the following table:

Table 5. Leisure Activities

Activities	Hours per Person and Day		
	Male	Female	Average
Social Activities	0.32	0.15	0.23
Visiting of Cultural Institutions	0.22	0.18	0.20
TV and Radio	1.67	1.23	1.43
Listening to Records and Tapes	0.05	0.02	0.03
Reading	0.38	0.25	0.32
Recreation with Special Activities	0.18	0.18	0.18

Source: Lebensweise und Lebensniveau im Sozialismus (E. Berlin: Die Wirtschaft, 1977) p. 150

The predominance of television and radio as leisure time activities is as evident as the relatively bad situation of women, who--this should be added--do twice as much housework as men. If we inquire about the media programming, we learn that the GDR audience places the most value on "entertainment" and "information." Regarding "entertainment," I would like to quote the leading East Berlin culture expert, Professor Hans Koch: "Nicht wenige Menschen . . . mögen mit dem Sozialismus politisch einverstanden sein, durch ihre Arbeit und gesellschaftlich-politischen Aktivitäten bewußt zu seiner Gestaltung beitragen. Aber künstlerisch-kulturell leben sie in dem (falschen) 'Bewußtsein', als gehe hier die Dynamik der Entwicklung von der kapitalistischen Welt aus."[16] As for "information," one sometimes encounters

11

self-critical sentences like the following about the GDR news program, Aktuelle Kamera: "Manches an unserem Sozialismus-Bild in der AK ist noch zu glatt, zu oberflächlich."[17] A more trenchant criticism was put forward by the East Berlin poet Stefan Heym: "Die Struktur der Sendungen ist unkompliziert und gleichfalls von beruhigender Einförmigkeit . . . Hofnachrichten."[18] But that is not all there is. Critical documentary films are shown both on TV and in the cinemas, for example. There is certainly more than just apolitical programming. One leisure time activity where criticism was possible was the so-called singing movement. A pamphlet on youth in the GDR states that the membership of the singing movement increased from 31,726 in 1970 to 43,000 in 1976. Unfortunately, the authors do not mention that in 1973 there were 63,796 members.[19] This sharp decrease is reason to reflect on the contents of leisure time as well as on the tendency towards apolitical behavior mentioned earlier.

Another point of departure for the investigation of leisure time is physical consumption. Without being an ascetic, one can question whether the rapidly increasing consumption of alcohol and tobacco indicated in Table 6 is only an indication of joie de vivre:

Table 6. Per Capita Consumption of Some Foodstuffs and Semi-luxuries

Product	1965	1975	1979
Meat (kg.)	58.7	77.8	88.6
Butter (kg.)	9.6	10.3	10.8
Cocoa Products (kg.)	2.1	3.0	3.4
Cigarettes	1,123	1,451	1,732
Wine/Champagne (l.)	4.2	7.4	9.3
Beer (l.)	80.6	119.7	134.3
Spirits (l.)	4.7	8.6	11.3

Source: Statistisches Taschenbuch der Deutschen
Demokratischen Republik (E. Berlin:
Staatsverlag, 1980), p. 103

The significance of these rising consumption levels is underlined by discussions among East German medical students about the relationship between smoking, alcohol consumption, and use of
"speed pills" and tranquilizers, on the one hand,
and the increasing number of heart infarctions
and diseases of lungs and liver, on the other.

But there is more to the discussion of leisure time than these medical aspects. In 1978
the student journal Forum provoked a lively discussion by printing a hypothesis of the GDR sociologist Professor Jürgen Kuczynski, that "Freizeit
ist . . . der Maßstab allen gesellschaftlichen
Fortschritts."[20] He was attacked for various reasons, especially because he was said to have neglected the "im Sozialismus bereits qualitativ um-
gestaltete Beziehung von Arbeit und Nichtarbeit."[21]
The discussion was closed with a statement by
Lothar Kühne that individuals who do not experience full personal development in their work have
a tendency to develop "eine kompensierende Frei-
zeitbeschäftigung."[22] Even though these tendencies in the spending of leisure time are not very
pleasing, the mere fact that they are the subject
of discussion leaves us not entirely without hope.

Tendencies in Art and Literature

Among leisure time activities reading is in
second place. A vast increase in museum attendance has been recorded in recent years. In 1978
the exhibit of GDR art in Dresden was visited by
more than one million people. The series Poesie-
album, which often contains provocative poems, is
bought each time by 100,000 readers. The strong
interest in arts and literature can be accounted
for by the need for entertainment. But this is
probably not the only answer. To quote Kuczynski
again: "Wenn man in hundert Jahren über die so

13

großartig widerspruchsvolle Realität unseres sozialistischen Aufbaus, sagen wir, von 1967 bis 1976
nachlesen will, dann wird man zu unseren Romanen
aus dieser Zeit greifen, die wirklich die ver-
schiedensten Züge des Lebens der verschiedenen
Schichten der Werktätigen widerspiegeln, die ern-
ste Probleme konkret aufgreifen, denn man wird
nur wenige gesellschaftswissenschaftliche Werke
finden, die sich nicht in der Glätte der Abstrak-
tion oder in samtiger Schönfärberei verlieren."[23]

Taking this for granted, one is, I believe,
justified in looking at GDR literature not in regard to formal aspects but rather with the question: which understanding of society is expressed
by a particular author? This question alludes to
the current controversy over whether GDR society
is a society "after the revolution" or a society
"within the unfinished revolution." Exponents of
these positions are Peter Hacks and Volker Braun.
Hacks regards GDR society as post-revolutionary.
In his view, the essential changes have been completed. The main subject of art should be the relationship between utopia and reality. Art stimu-
lates the imagination; the world can be made into
a poem. Wolfgang Harich supported Hacks (and one
should bear in mind that even after leaving the
GDR Harich is fond of its authoritarian political
system): "Hacks lotet sehr produktiv die Bedingun-
gen einer nachrevolutionären Klassik aus, die mit
Langzeitwirkung fundamentale, sozusagen 'ewige'
Menschheitsprobleme aufarbeitet."[24]

The antipodal position is held by Volker
Braun, who regards the theory of Peter Hacks as
"bürgerlichen Humanismus mit sozialistischem Rost-
anstrich." He believes GDR society to be in the
state of an unfinished revolution: "Wir müssen die
Verhältnisse bis zum Ende vom Kopf auf die Füße
stellen, und nicht auf den Bauch legen."[25] Braun
explains his interpretation in various works, in
poetry, in his prose ("Unvollendete Geschichte"),
and several plays. His last play, called Großer
Frieden, is set in ancient China, yet deals with
revolution and, according to Braun, with the fol-

14

lowing essential problem: "Die neuen Lösungen in
Tschin sind nämlich nicht die alten, aber der ökonomische and soziale Fortschritt geht im alten Geschirr der Unterdrückung."[26]

In 1976 a new literary journal, temperamente,
was created by the official youth organization.
This journal appeared to be very sympathetic towards the position of Volker Braun. The first
three issues concentrated on the literary traditions of Soviet Russia in the twenties (especially
Mayakovsky), the German heritage (e.g., Kleist),
and new documentary literature on everyday life in
the GDR (both work and leisure). The editorials
and aphorisms were quite amazing. From my point
of view, they showed a steady decline in optimism
about the GDR. The first editorial in 1977 began
with the sentence: "Die Kunst braucht Raum, die
Kunst schafft Raum." The last edition prepared by
the original editorial board ended: "Es gibt einige wenige [Bücher], die auf geheimnisvolle Weise
als Mitteilungsträger gekennzeichnet sind. Ich
fühle mich angenehm entdeckt und schweige zumeist.
Aber seit gestern ist alles beängstigend anders."
After this issue the complete editorial board
changed--without a word of explanation. temperamente 2 (1978)--the first made by the new editorial board--expressed "confessions of love to our
socialist fatherland." Nevertheless, it contained
some criticism and "socialist feminism," facts
which indicate that there is some continuity and
no complete break. There may be some hope that
temperamente has not been deprived of all of its
temperament.

I think that the emerging women's literature
more or less supports the "unfinished revolution"
argument, reflecting the actual situation of women
in the GDR, which is characterized by both progress and stagnation. Consider the following question from Irmtraud Morgner's Trobadora Beatriz:
"Kann eine Frau, deren Körper in Valeskas Land bis
zum Erlaß des Gesetzes über die Unterbrechung der
Schwangerschaft am 9. März 1972 vom Staat verwaltet wurde, plötzlich ein Gefäß ihrer selbst sein?"[27]

15

The answer is probably no. But even in this case one should ask what the preconditions for this question were. A few hints: about 86% of the women in the GDR work; one third have leading middle echelon positions in economics and politics. I made some remarks earlier about the problems of women in regard to the structuring of leisure time. Now I would like to add some information about sexuality:

Table 7. Female Orgasms in the GDR

Orgasms of women during sexual intercourse
(in % of sample)

Never	Rarely	Occasionally	Often	Usually	Nearly Always
9	16	19	12	17	27

Source: Siegfried Schnabl, Mann und Frau intim (E. Berlin: Volk und Gesundheit, 1978), p. 15

Considering the sexual problems of men also, there is no reason to assume that the revolution is over, least of all in the field of sexuality. The joy and bitterness of sexuality are probably better discussed in literature than in scholarly books on politics and culture. Equally interesting are the fine arts in this respect. I am thinking especially of the vitalist paintings of Willi Sitte, the sensitive portraits of Ursula Mattheuer, or Sighard Gille's painting Brigadefeier. This painting shows workers at a fete: not very handsome, not very decent, not very sober. It was attacked and defended after its exhibition, but it was not suppressed.

The present wave of suppressions indicates hard times for the advocates of an "unfinished revolution" wishing to express themselves in arts and literature. Their contribution to political culture in general and to communist goal culture in particular is of great importance because, due to the given structure of the mass media, political dialogue often has to take place in literature, and because "culture" itself has a high rank in communist goal culture: "Die Politik ist das Mittel, die Kultur ist das Ziel."[28]

Summary and Conclusions

It may be useful to adopt the term "political culture" for the study of the GDR because it overcomes the narrowness of analysis based on the observation of institutions. Nevertheless, political culture must be understood as being closely related to its historical, political, and socioeconomic preconditions. On its own it explains nothing. The few data on mass cultural activities and literature given here indicate that there are sharp contradictions within the political culture of the GDR. While some goals have been achieved, like the changing of the structure of job qualification, the SED has not been successful in other fields of political culture. Perhaps one can ask whether a boring style of political propaganda is responsible for a certain apolitical attitude. On the other hand, there is a tendency towards taking the democratic and socialist claims of the leadership more seriously. This inevitably leads to the issue of the "unfinished revolution."

Freie Universität Berlin/Universität Bielefeld

Notes

[1] Gabriel A. Almond and Sidney Verba, The Civic Culture. Political Attitudes and Democracy in Five Nations (Boston: Little, Brown, 1965), p. 12.

[2] Frederick C. Barghoorn, Politics in the USSR (Boston: Little, Brown, 1972), p. 20.

[3] A.H. Brown, Soviet Politics and Political Science (London: Macmillan, 1974), p. 101. See also Volker Gransow, Konzeptionelle Wandlungen der Kommunismusforschung. Vom Totalitarismus zur Immanenz (Frankfurt/New York; Campus, 1980).

[4] Archie Brown and Jack Gray, eds., Political Culture and Political Change in Communist States (London: Macmillan, 1977), p. 1.

[5] Robert C. Tucker, "Culture, Political Culture and Communist Society," Political Science Quarterly, 88, No. 2 (1973), 188.

[6] Frederic Fleron, Jr., "Technology and Communist Culture," Technology and Culture, 18, No. 4 (1977).

[7] DDR. Das politische, wirtschaftliche und soziale System, ed. Heinz Rausch and Theo Stammen (Munich: Beck, 1974).

[8] Christa Ziermann et al., Die geistige Kultur der sozialistischen Gesellschaft (E. Berlin: Dietz, 1976).

[9] John M. Starrels and Anita M. Mallinckrodt, Politics in the German Democratic Republic (New York: Praeger, 1975).

[10] Arthur M. Hanhardt, J. and Gregory P. Swin, "Literature and Political Culture," in The German Democratic Republic. A Developed Socialist Society, ed. Lyman H. Legters (Boulder: Westview, 1978).

[11] See Gero Neugebauer, Partei und Staatsapparat in der DDR (Opladen: Westdeutscher Verlag, 1978).

[12] Statistics taken from Zur gesellschaftlichen Stellung der Frau in der DDR (Leipzig: Verlag für die Frau, 1978), p. 222.

[13] Isolde Dietrich, Kulturvoll leben (E. Ber-

lin: Tribüne, 1975), p. 115.

[14] Harald Bühl et al., Beiträge zur sozialistischen Arbeitskultur (E. Berlin: Tribüne,
1973), p. 8.

[15] Helmut Hanke, "Zu Fragen der sozialistischen Lebensweise und Kultur," Weimarer Beiträge,
24, No. 8 (1978), 19-20.

[16] Hans Koch, ed. Zur Theorie des sozialistischen Realismus (E. Berlin: Dietz, 1974), p. 234.

[17] In Neue Deutsche Presse, No. 9 (1976).

[18] Stefan Heym, Wege und Umwege. Streitbare
Schriften aus fünf Jahrzehnten (Munich: Bertelsmann, 1980), p. 347.

[19] See Jugend in der DDR (E. Berlin: Panorama,
1974), p. 59; Junge Leute - hier und heute (E.Ber-
lin: Panorama, 1977), p. 62.

[20] In Forum, 32, No. 8 (1978).

[21] Forum, 32, No. 16 (1978)

[22] Forum, 32, No. 17 (1978)

[23] Jürgen Kuczinski, "Leserbrief," Sinn und
Form, 29, No. 4 (1977), 880.

[24] In Stern, No. 37, 1977.

[25] Volker Braun, Es genügt nicht die einfache
Wahrheit (Leipzig: Reclam, 1975), p. 112.

[26] Quoted from Die Neue, 5 May 1979.

[27] Irmtraud Morgner, Leben und Abenteuer der
Trobadora Beatriz (E. Berlin: Aufbau, 1976), p.
649.

[28] Georg Lukács, 1919.

19

Socialist Personality and
Workers' Culture in the GDR

Christiane Lemke

Workers' culture has a long tradition in the
labor movement in Germany. The prime period of
workers' culture came in the 1920s when it developed as a proletarian counter culture (<u>proleta-
rische Gegenkultur</u>). It was understood as the
cultural expression of a certain social class in
opposition to the culture of other classes and
groups in society. Workers' clubs for sports,
music, and other social activities, as well as
special workers' theaters, film companies, and
study groups were manifestations of this type of
workers' culture.

The democratic reconstruction of Germany after World War II did not include the revival of
traditional proletarian culture, which had been
completely destroyed by fascism. The situation in
the Federal Republic has even given rise to the
questions of whether workers' culture has not come
to an end and whether class consciousness and the
labor movement in general aren't things of the
past. This question has yet to be answered empir-
ically. Another hypothesis, developed by the Italian Marxist Gramsci, seems more reasonable: that
in the capitalist western societies not a disso-
lution of workers' culture, but rather a fundamental change in its appearance should be assumed.[1]

The social and political development in the
GDR differs fundamentally from that of the Federal
Republic. Nevertheless, there was no revival of
the traditional type of proletarian culture in the

GDR either. The cultural heritage, of course, included proletarian literature, etc., but the idea
of an oppositional proletarian culture does not
determine cultural concepts and policy.

One of the basic concepts in the cultural policy of the GDR today is that of a specific socialist type of personality. The idea of the socialist
personality has gained importance in all socialist
countries, both as a main issue of ideological dispute and as the basis for various political decisions. What consequences does this concept have
for workers' culture? Does it take the place of
the traditional class concept of workers' culture
as a proletarian culture?

With the following remarks I shall try to
give an answer to these questions. First, I would
like to explain the concept of socialist personality. Then I shall try to outline how this concept
is influencing the present discussion about culture, especially with regard to workers' culture.
Some basic questions which result from the inter-
connection of socialist personality and workers'
culture will be considered at the conclusion of
these remarks.

The concept of personality in the GDR is
based on Marxism-Leninism. In the history of
Marxist theory there has always been a dispute
over what function a theory of personality could
have, and how its subject should be defined. As
Marx and Engels showed, the key to the understanding of personal development, from the materialis-
tic point of view, is to be found through analyzing the social system. But how does one proceed
from here to the _individual_ forms of living and
acting? This question has been answered in different ways. In the socialist countries Marxist
theory has suffered an over-simplification since
the Stalin era. The discussions about alienation
and about the character of labor in socialism show
how difficult it was—and compared to Western
European discussion still is[2]—to develop a Marxist theory of personality.

In the GDR the first efforts in this direction were made in the field of psychology.[3] In the early sixties the well-known social psychologist Hiebsch suggested that research be done on the behavior and consciousness of the personality. His research was influenced by the work of the Soviet psychologist S.L. Rubinstein. Other social scientists followed suit as increased significance was attached to social science during the sixties in the GDR. The question of personality soon became one of the main issues in philosophical, psychological, and sociological research. Official policy supported this process. Its full importance wasn't realized however until the early seventies, when new economic and social goals were developed.

Despite debates within the various disciplines, the following aspects may be said to constitute the essence of the concept of personality presently held in the GDR. First of all, history is thought to play a role in the development of personality. It is assumed that personality develops from different historical conditions, that every social system produces its own types of personality. The social scientists reject the thesis of a general type of human personality; instead they distinguish between different historical stages. From this point of view, the socialist society produces the historical preconditions necessary for the development of personality. Complete personality development is the main goal of this society.

The second aspect of the concept of personality is the social one. Several studies point out that the social conditions of working and living are most important for personal development. It is not possible, therefore, to understand the personality without considering social conditions, including social relationships. At the same time, social reality contradicts the development of the idealized type of personality. Personal development is much more differentiated.

Of all social determinants the most decisive one is labor. From the GDR point of view, the

social characteristics of labor shape the social
system, including the individual conditions of
working and living.[4] Various qualities of socialist personality, such as social activity, sense of
responsibility, creativity, etc., are said to be
formed primarily during work. For social, as well
as political reasons the members of the working
class are the focus of research concerning the
concept of personality. This suggests the importance of workers' culture.[5] A breakdown of the
social stratification of the 8.6 million working
persons in the GDR is of interest here. In 1978
89.3% were classified as workers and employees,
including about 15% intelligentsia; 8.6%, as members of production cooperatives; 0.3%, as general
partners and commission merchants; 1.8%, as private merchants, freelancers, and others.[6] The core
of the working class are the industrial workers.

The third characteristic of the concept of
personality is a political one. From the GDR
point of view, there can be no socialist personality without political consciousness and political
activity. Quite often one finds that a certain
code of political and moral behavior is not only
considered important for political work but also
for goals in culture and education. Unfortunately, very few empirical studies have been published
about the shaping of political consciousness.

Last, but not least, the concept of personality can not be understood without the individual
aspect. The GDR concept of personality makes al-
lowances for the fact that it is always the individual human being who develops into a personality. Although society is considered the most important factor in personal development, the individual preconditions are nevertheless of great
interest. How else can one explain the fact that
even if two people live under similar social circumstances they will not have the same personality? This last aspect includes not only the individual psychic and physical conditions but also
the improvements in education, cultural opportunities, and the extension of leisure time, which are

24

said to be preconditions for personal development.

These are the main issues of the concept of personality. They are accepted in all social and cultural theories even though the various disciplines have set up different priorities for their research. One also encounters the concept of an idealized personality, but the basic approach is the socially determined one.

What sort of influence does the concept of personality have on the discussion of workers' culture? Some western scientists suggest that the discussion of socialist personality is primarily an ideological one which serves to stabilize present political power in the GDR by propagating a "model" personality. This, however, does not explain why the concept has become so important, especially since the early seventies, and why cultural scientists, psychologists, and sociologists concerned with personality research stress the difficulties and social contradictions of personal development. Therefore I recommend analyzing the social and political substance of the existing GDR studies on personality.

Although the working class is the focus of attention in cultural and social research, there are very few studies which analyze workers' culture with regard to socialist personality. This seems to be quite a new subject in the discussion of culture. In her study on the "biological constitution of personality," the cultural scientist Irene Dölling, on the faculty of the Humboldt University in (East) Berlin, presents some basic ideas on workers' culture and personality, which I would like to review here.[7]

Irene Dölling discusses how personal development is shaped by working conditions; she also examines the stimulating and the oppressive aspects of these conditions. In reference to sociological surveys she asserts that, in spite of improvements in working conditions, education, and social benefits, about 75% of the industrial workers still do physical labor and about half, hard work; that in 1976, 16.6% worked in two shifts, that the amount of shift work is still increasing;[8] and that as late as 1973, 20% of the industrial workers suffered due to unhealthy working conditions, especially noise disturbance.

Hard and unhealthy work is often done by unskilled or semi-skilled labor. As different sociological studies have pointed out, this causes a lower interest in education, also continuing education, and in cultural activities. What does this imply for the cultural forms being developed by the working class?

On the one hand, cultural activities are much more varied now than, for example, during the fifties. The extension of free time, the development of the mass media, and new cultural facilities changed the possibilities and the forms of culture for social classes and groups. On the other hand, class- and strata-specific characteristics are significant. Studies on life style support this assumption. The main question, therefore, is how cultural opportunities can be structured to correspond with the demand of the workers for relaxation, entertainment, and creative expression.

It is of great interest to me that Irene Dölling, for example, regards it as fundamentally wrong to distinguish between "higher" and "lower" forms of culture. Workers' culture includes more activities than those usually attributed to the "higher" forms of culture, such as intellectual or artistic-aesthetic activities. In her view, the main point is the ways in which the members of the working class are able to develop their abilities and cultural needs, taking into consideration the concrete stress of labor. Therefore the traditional forms of cultural life in the GDR, such as the Kulturhaus with its various groups, or the lectures organized by Urania, all which require pre-existing special interests, mainly intellectual-receptive ones, need to be examined to see if they really correspond to the cultural demands of the working class.

For those specialists concerned with workers'
culture the concept of personality seems to have
two primary functions: first, it serves to discuss
the future development of culture and thus gives
an orientation to cultural work and its conception;
secondly, the concept of personality is confronted
with reality. This raises the questions: Do the
working and living conditions of the working class
promote the complete development of personality,
and how can this ideal be achieved?

Given the fact that the concept of personality
is presently influencing the discussion of workers'
culture in the GDR, some essential questions can be
posed regarding the possibilities for the development of workers' personality. I would like to sum
up some of the questions which should be discussed
in regard to research work on workers' culture in
the GDR.

I have already mentioned that working conditions are quite important for personal development.
Labor has its positive, attractive aspects, but
also negative, repulsive ones. How important to
the individual is labor, as compared to free time?
Which is of greater importance for workers' personality? This leads to the question of where to put
the emphasis in cultural work. Does culture,
which is mainly organized during free time, have a
compensatory function, that is, does it compensate
for stress at work? Or does it have a supplemen-
tary function? Or are free time and leisure more
important for promoting workers' personality than
labor?

Since about half of the working population
is made up of women there is of course a sex-specific aspect of workers' personality. Studies
about working conditions, time-budget analyses, and
studies on free time and leisure point out significant differences between men and women. Women,
for example, do twice as much housework as men,
although 87% of them are working. While male

27

workers have 4.1 hours per day of leisure time, women workers have only 3.1 hours.[9] Studies also point out the double stress women feel because of work and family tasks, especially women with children. The increasing signifance of women's literature--Irmtraud Morgner, Sarah Kirsch, and Maxie Wander, for example, have made traditional role patterns a topic of discussion--supports the argument of the sex-specific aspect of personality and development. The question is, then, do culture and cultural policy reinforce or dissolve the traditional division of labor between men and women?

Workers' culture is supposed to serve the process of developing all the abilities and needs of a worker. But who decides cultural needs and who organizes the cultural environment? Quite often there is a lack of cultural opportunities--in rural areas, for example, or for certain groups, such as young people. Furthermore there is the question of how the existing capacities are formed and organized, and how the different social groups participate in this structure. Of course, this is mainly a question of democracy and participation in the planning process.

The discussion of personality in the GDR primarily shows the subjective, individual problems of social change. It is based on a class-specific point of view. In regard to workers' culture, workers' personality is the focus of attention, and working and living conditions are analyzed as to whether or not they are conducive to the achieving of the ideal goal of a complete development of personality. With regard to this goal, various contradictions and difficulties can be said to exist in daily life in the GDR.

Freie Universität Berlin

[1] Gramsci developed the idea that the "super-structure" changes within the history of capitalist societies and that culture thus gets new appearances. He pointed out the importance culture had in Italy during the twenties in the fight against fascism. Antonio Gramsci, Philosophie in der Praxis. Eine Auswahl (Frankfurt/M.: Fischer, 1967).

[2] See, for example, Lucien Sève, Marxisme et théorie de la personnalité (Paris: éditions sociales, 1972).

[3] A review of the history of the theory of personality is given in: Christiane Lemke, Persönlichkeit und Gesellschaft. Zur Theorie der Persönlichkeit in der DDR (Opladen: Westdeutscher Verlag, 1980).

[4] This is evident, for example, in the definition given by the philosopher Alfred Arnold: "Der Begriff 'Persönlichkeit' bezieht sich in erster Linie auf die wesensbestimmenden Merkmale des Menschen, auf ihn als tätiges gesellschaftliches Wesen. Kriterien der Persönlichkeitsentwicklung eines Menschen sind die Art und Weise und die gesellschaftliche Wirkung seiner Tätigkeit - vor allem sein durch Arbeit geleisteter Beitrag zur Erzeugung gesellschaftlich nützlicher materiell-gegenständlicher oder geistiger Produkte - und sein soziales Verhalten." Alfred Arnold, Was formt die Persönlichkeit? (E. Berlin: Dt. Verlag der Wissenschaften, 1976), pp. 14f.

[5] See, for example, Fred Adler et al., Arbeiterklasse und Persönlichkeit im Sozialismus (E. Berlin: Dietz, 1977).

[6] Statistisches Jahrbuch der DDR 1979 (E. Berlin: Staatsverlag der DDR, 1979), p. 84.

[7] Irene Dölling, Naturwesen - Individuum -

Persönlichkeit. Die Menschen und ihre biologische
Konstitution in der marxistisch-leninistischen
Kulturtheorie (E. Berlin: Dt. Verlag der Wissen-
schaften, 1979), Chaps. IV and V.

[8] In 1977, 14.3% of the industrial workers
in centralized industry worked in two shifts;
28.2%, in three shifts.   Source: Statistisches
Jahrbuch der DDR 1978, p. 124.

[9] Helmut Hanke, Freizeit in der DDR (E. Berlin: Dietz, 1979), p. 64.

Consumer Policy in the
German Democratic Republic:
Changes Ahead for the 1980s?

Barbara A. Dooley

In the thirty years since its creation, the
German Democratic Republic has become one of the
world's leading industrial powers and the most
successful follower of the Soviet model of central
planning in Eastern Europe. At the same time, its
unique historical experience as part of highly industrialized pre-war Germany, and its geographical
location, which allows a relatively unobscured
view on the West, have made it particularly vulnerable to economic comparisons with one of the industrialized West's great economic powers, the Federal Republic. As a result, the GDR has long been
confronted with the issues of living standards and
consumer welfare. A significant realignment of
economic priorities after the Eighth Party Congress
in May 1971, coupled with improved relations with
the Federal Republic after the signing of the Basic Treaty in 1972, resulted in a greater emphasis
on satisfying the needs and desires of GDR consumers, a trend which continued throughout the 1970s.
Internal and external factors, however, have made
it increasingly difficult, and increasingly costly,
to continue these policies without modification.
Events and policy changes which took place in 1979
may well be an indication of the emphasis of policies for the coming decade.

As the Hungarian economist Bela Belassi has
noted, every economic system can be evaluated by
certain goals or "success criteria."[1] Some of
these criteria are economic goals such as efficien-

cy, equilibrium, and growth. There are other criteria, however, which lie outside of strictly economic assessments and which may conflict with economic goals. For socialist economies such as the GDR, some of these goals are full employment, the growth of the economy without "capitalist cycles," and the continual improvement of living standards.[2] In addition, developing socialism in the GDR has further identifiable goals, for example, the full use of the possibilities of the "scientific-technical" revolution, the improvement of management principles, the development of socialist democracy, and the enhancement of the leadership role of the SED.[3] While all these criteria, both economic and non-economic, are important, the GDR has taken the position that, at least theoretically, the most important is "real income, which to us comprises, simply said, the goods and services which people are able to buy in money terms from their earnings and the benefits which they receive through public funds which is a form of indirect income."[4]

Consumption, as implied by the preceding quotation, is usually divided into two categories: personal consumption, consumption out of disposable income, which includes wages and salaries, bonuses, grants and transfer payments; and social consumption, that is, goods and services received from the state and not purchased on the market from wage earnings. (In the GDR this includes such things as education and health benefits, culture and sports activities, housing maintenance, vacation facilities, and subsidies for such basic necessities as housing, food, and mass transit.) In the centrally planned economy of the GDR, the state controls consumption through policy (Konsumpolitik) outlined generally in the Five Year Plan and more particularly in annual plans, which state how much of the national income produced will be devoted to consumption and how much to investment (i.e., the ratio between consumption and accumulation), as well as the ratio between social and personal consumption, the amount and types of goods and services which will be produced, and the

32

quality and prices of these goods and services.

In addition, social policy (<u>Sozialpolitik</u>) sets goals in such areas as worker productivity, the price system, health and welfare, etc. An official GDR acknowledgment of social policy is, however, relatively recent. In the past, social policy was considered a reactionary attribute of capitalism and, therefore, unnecessary in a socialist society such as the GDR.[5] The institutional groundwork for social policy was laid at the Seventh Party Congress in 1967. It was at the Eighth Party Congress in 1971, however, that the unity of economic and social policy, and the aim of increasing consumer welfare were officially proclaimed. In the new policy, "the economy is a means to an end--that end being to continually raise the population's living standards and cultural level."[6] This change in emphasis has led to what has been called Honecker's "Konsum Kommunismus," which critic Robert Havemann has decried as "goulash communism" and political scientist Melvin Croan has described as "consumeristic authoritarianism."[7] In other words, the GDR consumer was to be satisfied without affecting, or in order not to affect, the political power of the SED.

The roots of the GDR's consumer welfare policies in the 1970s are deep. Although living standards have steadily increased since the creation of the new state, the GDR in the 1950s and most of the 1960s built its economy along Soviet lines, emphasizing self-sufficiency and capital goods industries, and giving low priority to consumer goods. This low priority influenced in particular such important industries as textiles and durables, which received few investment funds to improve or modernize, causing repercussions lasting to the present-day.[8] The slogan of this period "Wie wir heute arbeiten, werden wir morgen leben" represented the conscious policy of restricting consumption, while holding out hope for a better future. The New Economic System of Planning and Management (NES), which was introduced in 1963 under Ulbricht, promised to satisfy demands both for substantial

economic growth and improved living standards.
Although the NES was not a success and the GDR
soon returned to more traditional and centralized
planning, the attempted reforms and ambitious
plans for economic growth left a legacy of increased consumer demand.[9] To ignore serious consumer
discontent might not only risk political instability and challenges of the SED leadership (workers'
protests in Poland in 1971 and again in 1976 were
warning signals to the Party), but might directly
influence worker productivity and, therefore, overall economic growth. It was not really surprising
then that, when Honecker took control at the Eighth
Party Congress in May, 1971, he stressed a new economic policy emphasizing consumption and higher
living standards, without, of course, softening
the demand for higher productivity and increased
economic growth. In concrete terms, the SED committed itself to improvements in such areas as
housing, wages, pension reforms; and it reaffirmed
its commitment to stable consumer prices. In addition, improvements in the supply, quality, and
variety of consumer goods were promised. The
Ninth Party Congress in May, 1976 repeated these
same objectives. (At the same time, however, the
Ninth Party Congress signaled a change away from
increasing direct investment goods to an emphasis
on the production of goods for export, a step
which was intended as a means of improving the
GDR's worsening position in international trade
and of increasing its hard currency balances to
pay for needed investment goods as well as the increasing amounts of consumer goods being imported
from the West.)

        At the same time that Honecker was proposing
policies which in effect realigned the priorities
of the economy, external factors began to exert
increasingly powerful influence on the domestic
economy. Rising raw material prices as well as
the world energy crises had significant economic
repercussions in the GDR, as in other industrialized nations. In addition, the 1970s witnessed
the opening of the GDR to the West, particularly
to the Federal Republic. West German influences

on the GDR economy proved to be great--partly as a result of the 1972 Basic Treaty, partly as a result of the ensuing accords in trade and tele-communications, etc., and partly as a result of increasing cultural and personal contacts. Intra-German trade grew from DM 4548 million in 1970 to DM 1100 million in 1979.[10] The increased personal contacts, coupled with the effects of West German radio and television (which can be received all over the GDR except in small areas of the south-east and the northeast Baltic littoral), have served to fuel consumer demand, particularly for luxury items.[11]

Two of the most tangible consequences of the developing intra-German relationship for the GDR have been, without a doubt, the increased import of high quality and luxury consumer goods from the West, and an increase in hard currency in both private and state hands.[12] Hard currency in the hands of GDR citizens has led to new problems and new domestic tensions, seen most clearly in the Intershop and "second economy" difficulties. Intershops were created for West German and other foreign tourists, who could buy high-quality western goods with hard currency, often at prices lower than at home. In 1973 the privilege of holding hard currency, and thus shopping in Intershops was extended to GDR citizens. Expensive consumer durables became available for GDR citizens with access to hard currency through a special organization called Genex. To satisfy the demands of those without western currency (for example, SED members with no western contacts), Delikat and Exquisit shops were introduced which offer goods in exchange for GDR marks (although at much higher prices than in the Intershops).

One example may help to illustrate the social and economic problems which have resulted. Through Genex GDR citizens are able to purchase cars that are generally not available in the GDR (West German models, for example), or domestic models at a cheaper price. A Trabant, the most common GDR car, costs DM 5,000 rather than 8,000 M.; a Wartburg,

DM 8,500 rather than 17,000 M. In addition, it is not necessary to wait the customary four to twelve years (averaging about seven) to receive the car.[13] It has been suggested that in the GDR the attainment of a private automobile is "a bigger event than birthday, youth consecration and wedding combined."[14] In comparison to other East bloc countries, the GDR is relatively well-supplied with private automobiles. In 1975, for example, 1 out of 9 GDR citizens owned an automobile, compared to 1 in 19 in Czechoslovakia, 1 in 19 in Hungary, 1 in 23 in Bulgaria, 1 in 32 in Poland, 1 in 66 in the Soviet Union, and 1 in 91 in Romania. By 1978 the ratio in the GDR had improved to 1 in 7. Nonetheless, the standard for comparison of living standards has not been the East bloc but the Federal Republic, which boasted a ratio of 1 automobile per 4 inhabitants in 1975. Unless current production rates are increased in the new 1981-85 Five Year Plan (approximately 175,000 autos were produced domestically and 100,000 imported annually in 1976-80),[15] the GDR by the end of 1985 will not even reach the 1975 Federal Republic level (at least a half million short). The current estimate is that by the year 2010 the ratio will be 1 per 3.5 inhabitants, the greatest growth being anticipated in the next two decades.[16]

The second area greatly affected by the increases in hard currency has been the so-called "second economy," the artisan, spare parts, and service sectors, much activity of which is carried out extra-legally. Citizens without hard currency have found it increasingly difficult to receive services, since payment has come to be expected in DM. The Deutsch Mark has become in effect a second GDR currency, the possession of which distinguishes the privileged individuals from the non-privileged masses.[17] The inequities of such a "two-class" system and the resulting consumer dissatisfaction became a source of political embarrassment to Honecker. The resulting actions were strong: the spread of the Intershop system was halted in 1979; Exquisit and Delikat shops increased in number; and, since April 1979, it has again become illegal for GDR citizens to hold foreign currency. Hard currency must now be exchanged for vouchers, which may be used for purchases in the Intershop and Genex stores.[18]

Another recent change in policy, and one which strikes at the heart of the GDR's commitment to consumer welfare, is the new official consumer price policy, announced by Honecker at the 11th meeting of the Central Committee of the SED in December, 1979.[19] Five year plans have regularly contained stipulations that no increases in retail prices may be introduced and that supplies in the lower price brackets will be guaranteed in keeping with demand.[20] (When price changes for consumer goods have occurred they have been justified with product changes and shifts in the range of goods.) The lowest price category has traditionally included staples, children's and occupational clothing, service charges, rents, and transport fares. The stability of these prices can be seen below:

Table 1. Prices of Selected Consumer Goods
(in Marks)

	Unit	1960	1975
Milk (2% fat)	l.	0.72	0.72
Butter	kg.	10.00	10.00
Eggs	one	0.37	0.34
Rye bread	kg.	0.52	0.52
White bread	kg.	1.00	1.00
Sugar	kg.	1.64	1.64
Beef (boneless)	kg.	9.80	9.80
Pork cutlet	kg.	8.00	8.00
Potatoes	5 kg.	0.65	0.85
Brown coal briquettes	50 kg.		
ration		1.70	1.70
non-ration		3.66	3.51
Children's shoes	pair	16.30	18.00
Rail ticket (2nd class)	50 km.	4.00	4.00
Streetcar ticket		0.20	0.20
Electricity (household)	kWh.	0.08	0.08
Gas (household)	m^3	0.16	0.16

Source: Deutsche Demokratische Republik. Handbuch
         (Leipzig: VEB Verlag Enzyklopädie, 1979),
         p. 419

Low and stable prices have been made possible
through large subsidies in the state budget. In
1979 a series of planned price increases at the
enterprise level reached the level of finished
products, thus necessitating even higher subsidies.
In addition, the worsening economic performance,
the rising, yet unfulfilled expectations of the
population, and its excess purchasing power (per
capita savings exceeded 5400 M. in 1978)[21] have
exerted strong, upward pressure on prices. As a
result, both prices and the availability of consumer goods have been affected.

While official price indexes show a stable or
even declining cost of living through 1978 (based
on 1970 prices),[22] the statistics do not take into
account such matters as the composition of the
market basket, price increases of new or improved
goods, or other types of "hidden inflation."[23]
For example, while prices of the goods included in
the market basket have been low and stable, consumer durables and "luxuries" have always been relatively expensive. Higher prices for textiles
have been officially explained as stemming from
the introduction of new fibers and fabrics. The
price of many foods has been raised by means of
new packaging or reductions in package content.

Rumors of general price increases circulated
in the GDR throughout 1979. It was reported in
the West German press that an actress playing a
discontented French worker in an Offenbach opera
staged by the East Berlin Komische Oper was
greeted with laughter and applause when she sang
the refrain, "Und überall steigen die Preise."[24]
Stories about inflation in other bloc countries
appeared in the GDR press and, interpreted as being intended to prepare GDR citizens for imminent
price increases, may have helped spur "panic buy-

ing," resulting in shortages of many cheap consumer goods. Even though the state tried to combat hoarding by emphasizing the stability of "basic necessities," and by blaming "adversaries" for the rumors, it was obvious that price increases could not be avoided.[25]

Sudden huge price increases in the fall of 1979 (for example, men's suits increased in price 50-150%; leather goods, 50-100%; furniture, 150%; bed linen, 50-100%; bicycles, 300%) were met with protest, some of which even appeared in the GDR press.[26] In response to consumer discontent, the price increases for some items were subsequently rescinded because they were considered "unjustified."[27] Nonetheless, it has been estimated that prices have been increased between 10-20% in the clothing sector and that the range of many durable goods (major household appliances, furniture, etc.) has been shifted and prices increased.[28] The December 1979 policy confirmed this trend by declaring that, while the prices of basic foods, rent, and transport fares would remain stable, all other prices would be allowed to increase, based allegedly on improvements in quality and utility value. In March, 1980 the legal basis for sweeping increases in both consumer and industrial prices was provided by the Council of Ministers, which declared the need to further "strengthen democratic centralism in the field of prices" and to ensure "that prices continue to be firmly in the hands of the socialist state."[29]

Whether termed "Konsum Kommunismus," "goulash communism," or lauded in the rhetoric of Party congresses, Honecker's policies faced serious challenges in the 1970s. On the economic front, the world energy crisis, rising prices for raw materials and imports, and increasing foreign indebtedness[30] have strained the domestic economy. Increases in labor productivity have not been meeting plan targets, and overall economic growth in 1976-80 will fall quite short of the 5.2% annual increase planned in the FYP directives.[31] The commitment to stable consumer prices has proved to be an increasing burden as the state budget subsidies increase from year to year. Even with price increases in certain areas officially confirmed, the subsidies needed to maintain prices in the now more limited number of areas will amount to 16.4 billion M. in 1980, only slightly less than the amount allocated for housing construction and housing (a priority investment area since the 1960s) for this year.[32] Increased amounts of consumer goods and hard currency have fostered rising expectations and discontent. In addition, Honecker's policies have been criticized on both economic and ideological grounds by conservative, hard-line cadres as well as by opposition intellectuals such as Havemann, Harich, and Bahro, who have challenged the legitimacy of capitalistic consumption values in socialist, and particularly GDR, society.[33]

What is ahead, then, for the GDR in the 1980s? As the GDR plans for the Tenth Party Congress to be held in April, 1981, and begins to formulate policy for the 1980s, a reevaluation of policies directly affecting consumers is certain to take place. While it is risky to make specific predictions, certain possibilities come to mind.

It is doubtful that the Tenth Party Congress will change its commitment to increase living standards and consumer welfare; however, changes in emphasis may be anticipated in the 1981-85 FYP and in the coming decade. There will likely be a change in planning priorities away from consumer areas, not only to production for export for hard currency, but also increasingly to the East bloc. The recently signed agreement between the Soviet Union and the GDR will guarantee the GDR's energy supplies for 1981-85 only at 1976-80 levels. Additional purchases will have to be made on the open market for hard currency. In addition, the commitment to "socialist economic integration" (with the CMEA trading bloc by 1990) may increasingly influence the GDR's trading pattern. The program of the Thirty-third CMEA Session included, for example, plans for integration in five spe-

cific, important consumer goods industries.[34] The
GDR has export markets within the socialist trading bloc already, which may improve its situation
in the short run, but it must balance this gain
with the possibility of a long-term loss of technological competitiveness if its foreign trade is
conducted almost totally within the bloc. Moreover, the GDR leadership may well have to face the
prospect that the population's desire to "catch
up" with the Federal Republic is not only economically unsound but that the satisfying of this desire becomes a cause of tensions within the socialist bloc, whose integration policies call for the
equalization of living standards, made more difficult by the GDR's already high standard.

Price increases may be expected, both "con-
cealed" and straightforward, as more and more
goods are moved from the low, subsidized price
level to the middle and high price categories.
These price increases will not only help drain
excess purchasing power from the hands of GDR consumers, but may also allow the state subsidies for
consumer welfare to decline, or at least increase
at a slower rate, thus freeing funds for investment purposes. Areas of piecemeal reforms, such
as pensions, will probably receive less attention.
There will likely be a strong attempt to widen
the gap between increases in wages and increases
in worker productivity, thus improving the overall economic picture and, again, freeing funds
for investment. While it would be economically
advantageous to promote some of the anti-consump-
tion critics' suggestions, especially regarding
"conspicuous consumption" and luxury items, the
political implications are, it would seem, too
potentially destabilizing to merit serious consideration at this time.

Honecker's policies have at times been criticized as "half-hearted" in their attempts to reconcile such goals as cooperation and delimita-
tion, ideology and pragmatism, security and freedom. The consumer policies of the 1970s have been
similarly contradictory as political pragmatism

has met increasinly harsh economic realities. While it remains to be seen what specific policies will be proposed for the 1980s, more conservative plans for economic growth and slower increases in living standards and consumer welfare can certainly be predicted.

University of Kansas

Notes

[1] Bela Belassi, The Hungarian Experience in Economic Planning (New Haven: Yale Univ. Press, 1959), pp. 5-24.

[2] Roy E. Mellor, The Two Germanies: A Modern Geography (London: Harper & Row, 1978), p. 178.

[3] Wolfgang Behr, Bundesrepublik Deutschland und Deutsche Demokratische Republik, Systemvergleich: Politik-Wirtschaft-Gesellschaft (Stuttgart: Kohlhammer, 1979), p. 102.

[4] Karl-Heinz Arnold, Policies which put people first, Panorama DDR (Dresden: Verlag Zeit im Bild, 1976), p. 37.

[5] Wolf-Rainer Leenen, "Sozialpolitik in der DDR (I): Theoretische Probleme," Deutschland Archiv, 8, No. 3 (1975), 259.

[6] What is life like in the GDR: The way of life and the standard of living under socialism, Panorama DDR (Dresden: Verlag Zeit im Bild, n.d.) p. 20.

[7] See for example the series of articles in Der Spiegel, 1 Oct. 1979, pp. 102-121; 8 Oct. 1979, pp. 102; 15 Oct. 1979, pp. 105-129. Havemann is discussed in Karl H. Kahrs, "The Theoretical Position of Intra-Marxist Opposition in the GDR," East Central Europe/L'Europe du Centre-

Est, 6, No. 1, Pt. 2 (1979), 150.

[8] Mellor, p. 369.

[9] When planning is overambitious or "taut" in economists' terms, unmet plan targets and supply and/or distribution bottlenecks frequently bring about insufficient inventories. Unsatisfied demand, which can be likened to inflationary pressure, builds up in the economy. However, when prices are fixed or stable this inflation is repressed, and queuing and shortages result.

[10] Bundesministerium für innerdeutsche Beziehungen, Zehn Jahre Deutschlandpolitik: Die Entwicklung der Beziehungen zwischen der Bundesrepublik Deutschland und der Deutschen Demokratischen Republik, 1969-1979, Bericht und Dokumentation (Melsungen: A. Bernecker, 1980), p. 29.

[11] "Television Goes Through the Wall," The Economist, 30 Sept. 1978, p. 57, noted in Phillip J. Bryam, "The GDR in the International Economy," East Central Europe/L'Europe du Centre-Est, 6, No. 1, Pt. 2 (1979), 143.

[12] Including such publicized examples as 10,000 VW Golfs and 800,000 pairs of American blue jeans. The young people's preference for western consumer goods was documented in May, 1979 for the SED by the Zentralinstitut für Jugendforschung, Leipzig. See Der Spiegel, 15 Oct. 1979, p. 115.

[13] Marlies Menge, "Warten auf Trabbi," Die Zeit, 16 Nov. 1979, p. 69.

[14] Menge, p. 69.

[15] Deutsches Institut für Wirtschaftsforschung Berlin, Handbuch DDR-Wirtschaft (Reinbek bei Hamburg: Rowohlt, 1977), p. 243.

[16] Fritz Müller and Hans-Werner Schleife, "Der Personenverkehr--Leistungen, Aufgaben, Tendenzen," DDR Verkehr, 10, No. 10 (1979), 361.

43

[17] Kurt Sontheimer and Wilhelm Bleek, _Die DDR: Politik_, _Gesellschaft_, _Wirtschaft_, 5th rev., enl. ed. (Hamburg: Hoffmann & Campe, 1979), p. 216.

[18] It is interesting that the April 1979 action against West German correspondents was initiated soon after man-on-the-street interviews in East Berlin were published and broadcast about the problem. See _Der Spiegel_, 23 April 1979, pp. 19-22.

[19] _Neues Deutschland_, 14 Dec. 1979, p. 5.

[20] _What is life like in the GDR?_, p. 24.

[21] _Statistical Pocketbook of the German Democratic Republic 1979_, p. 86.

[22] _Statistical Pocketbook of the German Democratic Republic 1979_, pp. 88-89.

[23] For a discussion of many of the issues associated with price increases and inflation, see Karl-Hans Hartwig, "Preiserhöhungen in der DDR," _Deutschland Archiv_, 13, No. 3 (1980), 246-251.

[24] "Inflation à la DDR," _Frankfurter Allgemeine Zeitung_, 20 Nov. 1979.

[25] "Gerücht über Preiserhöhungen," _IWE-Wirtschaftsdienst_, 20, No. 33/34/35, 21 Sept. 1979, 2-3.

[26] "DDR-Zeitung zur Preissituation auf dem Konsumgütersektor," _Informationen_, No. 20, 1979.

[27] "Wachsende Unruhe über Preiserhöhungen--Warnung vor Hamsterkäufen," _Der Tagesspiegel_, 17 Nov. 1979.

[28] Doris Cornelsen, "GDR: Economic Reforms," Colloquium 1980 on Economic Reforms in Eastern Europe and Prospects for the 1980s, NATO Economics Directorate, Brussels, 16-18 April 1980.

[29] "Verordnung über die staatlichen Kontroll-
vollmachten und Aufgaben des Leiters der Abteilung
Preise in volkseigenen Kombinaten," Gesetzblatt
der Deutschen Demokratischen Republik, 1, 3 March
1980, pp. 58-63.

[30] Swing credit increased greatly in the
1970s and is approaching the 850 million DM maximum. See Zehn Jahre Deutschlandpolitik, p. 29.

[31] Actual growth has been as follows (plan
targets in parentheses): 1976, 3.5 (5.3); 1977,
5.2 (4.8); 1978, 3.8 (5.0); 1979, 4.0 (5.1); 1980,
4.8 (5.0). Figures taken from Doris Cornelsen,
"The GDR in the Period of Foreign Trade Difficulties: Development and Prospects for the 1980's,"
Joint Economic Committee East European Economic
Assessment, Part I. Country Studies, 1980 (Wash-
ington, D.C.: U.S. Government Printing Office,
1981).

[32] "Staatshaushaltsplan 1980," Gesetzblatt
der Deutschen Demokratischen Republik, 1, 21 Dec.
1980, 462.

[33] Harich's views are discussed in Wolfgang
Harich, Kommunismus ohne Wachstum? (Reinbek:
Rowohlt, 1975); Der Spiegel, 9 April 1979, p. 133;
Kahrs, pp. 253-54. For a more complete discussion
of Bahro, see Rudolf Bahro, Die Alternative (Cologne: Europäische Verlagsanstalt, 1977); in English, The Alternative in Eastern Europe (London:
NLB, 1978); and the Bahro interview in Der Spiegel,
22 October 1979. For Havemann, see Note 7.

[34] "RGW-Zielprogramm: Abgestimmte Maßnahmen
zur Erhöhung und Verbesserung der Konsumgüterpro-
duktion," DDR Außenwirtschaft, 8, No. 7 (1980),
1.

The German Democratic Republic:
A Partner in Comecon

Lucie Pfaff

After World War II, socialist governments with leaders loyal to the USSR took power throughout eastern Europe: in Albania, Bulgaria, Czechoslovakia, East Germany, Hungary, Poland, and Rumania. These political changes initiated major economic realignments. It was in the interest of the USSR, which had suffered from slow economic growth before WW II, to develop a "second world market" vis-à-vis the capitalist world. Eastern Europe was to provide a group of friendly nations with which the USSR could have mutual trade relations. Prior to the war, the USSR had had almost no economic ties with the nations of eastern Europe, whose major trade partner had been Germany. The defeat and collapse of Germany in 1945 left a vacuum, which was, within a few years, largely filled by the USSR.

The newly developed ties within eastern Europe were formalized in 1949 with the establishment of an organizational framework: the Council for Mutual Economic Assistance. The formation of the CMEA or Comecon, as it is referred to in English language publications, has to be seen in part as a response to the Marshall Plan, the concomitant development of the Organization for European Economic Cooperation (OEEC, now OECD), and the division of Europe into two political camps.[1]

At its inception the Council consisted of Albania, Bulgaria, Czechoslovakia, Hungary, Poland, Rumania, and the USSR. The German Democratic Republic (GDR) joined in 1950. Albania ceased to participate in the activities of the Council at the end of 1961 due to political tensions. In 1962, the Mongolian People's Republic was admitted. The Republic of Cuba acceded to Comecon in 1972, followed by the Socialist Republic of Vietnam in 1978. In the following, the discussion will concentrate on the European members of the Council.

The aims of Comecon as stated in the charter are to unite and coordinate the efforts of the member countries in order to further the development of socialist economic integration. This is to be done by promoting economic planning and economic and technical progress in these countries, especially in countries with less developed industries. Comecon is pledged to work towards a steady growth of labor productivity and a balanced level of development in the different regions, as well as towards the steady increase in the standard of living in the member countries.[2]

The institutional framework of Comecon is made up of the Council, the Executive Committee, the Standing Commissions, and the Secretariat. The Council is the supreme organ of Comecon. According to the charter, delegations from all the member countries take part in the Council sessions. The composition of the delegations is determined by the governments of each country concerned. The Council discusses proposals received from member nations, the Executive Committee, the Committee for Cooperative Planning, the Committee for Scientific and Technical Cooperation, the Standing Commissions, and other bodies. It considers economic, scientific and technical collaboration and determines the program of action of Comecon. The powers of Comecon are narrowly circumscribed. The various institutions cannot make binding decisions, but only recommendations, which the member states can approve or reject. All decisions have to be arrived at by unanimous vote.[3] Once recommendations are accepted, they take on the character of mutual economic agreements.

Comecon, in its structure, does not fall into

the category of a customs union or a common market. It has neither the external tariff wall nor the quota restrictions characteristic of the customs union. Integration policies do not apply to the movement of capital or labor. Although the charter speaks of international integration (referring to internal affairs), the national character of the member countries and their autonomy in trade with outside countries is still upheld. Comecon concentrates on the intra-regional specialization of production and comprehensive economic development of the individual socialist countries. Coordination between member countries is achieved by the process of simultaneous bilateral and multilateral consultation. The association is thus an instrument for the coordination and clarification of national production planning, and its activities have been geared to international specialization and cooperation in production, standardization and coordination of scientific research, statistical methodology, contacts with international and scientific organizations, and the creation of joint ventures between the participating countries. It is not an organ for the promotion of competitive trading conditions between member states of a common market.[4] Comecon is therefore merely a consultative, not a supra-national body.

In the economies of the socialist countries exports do not have the same priority as in western countries. There exist certain tendencies towards autarky, and, even between themselves, the Comecon countries limit trade to those needs which cannot be satisfied from domestic production. They export generally just enough to cover imports. Trade between Comecon countries is on the whole based on bilateral exchanges, although attempts are being made to expand to multilateral agreements, at least in the area of payments and concerted actions. If socialist nations sell to western countries, it is only because they need to buy. In their trade exchanges they try to achieve equilibrium in their balance of payments with each of their partners. But at all times foreign trade remains subordinated to the needs of the domestic

49

plan. Commodity flows are mainly planned, and
purchases by foreign countries are therefore limited.

This digression into the operation of Comecon
was necessary before evaluating the GDR's part in
this economic organization. Seldom has a period
of a few decades witnessed such a dramatic change
in economic relations as that which has occurred
since 1938 in the three Comecon countries situated
in the northern European region of the bloc: the
GDR, Czechoslovakia, and Poland. These changes
took place under the combined impact of a number
of factors: a far-reaching transformation of socioeconomic structures and of institutions; the sev-
erance of historically developed economic ties and
the forging of new ones; and, above all, the primary importance placed on the political and economic philosophy. Of these three countries the GDR
had to make the most dramatic adjustments.

The GDR suffered severe economic losses due
to the reparations it had to pay to the USSR. Although a fellow People's Republic, it had to carry
the heavy burden of being a former enemy nation.
The Russians were entitled to reparations as a result of political settlements made after the war.
The reparations took two forms: dismantled plant
and deliveries of commodities. It is estimated
that the Soviet Union took $12 billion worth of
plant and $4 billion worth of commodities from the
GDR.[5] In addition to the loss of plant and the
large annual reparation payments in the form of
commodities, the GDR was obliged to support approximately twenty divisions of Soviet troops station-
ed within its borders. Another means of gaining
reparations was through the establishment of joint
stock companies. These companies were supposedly
financed half by the host nation and half by the
Soviet Union. The share of the USSR generally consisted of captured German or other western invest-
ments in the host territories. It is suspected
that the USSR took far more than a fair share of
profit out of these joint ventures.[6]

In addition to these factors, the loss of specialized trade with West Germany and access to pre-war markets, as well as changes in the structure of production, delayed the recovery of the GDR economy. It was not until 1959 that the GDR regained its 1939 level of economic development.[7] The changeover to the framework of a command economy was introduced by degrees. During the period of 1945-1948 large agricultural holdings were broken up and divided among the farm population, and large-scale industries, trade, and finance were nationalized. By the end of the 1940s industry consisted almost entirely of state enterprises. Formal economic planning went into effect with the introduction of a two-year plan in 1948. In agriculture, collectivization proceeded at a slower pace. Up to the mid-1950's, vestiges of an independent farm population contributed a share of the food supply. As the state control of the economy became more absolute, the SED pushed for greater collectivization, and by 1961 almost all farmers were in collectives. For private businesses a partnership was established with the state, or they were nationalized outright. The result was that more than 50% of private enterprise moved into a semi-state category in 1958-59.[8]

All these factors put a tremendous strain on the GDR economy. In order to ease the situation somewhat, the USSR agreed in 1950 to reduce the reparation debt by 50%. The rebellion in the GDR in June 1953 effected a cancellation of reparation payments and the return of about two-thirds of the factories which had been dismantled. The troop maintenance payments were reduced in 1953 and finally eliminated in 1959.[9] Most of the joint stock companies were also dissolved in the aftermath of the uprisings and unrest of 1953 in the GDR and in 1956 in Poland and Hungary.

Under the impact of the uprisings, the USSR modified its economic policy towards the Comecon countries and, in the case of the GDR, started to extend loans to ease the economic dislocation. Although the progress was slow, intra-bloc trade

increased, partially because the countries were
growing, but also because of increased Comecon
activity. In 1948, trade among the Comecon member
states had been only 5%.[10] By the mid-1950s, due
to the efforts of the Comecon agency and the influence of the USSR, 80% of their total export
trade was with each other. This receded to 63% by
1966 and then remained steady in the 65% range into the 1970s.[11] Trade with the West showed a constant increase throughout the 1960s and 1970s, so
much so that the percentage of their mutual trade
dropped again below 60% by 1978.[12]

The attempt by the USSR to increase the ef-
fectiveness of the Comecon agency was supported by
the conservative leaders--Ulbricht in the GDR and
Gomulka in Poland, who wanted integration for political reasons. Much like the Russians, they be-
lieved that integration would make the eastern
bloc more monolithic.[13] The GDR was less interested in trade benefits: it was able to satisfy
most of its trade needs on a bilateral bargaining
basis with its two major trade partners, the USSR
and the FRG. The GDR opposed internal reforms
aiming at a program for the furtherance of unplan-
ned trade, the development of a "collective currency" which would eventually be convertible into
national currencies, and a study of foreign trade
pricing.[14]

As a result of extended Comecon activities,
some major innovations in joint investment and
joint enterprise agreements took place in the late
1950s. The GDR helped finance the building of new
mines in Poland, taking repayment and interest in
coal deliveries rather than currency. Hungary and
the GDR partially financed chemical projects in
Rumania. None of the joint investment projects
involved the USSR. All agreements were bilateral
or trilateral and were negotiated without substantial assistance from CMEA agencies.[15]

The GDR, like the other East bloc nations,
had to make adjustments in its former production
patterns. During the years of heavy Soviet con-

trol, central plans which set the guidelines for what was to be produced and what to be traded were developed for each country. These plans made it necessary for some of the countries to reorganize their established production and trade patterns. In the case of the GDR and Czechoslovakia, it is obvious that industrialization was geared into channels most beneficial to the Soviet Union. East German engineering, for example, had traditionally been oriented towards production of highly finished equipment, such as precision and optical instruments, printing, and food processing, for which material was imported from the western part of Germany. But to meet the preferential demand of the USSR during and after the reparation period, the GDR had to shift its output pattern towards heavy machinery and equipment. In 1975, this category constituted 50% of the GDR's total exports.[16] Before WW II, manufactured consumer goods had held the leading place in exports. They receded now into second place (15% of total exports in 1975) behind machinery and equipment. The predominance of capital goods exports has been influenced by pulls in two opposite directions: on the one hand, by the internal demand for investment goods; on the other, by the demand in foreign markets and the need for foreign currency.

On the import side, there is heavy reliance on foreign raw materials, consisting of primary products such as food, fuel, and other basics. The GDR's dependence on imports of basic growth materials, such as rolled steel, non-ferrous metals, hard coal, and metallurgical coke for vital industries, makes the GDR very vulnerable. Imports of fuels and raw materials constituted 5% of the total imports in 1975; food stuffs imports amounted to 22.6% of total imports, a trend which has not changed significantly in the second half of the 1970s.[17]

Due to the separation from West Germany, the GDR had to redirect her trade towards eastern Europe. It renewed some of the old trade links with Czechoslovakia and Poland, and opened a certain amount of exchange with the Balkan states. As mentioned above, the USSR became the major trade partner of the GDR. The political isolation of the GDR's regime in the world outside the bloc, especially in the 1950s and 1960s, and the increasingly complementary nature of the economies of the Soviet Union and the GDR tended to extend the GDR's dependence on intra-bloc trade. In return, the GDR has occupied the first place among the Soviet Union's customers since the 1950s. The USSR, however, mostly supplies the Comecon area with raw materials rather than industrial commodities. In spite of all the drawbacks and obstacles, the GDR has become the principal intra-bloc exporter.

When discussing the trade of the GDR, the special arrangement with the Federal Republic of Germany cannot be overlooked. The so-called Berlin Agreement of 1951 gave special status to the trade between the two Germanies. Their trade relations are treated as if they were intra-German trade, although all commercial dealings need special permission according to the Berlin Accord. This agreement, amended in 1960 and 1968 in consideration of later developments, is still the basis for all intra-German trade.[18] When the Rome Treaty for the European Economic Community (EEC) was set up in 1957, the trade between the two German states received special treatment. Under the protocol of the Rome Treaty, trade with the GDR is technically classified as "intra-German" and is therefore exempt from tariffs and levies which fall on trade with other non-EEC countries.

The Berlin Agreement between the two Germanies states that only goods produced in the currency areas of the Deutsche Mark (DM) or the Mark of the GDR can be exchanged. The settling of accounts between the two currency areas is conducted in bilateral clearing by the two central banks. The clearing is not executed in the currencies of the two states, but in units of account (1 UA = 1 DM).[19] The prices of intra-German trade are based on the market prices of the FRG.

In the process of clearing, the accounts can
be overdrawn free of interest up to a certain
amount. This credit arrangement is referred to as
the Swing. The Swing has been repeatedly increased since 1950. In June 1968 a new arrangement for
the determination of the size of the credit went
into effect. The new agreement, effective until
1975, stipulated that the size of the Swing be determined at the beginning of each year as 25% of
the amount of payments made in the previous year
by the GDR. In 1974 this agreement was extended
until 1981; however, a ceiling of 855 million UA
was established.[20] In the past, only the GDR has
taken advantage of this credit availability by
overdrawing on the account. Because the trade between the GDR and the FRG does not constitute foreign trade, commercial goods and agricultural products imported from the GDR can enter the FRG free
of tariffs. In the same way, the GDR does not
levy tariffs on imports from the FRG.

As a result of the special consideration given
intra-German trade in the Treaty of Rome, the GDR
enjoys great privileges within the European Economic Community. Its products can enter the Community free of tariffs and quotas through the FRG.
Other EEC members have viewed this arrangement,
which also gives FRG goods privileged access to the
GDR, with misgiving, but have been unable to persuade the FRG to drop it. Several EEC members have
protested especially in the area of agricultural
products. Since only products produced in the GDR
can enter EEC markets through the FRG, the GDR has
exported many of its farm products to the FRG and
filled its domestic needs by purchases from other
socialist countries. Thus other Comecon countries
have also indirectly benefited from this intra-
German trade.[21] But just as the EEC members question the intra-German arrangement, the other Comecon nations also protest that the GDR has an advantage by being able to export tariff-free to the
FRG and thus to the EEC, while the other Comecon
nations face the EEC tariff and quota walls.

The intra-German trade, however, must be brought into perspective by comparing it to the total trade volume of the FRG. In 1978, trade with the GDR amounted to about 1.8% of the total external volume of the FRG.[22] Among all the trade partners of the Federal Republic, the GDR is only in 10th place. For the GDR, however, the Federal Republic is, after the Soviet Union, the second largest trade partner; trade with the FRG represents approximately 9% of the total trade volume of the GDR.[23]

Although the GDR is trying to become less dependent on the Federal Republic, this special arrangement with the FRG enables the GDR to pay less attention to trade with the European Economic Community and the West in general than is the case for the other East bloc nations. The intra-bloc-oriented view of the GDR is not necessarily shared, at least not to the same extent, by the other members of Comecon. Poland and Rumania, for example, are actively seeking trade agreements through GATT (General Agreement on Tariffs and Trade). Rumania is the most outwardly oriented of the group and the only Comecon member belonging to the International Monetary Fund.

Most of the Comecon members are actively trying to obtain improved trade relations with the EEC. Before 1973, most commercial agreements between Comecon and EEC members were between individual nations. However, EEC regulations which went into effect in 1973 prevent any further bilateral trade deals between Comecon countries and the individual members of the EEC; EEC countries now have to negotiate and settle agreements with the socialist states collectively. As a result, the negotiations between Comecon and the EEC on an institutional basis were stepped up, with the hope of reaching a basis for agreement in 1980. The greatest difficulty in reaching any kind of accord springs from the fact that, on the one side, Comecon has never officially recognized the EEC, and, on the other, that the EEC claims that Comecon lacks the legal power to speak for its member coun-

tries or sign trade contracts for them. The EEC
insists that any trade deals would have to be
signed between the EEC and the governments of the
East European nations.

As we have seen, the GDR holds a special position within the Comecon camp. This special position and the political philosophy of the leadership contribute to an attitude of aloofness in
this dispute between Comecon and the EEC. All indications seem to suggest that the policy of the
GDR leadership will not change very much in this
respect. Most likely, the GDR will remain more
Comecon- and intra-bloc-oriented than the other
European members of the bloc. It will probably
also side with the USSR in a more conservative attitude and reluctance towards reform and innovation in regard to trade policies and greater involvement with the West. Reforms which would de-
centralize operations might increase the influence
of economic professionals and erode government
control. Furthermore, there is the danger that
economic liberalization would bring political and
intellectual liberalization in its wake. Neither
the Soviet Union nor the GDR are interested in any
measures which might reduce intra-bloc economic
interdependence and cause a shift in imports from
the eastern bloc to western markets. Nevertheless,
given the economic developments in Europe during
the 1970s, interdependence and interrelatedness
between all these countries, socialist or capitalist, are bound to grow, unless there are drastic
developments in world politics.

Fairleigh Dickinson University

Notes

[1] Franklyn D. Holzman, International Trade
Under Communism - Politics and Economics (New
York: Basic Books, 1976), p. 68.

57

[2] _Europa Year Book 1979_ (London: Europa Publications Ltd.), I, 162.

[3] K. Weisskopf, "Progress of the Comecon Integration Programme," in _Comecon: Progress and Prospects_, Colloquium March 16-18, 1977 (Brussels: Nato-Directorate of Economic Affairs, Series No. 6, 1977), p. 27.

[4] Barry Bracewill-Milnes, _Eastern and Western European Economic Integration_ (New York: St. Martin's Press, 1976), p. 194.

[5] Holzman, p. 75.

[6] Holzman, p. 75.

[7] Martin Schnitzer, _East and West Germany: A Comparative Economic Analysis_ (New York/Washington/London: Praeger, 1972), p. 22.

[8] Schnitzer, p. 22.

[9] Holzman, p. 76.

[10] Michael Kaser, _Comecon: Integration Problems of the Planned Economies_ (London/New York/Toronto: Oxford University Press, 1967), p. 142.

[11] Marie Lavigne, _The Socialist Economies of the Soviet Union and Europe_, trans. T.G. Waywell (White Plains, N.Y.: International Arts and Sciences Press, Inc., 1974), p. 34. Cf. Z.M. Fallenbuchl, "The Commodity Composition of Intra-Comecon Trade and the Industrial Structure of the Member Countries," in _Comecon: Progress and Prospect_, p. 109.

[12] _United Nations Yearbook of International Trade Statistics and Department of Commerce 1979_ (New York: United Nations, 1980).

[13] Wolfgang F. Stolper, _The Structure of the East German Economy_ (Cambridge, Mass.: Harvard University Press, 1960), p. 11.

[14] Holzman, p. 119.

[15] Holzman, p. 82.

[16] Fallenbuchl, p. 111.

[17] Fallenbuchl, p. 111. Trade statistics recently released by the U.N. still report 1974 levels for the GDR. Some insight can be gained by analyzing the statistics reported by the major trade partners of the GDR, which suggest that the trend has not changed significantly.

[18] "Innerdeutscher Handel," Unterrichtung durch die Bundesregierung, Deutscher Bundestag, 7. Wahlperiode, Drucksache 7/420, March 28, 1973, p. 17.

[19] Unterrichtung durch die Bundesregierung, p. 17.

[20] Siegfried Kupper, "Innerdeutscher Handel," DDR Handbuch, ed. Peter C. Ludz (Cologne: Wissenschaft und Politik, 1979), p. 535.

[21] "The Hidden Tenth," The Economist, Nov. 6, 1976, p. 70.

[22] Hansjürgen Schierbaum, Intra-German Relations, Reihe Politologie/Soziologie (Munich: tuduv Verlagsgesellschaft, 1980), p. 52.

[23] Schierbaum, p. 52. For detailed statistical data, compare BMWI (Mitteilungen des Bundesministers für Wirtschaft), Tagesnachrichten, Aug. 24, 1979, pp. 2-8.

Rudolf Bahro's <u>Die Alternative</u> and the
Concept of <u>Cultural Revolution</u>

James Knowlton

The 1977 West German publication of Rudolf
Bahro's radical critique of GDR society caused an
unusually strong reaction on the part of GDR officials.[1] Bahro was arrested, charged with espio-
nage activities, and sentenced to a prison term of
eight years. After having served a little more
than two years of his sentence, he was released in
a general amnesty. He is now living in the Federal Republic.

The initial severity of the GDR's reaction is
no doubt a result of the book's political ambition.
Bahro doesn't stop at a historical-critical analysis of his society, but rather offers a radical
alternative: the revolutionary restructuring of
GDR society carried out under the guidance of an
envisioned new "League of Communists" (<u>Bund der
Kommunisten</u>).

Another unusual aspect of the Bahro affair is
Bahro's background. Bahro was not only a member
of the artistic-scientific-academic elite, but also a member of the SED apparatus, a party member
and economic functionary.[2] The importance of
Bahro's political background should not be overlooked, for it has provided him with the technical
insight necessary to design a radical alternative
and to support it with first-hand knowledge and
experience.

This point of departure is of considerable
importance as Bahro's book not only attempts to

61

challenge the self-understanding of "really existing socialism";[3] it offers a fundamental and im-
manent critique of Marxism-Leninism in practice--
a critique capable of reopening the Marxist realm
of discourse within a philosophical framework able
to transcend the officially sanctioned version of
dialectical materialism and to clearly illuminate
the gap between concrete socialist potential and
everyday GDR reality.

For Bahro, really existing socialism, his
word for the social formations in the Soviet-inspired countries, has only achieved a superficial
transformation of capitalism. The domination of
man over man has remained unchanged, alienation
and subalternation (Subalternität) among the working masses are still a widespread affliction.
How, asks Bahro, could a societal structure claim-
ing to overcome capitalism have preserved so many
of the negative aspects of capitalist society? It
must be noted that Bahro avoids the pitfalls of
the "new class," i.e., the primarily bureaucratic
explanation, nor does he seek an answer in a kind
of deformation theory.[4] For Bahro, the shortcomings of really existing socialism are the result
of an intensified and rigid division of labor.

Bahro elucidates his point with a hypotheti-
cal situation well worth quoting: "Let's assume
the necessary quantity of produced goods were
available; let's also figure with the demise of
the capitalist system of production. Then we can
see with all clarity that equality in the distribution of material goods and educational opportunities is not an adequate lever to produce an abun-
dance of free individuals."[5] Freedom and unfreedom are not determined by the possession of goods
or the availability of education. Alienation and
subalternation can clearly not be overcome by a
more equitable distribution of wealth and social
mobility. The negative manifestations apparent in
capitalist and socialist societies are evidently
rooted in a deeper structure inherent to both societal formations.

62

Alienation and subalternation must be seen in the total context of the social reproduction process. Alienation, after all, is the estrangement and exclusion from the complex totality of society, a process which manifests itself in the inability to mentally reproduce those relationships which together constitute a given society. The inability to mentally mediate between the individual as subject and the objective whole leads, objectively, to social fragmentation and, subjectively, to a feeling of hopelessness and passivity, of unfreedom.

The root of these problems can be found in the division of labor and its reflection in the consciousness of the members of society. For Bahro, people who have to concentrate all their energies each and every day on activities which require "relatively low degrees and isolated fields of mental coordination" (p. 208) must, by necessity, be excluded from high-level decision-making processes, as they have never been able to develop the requisite ability to apprehend and think abstractly. These people "fundamentally belong to the oppressed of a given society" (p. 208).

By definition, social classes in really existing socialism no longer stem from the private ownership of the means of production. Yet, according to Bahro, the GDR is clearly a society which is characterized by the existence of classes: "As long as work takes up all or almost all the time of its members, society is necessarily divided into classes. . . . The law of labor division is thus the basis of class division" (p. 164). Socialist revolution meant a transformation in the realm of ownership of the means of production as well as the socialization of those means. But socialization has not brought about an appropriation of the totality of the social connections by the people. Instead, the capitalist managerial functions were taken over by an educated elite, leaving the essential societal relationships fundamentally intact, while at the same time eliminating private ownership of these means of production.

The universal nationalization which led to the present social formation in the GDR resulted in the managerial functions of capitalist society simply being appropriated by the state in their existing form. The effect is a rigid hierarchy of power and social control which excludes members in the lower realms of the structure from the decision-making process by making inaccessible to them the flow of information needed to grasp the complex totality of society. The net effect is that the state has appropriated the means of production and consequently the power residing in them. "The elimination of private ownership of the means of production has by no means meant their transformation into public ownership. Instead, the entire society stands, without property, vis-à-vis its machinery of state" (p. 12).

For Bahro, the particular development of Soviet socialism under Lenin and Stalin--a development which became decisive for all Soviet-inspired countries--is not the result of a deformation of Marxist theory, but the necessary consequence of the pre-industrial stage of that country's productive forces.[6] "The state as disciplinarian of society" (Lenin) allowed a rapid breakthrough into the twentieth century. Bahro sees the Russian Revolution as the re-formation of pre-capitalist peoples for their own--non-capitalist--way to industrialism. Communism presupposes mature industrialism as well as the creation of an adequate material base for general socialization and public appropriation. State repression in the countries with really existing socialism is, in the last analysis, a function of those countries' industrial underdevelopment, "more precisely, the task of overcoming this underdevelopment actively by an 'anorganic' restructuring, while maintaining national identity" (p. 148).

The special role of the Party as the vanguard of the working masses has inevitably kept these masses in tutelage through the creation of an ideological and administrative apparatus which transcends the state (an Überstaatsapparat) and which,

64

in its hierarchial rigidity, has reinforced the social hierarchy already evident in the present form of social reproduction.

In describing the intricate linkage of Party and state, Bahro is fond of using church-related analogies: "The dictatorship of the Politburo is a disastrous exaggeration of the bureaucratic principle, since the party apparatus, which is beholden to it, is, at the same time, church hierarchy and super state [Überstaat] in one. The entire structure is quasi-theocratic. For the core of political power is state power, with the constant tendency toward inquisition, such that the Party itself is its own political police: the party apparatus as the core of state power can only mean a secularized civitas dei. . . ." (p. 288).

Thus the Party and its various extensions are among the decisive impediments to the development toward true emancipation. The Party is apologist and protector of the alienated social formation which Bahro sees in all countries with really existing socialism. Communists in such parties are, as he notes, "organized against themselves and against the people" (p. 294).

Bahro tends to view the phenomena of alienation and subalternation according to a cybernetic model. The relationship of individuals to the whole, of the various social strata to the state and its apparatus, can be subsumed in a model describing the flow of information in society: "The organized domination of social cooperation on the basis of the division of labor is, from the very beginning, an information problem, the problem inherent in a structure of consciousness which manifests itself as a relationship of persons to each other"(p. 177). The greater the degree of conscious cooperation within the social totality, the lesser the degree of alienation, of domination present. As long as individuals are not capable of gaining an overview of the whole, they must, by necessity, be excluded from higher levels of social synthesis.

65

The hierarchy in the division of labor is reflected in the hierarchy of information couplings performed on the various social levels. The entire process mirrors, as Bahro sees it, the structure of the material process of reproduction and is, in turn, mirrored by the hierarchically structured degrees of consciousness of this process present in the society. The character of class structure in GDR society is thus not solely a function of the social status level or type of work performed, but rather of conscious self-reflection, in varying degrees, of the social totality. Clearly, a better distribution of social wealth will not alter this kind of social structure, for consciousness as the decisive cause and effect of social structure can only be transformed by a radical change in the division of consciously reflected knowledge of the social reproduction process as a whole.

Really existing socialism is a societal form in which the great mass of people are readily susceptible to manipulation by the political upper echelon, which has hoarded and dominated the flow of information. "Independent of its concrete form and independent of the degree of social parasitism at the pole of social power, exploitation and repression consist of robbing the producers of the power of decision and control of their material life" (pp. 177f.).

Changing a hierarchical structure of consciousness that permeates all levels of society and determines the degree of alienation and subordination will not be a simple matter. The question arises: Which elements of society can be the motor of social change? Certainly not the working masses, who are bound up in virtual enslavement to the conditions of material reproduction. And not the existing Party. For the Party has a vested interest in maintaining the status quo as an assurance that its power will remain unbroken. In fact, Bahro views the Party with great bitterness. Should not the Party, he asks, which for over a hundred years has been the vanguard of emancipatory interests in capitalism, see its only task in overcoming alienation and social discontent? This would mean the appropriation of all governmental, managerial, educational, etc., functions by society itself, it would mean "the repeal [Rücknahme] of the state by society" (p. 44). It would mean closing the gap between party apparatus and people, "the positive expropriation of the bureaucrat," as Bahro calls it (p. 253).

In the third chapter of his book, Bahro elucidates the strategy of a communist alternative which could lead to general emancipation. The first step in this direction would be the creation of a new party which could attract oppositional interests and form a loose association of people dedicated to radically transforming their society.

We have seen that Bahro views his society in terms of a structure of consciousness. Clearly, only those in possession of a richly developed consciousness of the social totality will be in a position to understand the ills of their society and to formulate an alternative. Bahro describes two kinds of consciousness: surplus and absorbed. Absorbed consciousness is that which is thoroughly institutionalized in the existing apparatus of Party and state or in the work process, and thus not available for emancipatory interests. In contrast, there exists a large quantum of surplus consciousness, i.e. consciousness in excess of that absorbed in work and everyday life; this is found primarily among the academic-artistic elite, but also among disgruntled Party ideologists who see the hopelessness of present developmental trends. Where absorbed consciousness is thoroughly institutionalized, surplus consciousness is kept carefully dispersed and prevented from political articulation and organization. Acts of state repression in the last ten years are a good example of this.

Thus, although a number of oppositional intellectuals are in favor of change, there exists, as yet, no vehicle to represent their interests.

To alleviate this, Bahro suggests a loose organization of like-minded intellectuals, which he calls the "League of Communists"(<u>Bund der Kommunisten</u>). The League would not have as its goal the creation of a rigidly organized party structure--the danger would be too great that it would simply reproduce the existing party apparatus-- nor would it strive to take over governmental functions in their present form. The main task of the League of Communists would be to act as a catalyst for social change; it would "take aim not so much at the idea of the [old] Party, but at its apparatus, at its addiction to the state, which is embodied in the party apparatus"(p. 424). The new organization must begin by inspiring societal forces and organizations to become a counterforce to the state. As this counterforce grows, it will yield a major oppositional movement equipped with a specific revolutionary program.

The first point of the League's program will be to convince the populace that the existing Party has abandoned its position as a representative of emancipatory interests and thus has no true political constituency. The political power of the "statist," i.e., party apparatus side, must be split; the League of Communists must attempt to gain political and social hegemony.

Because of its undogmatic nature, the new party will have to cope with various political tendencies, and will, perhaps, even be divided into factions. But this represents no problem for Bahro, as long as the League does not assume an official state function. The League must be subject to direct societal control through a complicated system of feedback regulation.

The League cannot be a working class party, nor can it favor any one particular group over another, for a party of this kind must have the entire society as its constituency. In fact, Bahro envisions a near-metaphysical mission for the League: its goal must be to "mediate a linkage of the individual with a meaningful whole, to open

up space for self-realization in super-personal
historical dimensions" (pp. 444f.).

Once established, the party must strive to
organize for the transformation which Bahro calls
"cultural revolution"--a movement which will lead
to the socialization and democratization of the
entire social reproduction process. Bahro sees
the present GDR policy of actively forcing economic growth as achieving solely the reproduction and
petrification of social domination. The resultant
increase of material goods serves only to fulfill
what Bahro calls "compensatory gratification."
The need for compensatory gratification arises
from the sense of meaninglessness rampant in both
capitalist and socialist formations and reflects
the concrete impossibility of developing truly human interests. The cycle of increased production
and consumption serves to further tie the working
masses to their present condition, while solidify-
ing the grip of the apparatus.

Solutions cannot be found in a stepped-up attempt to satisfy compensatory interests, for this
can only lead to the reproduction of the very system which has created these interests and thus to
a more intense level of alienation. The net effect of this is the deadening of truly human interests and the increased destruction of our physical environment. One of the goals of the cultural
revolution must, then, be to break the cycle of increased production to fulfill the increased need
for compensatory gratification.

Since many of the problems confronting really
existing socialism are rooted in the vertical division of labor, one of the first points of Bahro's
program is an equitable distribution of work by
means of which all people would share tasks on all
functional levels of socially necessary work.
This might sound vaguely utopian, but the necessity is quite evident, since a redistribution of
work could produce levels of consciousness of and
responsibility toward the social whole sufficient
to begin eliminating alienation and subalterna-

tion. The universality and versatility of all
human beings is the guaranty for the presence of
the subjective--i.e., unrealized--forces of productivity necessary to transform the system of
really existing socialism into true socialism.
If the division of labor can be broken, the potential for the self-realization of human interests
can be developed, and the system of class division
and social fragmentation can be transformed. The
prerequisite is that all people enjoy the same
level of higher education presently available to
a limited number of people only.

Thus Bahro envisions a new type of worker,
who, although responsible for a specialized branch
of production or distribution, must dedicate himself for a specified amount of time to all functional levels at his place of work. And the same
principle is valid for people active in managerial, scientific or supervisory roles. They, too,
would be required to spend a specific amount of
time working directly in the operation of machinery or on similar functional levels. "Let's imagine . . . a uniform type of production worker, who,
within the framework of a given area of specialization, devotes himself, alternately, to all functional levels of work. People who occupy themselves with the development and design of machines,
technologies or products will be able to adapt
much more quickly to the demands of mass production if they are also active in operational technological supervision" (p. 331). And the relatively short time, perhaps one-third of the overall work time, devoted to operating production machinery will, in addition, be useful for the im-
provment of the work process.

Clearly, the prerequisite for all people participating on all levels of socially necessary
work would be a fundamental restructuring of the
educational system to allow--in fact require--all
people to acquire a general education on the university level. Bahro brushes aside questions of
whether society can afford the further years of
lost productivity for each person involved in the

70

education process by posing his own rhetorical question: Can society afford not to?

Under closer scrutiny, however, this problem begins to dissolve, since universal education could be realized successively and since the result would, no doubt, be an increase in labor discipline and productivity. The acquisition of a comprehensive philosophical, artistic, and scientific-technical education can open up access to any activity, thus enabling the person to participate actively on all levels of social synthesis, from the lowest forms of mass production to the highest levels of administrative and scientific-technical activity.

Of course, bureaucratic and statist elements will oppose these changes with all means available to them. As Bahro sees it, the impetus for real change must be initiated by increasing the number of disenchanted and disenfranchised intellectuals in the society, that is, those elements in possession of surplus consciousness. A large-scale increase of surplus consciousness can only be created by raising the educational level of the general populace, thus creating a pool of non-absorbed "accumulated qualification," which, stifled by the inflexible organization of really existing socialism, will militate toward change as a means of realizing its own established, but untapped potential. The dissident groupings will be, much as they are today, largely disorganized and fragmented, but the potential for change is clearly available and can be organized and directed by the League of Communists.

In the final chapters of his book, Bahro discusses the economics of cultural revolution. One of the first goals of the cultural revolution will be to shift interest from, as Bahro terms it, the production of quantity to the production of quality, from material goods as a saturation of compensatory interests to production aimed at the development of rich individuality and human realization. Instead of surplus value or product, disposable time, time for personal development will be the goal of socialized production.

The determination of need which today guides the process of production and distribution is based upon reification, the hopeless attempt to achieve meaning in life by increased material consumption, by surrounding oneself with material goods and projecting one's own individuality into these goods. "I am what I own" is the maxim of this kind of society, and the GDR is no exception to such trends. A redetermination of need such as that proposed by Bahro would allow a reduction in the necessary work time and thus free up available time for self-realization not bound to the consumption of material goods.

Alienation and subalternation are, as Bahro points out, results of estrangement from the social community. The alternative to perpetual alienation is, as Bahro sees it, the establishment of wide-ranging collectives and federations, in which people holistically pursue the specific goals of social reproduction which make up their lives. Here, decentralization and self-determination in small groups replace the present "centralistic organization, which is particularly hostile to individuality and private initiative" (p. 526).

What Bahro envisions here is more than a democratic reorganization of the structure of production and distribution. The communal system which he describes means the restructuring of the entire society in a form, which, viewed from today's perspective, might seem unthinkable, but would require from all individuals active social participation on all levels. "One can easily imagine how the population . . . would share the various activities from planning and statistics to cleaning and garbage collection, from applied research to shipping their products, from all types of teaching to repairing machinery, from constructing new buildings to the distribution of goods and services. . . ." (pp. 528f.). Each commune would be a social microcosm in itself as well as a ter-

72

ritorial unit with certain production goals measured and normed in terms of input and output. National governing functions would be assumed by representatives appointed by the communes to serve on a governing council and make decisions on national policy.

This kind of organization would allow for the liberation of women from their presently predetermined social roles and eventually lead to the decay of the nuclear family. Bahro sees the nuclear family as one of the ills of modern society. He calls it "the psychological structure factory" of society, the place where relationships of domination are produced, transmitted, and reproduced.[7]

In conclusion I would like to discuss briefly Bahro's own assessment of the concrete potential of his program being realized in the GDR. Bahro insists that the official rejection of his book masks a deeper interest which is wide-spread among members of the ruling apparatus. First, he points out that the State Security Service (Staatssicherheitsdienst, popularly called Stasi) knew quite well what he was writing and yet let him write for some five years without interruption--five years in which Bahro gave interviews to West German magazines and TV. And after his arrest the official interrogations quickly turned into discussions of Bahro's alternative conception. In fact, one Stasi officer admitted to Bahro that there were "Bahro fans even in this building."[8]

Before its publication in West Germany, Bahro distributed 75 mimeographed copies of his manuscript to friends and like-minded colleagues. The process of distribution and redistribution was assiduously investigated by the Stasi, but there were no official repercussions for those involved. Thus Bahro feels that, in his absence (he believes that his continued presence in the GDR would attract too much public attention and have a negative effect on the distribution of his ideas), his alternative view will find more adherents and begin to achieve fruition.

Notes

[1] Rudolf Bahro, <u>Die Alternative. Zur Kritik des real existierenden Sozialismus</u> (Cologne/ Frankfurt/M.: Europäische Verlagsanstalt, 1977). Bahro's book was not published in the GDR. It should also be noted that Bahro was arrested in 1977 following the publication of excerpts of his book by <u>Der Spiegel</u>. In an interview in <u>Der Spiegel</u> (22 October 1979, pp. 29-33) Bahro discusses details of his arrest, interrogation, and incarceration. See also <u>Rudolf Bahro: Eine Dokumentation</u> (Cologne/Frankfurt/M.: Europäische Verlagsanstalt, 1977.

[2] In the early 1960s Bahro edited the magazine <u>Forum</u>, organ of the Free German Youth. At the time of his arrest, he was bureau chief in the VEB Gummi-Kombinat, Berlin. See Hugh Mosley, "The New Communist Opposition: Rudolf Bahro's Critique of 'Really Existing Socialism,'" <u>New German Critique</u>, No. 15 (1978), p. 26.

[3] 'Really existing socialism' for the German 'real existierender Sozialismus' is perhaps an inadequate translation. In using this formulation I follow the tradition established by the <u>New German Critique</u>, where articles by David Bathrick ("The Politics of Culture: Rudolf Bahro and the Opposition in the GDR," <u>NGC</u>, No. 15 [1978], pp. 3ff.) and Hugh Mosley ("The New Communist Opposition") have consistently used this terminology.

[4] See David Bathrick, "The Politics of Culture," esp. pp. 19f.

[5] Bahro, <u>Die Alternative</u>, p. 144. All translations of Bahro are my own. Page numbers referring to <u>Die Alternative</u> are given in the text in

parentheses.

[6] See Bathrick, "The Politics of Culture," esp. pp. 19f. See also R. Bahro, "Die Herrschaft des Apparats muß gründlich unterminiert werden: Rudolf Bahro interviewt sich selbst," <u>Deutschland Archiv</u>, 10, No. 11 (1977), 1104-1112.

[7] In Bahro's discussion of the reorganization of society into communes, the idea of <u>Gemeinschaft</u> (community) is clearly implied, and it would be interesting to trace the development of the concept <u>Gemeinschaft</u>, which has played an important role from early anti-democratic and fascist ideologies, through early social democratic and Marxist thought to Bahro. Frank Trommler, in his article "Die Kulturpolitik der DDR und die kulturelle Tradition des deutschen Sozialismus," in <u>Literatur und Literaturtheorie in der DDR</u>, ed. Peter Uwe Hohendahl and Patricia Herminghouse (Frankfurt/ M.: Suhrkamp, 1976), pp. 13-72, indicates that there is such a tradition in German social democratic thought and sketches its development in the GDR.

[8] "Ich weiß, ich kann völlig abrutschen," <u>Der Spiegel</u>, 22 October 1977, p. 27.

The Kirchenpolitik of the
German Democratic Republic and the
Evangelical Churches, 1968-78

Robert F. Goeckel

This paper proposes to sketch the historical
background to the current church-state relationship in the GDR, analyze the motivations involved,
and discuss the effects of what may be called a
relationship of mixed conflict and cooperation.

I. "In Christ there is no East or West"---sometimes

In my remarks I shall focus on the primary
Protestant denomination in the GDR, i.e., the Evangelical (Lutheran) churches. Though the Roman
Catholic Church (11% of all religious identifiers
in the GDR) and the independent Protestant denomi-
nations (1-2%) pose in some ways more interesting
problems, the Evangelical churches (87%) without
doubt bulk most heavily in the state's Kirchenpolitik.

The structure of the Evangelical churches consists of eight provincial churches (Landeskirchen),
reflecting the strong Länder tradition in German
history. In turn, dating from the Prussian drive
for German unification in the nineteenth century,
five of the eight together form the Evangelical
Church of the Union (EKU). The remaining three
Landeskirchen, outside the Prussian sphere until
later in the nineteenth century, have retained
their particularistic, Lutheran traditions. In
1948 these eight Landeskirchen joined those in the
western zones in forming the loose umbrella organization, the Evangelical Church in Germany (EKD).

Until 1958 the GDR tolerated this all-German church organization. However, after the Military Chaplaincy Agreement between the EKD and the FRG army in 1958 and the building of the Wall in 1961, the state's wish for separation from the FRG churches became implicit. This did not take the form of a direct assault on the EKD, however, until 1966-67, when in the face of the first tentative moves toward Ostpolitik by the FRG under the Grand Coalition, the GDR recoiled. At that point, Ulbricht began sounding the death knell of EKD unity.

This campaign revealed two aspects of the pre-1969 tactics in the state's Kirchenpolitik. First, the Christian Democratic Union Party (East), long operating under the SED's discipline, served as the primary communicator and agitator of the state's policy to the church leadership and to the grass roots.

Second, the state sought to exploit the decentralized structure of the churches, using the willingness of Bishop Mitzenheim of Thuringia to deal with the state and make "progressive" pronouncements in order to pressure the other Landeskirchen, in this case toward separation from the EKD and Abgrenzung from West Germany.[1] This Mitzenheimpolitik in effect proved somewhat counterproductive, in that it alienated many church leaders and motivated them to seek to mitigate the danger from the state's "divide and conquer" strategy.

This motivation, though certainly a major factor in the churches' decision in 1968-69 to form the Federation of Evangelical Churches in the GDR (or Kirchenbund), does not provide the entire picture. Indeed, the formation of the Kirchenbund is better explained by the careful building of a fragile coalition of various often-conflicting factions of the church by the moderate tactician Bishop's Administrator Schönherr, future head of the Kirchenbund. For traditional Lutherans (Mitzenheim included), who had in December 1968 al-

ready severed ties with the all-German United
Evangelical Lutheran Churches in Germany, the ties
to the West German churches were weak; their Lutheran theology tended to deemphasize the link between organization and belief. The "progressive"
elements in the churches saw the separation from
the EKD in political terms, the prerequisite for
"intellectual new orientation" (Götting); though
concerned about the centralizing potential of the
Kirchenbund, they could not deny that the concur-
rent separation from the EKD represented progress.
The strongest opposition to the Kirchenbund developed in the EKU churches, especially in Berlin-
Brandenburg, for obvious reasons: for them, organization was more strongly linked to belief (especially since the Third Reich and the Barmen Declaration) and in practical terms their ties and dependence on the FRG churches were greater than the
Lutherans'. Yet, given their own Union tradition,
many saw in the formation of the Kirchenbund the
potential for overcoming the parochial organizational and the theological barriers characteristic
of the German Landeskirche tradition.

Although there appear to have been no direct
attempts at coercion by the state to force the
separation, there was no doubt a cooling of relations with certain church leaders, especially
those holding EKD offices (e.g., Bishops Krummacher, Greifswald, and Noth, Saxony-Dresden), and
harassment of inter-German church meetings. More
important than "punishment" in the churches' cal-
culations, it seems, was the denial of "rewards"
(e.g., state recognition of diaconical work, the
churches' right to retreats, church repair and
building of new churches, etc.) and the fear, based
on the ambiguity of the new 1968 constitution, of
discriminatory distribution of these "rewards" in
separate agreements with individual Landeskirchen.

The churches constituted the Kirchenbund officially on June 10, 1969. While protecting the
sovereignty of the individual Landeskirchen, the
Order of the new Kirchenbund formed a leadership
body commissioned to handle relations with the
state and the ecumenical relations of all eight

Landeskirchen. At its first synod in September 1969, the Lutherans, skeptical of the "Prussians" from the Union churches, concurred in Schönherr's selection as Chairman of the Conference of Church Leaderships (KKL) upon the selection of the Lutherans Oberkirchenrat Braecklein (Thuringia) and Bishop Noth (Saxony-Dresden) as speaker of the Synod and deputy to Schönherr, respectively, and a tacit commitment to a Lutheran successor to Schönherr.[2] The choice of Schönherr, it was hoped, would help persuade the doubting Thomases in the EKD and reassure the FRG churches (given Schönherr's symbolically important role in Berlin-Brandenburg-East and his personal ties with Bishop Scharf of Berlin-Brandenburg) of the continuing "spiritual community" delineated in Article 4,4 of the Order of the new Kirchenbund.

The state's initial reaction to the new Kirchenbund was a mixed one. On the one hand, it greeted the separation from the churches in the FRG and made salutatory statements regarding the Kirchenbund.[3] However, these were never unqualified endorsements; they were always couched in terms of satisfaction with the "continuing process among church leaders of clarification of their position in socialism" and coupled with admonitions regarding the interpretation of Article 4,4 and elimination of the remaining inter-German church ties (the EKU and the Landeskirche Berlin-Brandenburg).

There seem to have been three factors in the initial reluctance of the state to deal with the Kirchenbund. First, and clearly most important, the state was skeptical of the authenticity of the split with the EKD. Second, the state was unsure of the direction of the Kirchenbund in its relation with the state. Much depended on the leadership and control of the Kirchenbund. Though the choice of Schönherr no doubt reassured the state to a certain extent, it was unclear whether he would consolidate his position or what policy he would pursue in his new function. Finally, the state's Kirchenpolitik had until then been based

on a <u>Landeskirche</u> strategy, using the CDU and con-
ducting relations with the churches largely at the
regional (<u>Bezirk</u>) level. The state hesitated to
abandon the advantage and flexibility it had enjoyed with this approach. Nor could the inertia
inherent in this strategy be easily or readily
overcome (especially given the CDU's vested interest in it). Thus, for twenty months, until February 1971, the state withheld its blessings from
the new <u>Kirchenbund</u>.

II. <u>Socialist Blessings Bestowed</u>

On February 9, 1971, in a major address on
state policy, the Politburo member responsible for
<u>Kirchenpolitik</u>, Paul Verner, made the initial pub-
lic overture by the state to the new <u>Kirchenbund</u>.[4]
The Verner initiative is less important for its
substantive contribution to the state's policy,
than for its procedual breakthrough: the state's
quasi-recognition of the churches' new organization. The highly-publicized meetings of State
Secretary for Church Questions Seigewasser with
<u>Kirchenbund</u> and <u>Landeskirche</u> representatives in
February and March represent the official manifestation of this recognition.[5] The Verner-Seigewas-
ser initiatives represent the first steps on the
road to a rapprochement with the <u>Kirchenbund</u>.

Several factors contributed to the state's
forthcomingness toward the <u>Kirchenbund</u>: the continuing process of organizational separation from
the FRG churches; the entrance and developing of
profile on the ecumenical stage by the <u>Kirchenbund</u>,
the internal consolidation of the <u>Kirchenbund</u>, the
tactful diplomacy of its leadership, and the So-
viets' interest in détente with the FRG.

On the inter-German level, the GDR churches'
remaining ties with the FRG churches were further
loosened under state pressure. The EKU, under the
chairmanship of Bishop Fränkel (Görlitz), resisted
a total break in 1970, but did make some practical
moves at adaptation to the inter-German realities.
It became clear that other members in the EKU hi-

erarchy, notably Schönherr and Krummacher, would likely push for greater separation in the near future. Berlin-Brandenburg (East) under Schönherr's direction was also pursuing the path of gradual organizational independence. Finally, the Kirchenbund's interpretation of Article 4,4, implying only spiritual community and not intellectual community as well, eventually satisfied the state.[6] Moreover, the state became more willing to tolerate these remaining all-German links, since other priorities superseded the state's desire for "clear separation."

Related to this continuing process of formal separation from the FRG churches was the Kirchenbund's presence on the ecumenical scene. The Kirchenbund and the GDR National Committee now assumed responsibility for the representation of the GDR Landeskirchen in the World Council of Churches and the Lutheran World Federation, respectively. This transition did not proceed as smoothly as the formation of the Kirchenbund itself, since for the most part, ecumenical relations require state approval. The state objected to some individuals involved in exchanges. And ecumenical activity carried with it the risk of increased informal inter-German contact, which in fact turned out to be the case. Nonetheless, the state accepted the risks, since in 1969-70 its foreign policy interest in gaining international legitimacy by means of an independent GDR representation in these international church organizations took overriding priority. In fact, the Kirchenbund's ability in ecumenical forums to strike a profile independent of, and at times at variance with the EKD (e.g., the divergence of their positions on the Anti-Racism Program of the WCC), no doubt redounded to its credit in the eyes of the state.[7]

The internal consolidation of the Kirchenbund was also important for the modus vivendi with the state. Schönherr and his protégé Stolpe consolidated their positions in the KKL and the Secretariat of the Kirchenbund, respectively. More importantly, the Landeskirchen became somewhat overshadowed, as they deferred to the umbrella organization, the Kirchenbund, in dealings with the state. This was most evident in the case of Thuringia after 1970, where Braecklein, Mitzenheim's successor as bishop, proved to be a strong supporter of the Kirchenbund and thereby brought the Thuringian Way into alignment with that of the other Landeskirchen, thus denying the state and the CDU the opportunity to "play" Thuringia off against the other Landeskirchen.[8] The state realized that it had to play ball with the Kirchenbund.

Moreover, the diplomacy of the Kirchenbund leadership also led the state to see the Kirchenbund as useful. Criticism of the state was, for the most part, limited to the churches' direct interests and communicated in private discussions or in synodal reports, not in more provocative letters to congregations. In public expressions, the Kirchenbund and Schönherr underscored its role as the "church within socialism."[9] While this concept is vague and subject to varying interpretations, it gave the state media-makers good copy for the public justification of the improving relationship. Moreover, certain expressions supportive of GDR foreign policy by Schönherr in 1970 found positive resonance with the state, which began to view the Kirchenbund and Schönherr as useful levers against wayward bishops and as an influence on the often conservative clergy and laity.[10]

Finally, although remaining determinative in the Kirchenpolitik, the foreign policy dictates of the GDR changed. The GDR was forced to follow the Soviet foreign policy dictates of détente with the FRG. Relaxation of church-state tensions in the GDR was designed to show the FRG the concrete effects of détente and help win Bundestag approval of the pending treaties with Moscow and Warsaw.

It should be noted that the recognition of the Kirchenbund in February 1971 reveals a certain continuity across the Ulbricht and Honecker periods in this policy of rapprochement with the Kir-

chenbund. However, under Ulbricht the emphasis
was on consolidation in face of Ostpolitik; com-
promises on inter-German church questions were re-
luctantly made, most likely at Soviet behest. Under Honecker, on the other hand, Abgrenzung has
receded somewhat into the background of the Kirchenpolitik, superseded by a more pragmatic orientation.

III. "I'm OK, you're OK."

The immediate "blessings" to the churches
from the new relationship were meager. In fact,
just prior to the February initiative, the Interi-
or Ministry introduced the Events Ordinance (Ver-
anstaltungsverordnung), which required the churches
to notify the local police of all activities not
directly related to worship. This requirement was
disputed by the churches, which argued that worship
must be interpreted more widely (to include con-
certs, for example) and that indeed they alone
should make this determination. The enforcement
of the Events Ordinance revealed the continuation
of a multiple-track state Kirchenpolitik: despite
the certain rapprochement at the highest levels,
on other tracks the state continued policies which
adversely affected church interests. Other bu-
reaucracies, nominally independent of the State
Secretary's Office, pursued policies which caused
tension with the churches (e.g., the Ministry for
Technical and Higher Education, which, in formulating the Third Higher Education Reform in 1970-
71, sought to integrate the theology sections more
into the universities' Marxist-Leninist curriculum
and the FDJ). Lower levels of state authority (e.
g., Bezirk Rostock) often pursued "hard lines"
vis-à-vis the individual Christian.[11] These mul-
tiple tracks gave the State Secretary some bureaucratic "cover" when confronted by the churches.

Nevertheless, although the hoped-for agreements did not materialize initially (probably due
to a certain inertial caution surrounding Honecker's assumption of power in May 1971), eventually
the new relationship bore fruit. A first sign was

the state's approval of a license for a newsletter
for the Kirchenbund, the Mitteilungsblatt, in late
1971. This was followed in December 1972 by an
agreement on the Sonderbauprogramm for small construction and repair projects on current structures, to be funded in large part by the EKD in
hard currency. The diaconical works of the churches, long tacitly tolerated by the state, were officially recognized as part of the national health
care system in a formal agreement with the Ministry of Health in April 1973. The state showed for
the first time a willingness, albeit in small, con-
fidential forums, to brief the Kirchenbund on
broad policy issues, such as abortion and European
security. Finally, in perhaps the most notable
achievement of the Kirchenbund's solidarity, private agreement was reached in April 1973 with the
state on the Events Ordinance, after two years of
stubborn, often public contention over the issue.[12]
Church retreats would remain exempt from notifica-
tion; church events of more secular character
would be announced to the police. Under the tacit
agreement typical of the new rapprochement, the
state did not repeal the ordinance, but simply
left it unenforced, subject to re-enforcement at
any time.

On the international level, previously fostered ecumenical ties were furthered even more.
Contacts with the Russian Orthodox Church were allowed (e.g., exchanges in 1972 and 1973, leading
to the Sagorsk theological discussions in 1974).
And slowly, contacts with the FRG churches became
less taboo, as shown by the state's permission,
after repeated refusals, for a mutual exchange of
visitors between the Synods of the EKD and the
Kirchenbund in 1973.

The state, of course, benefited from this new
relationship as well. The hard currency from the
building and diaconical arrangements is no small
factor in this equation for the state, just as the
large subsidies of the current accounts of the GDR
churches by the FRG churches (estimated at over
100 million DM yearly) have long been "tolerated"

by the state. The <u>Mitteilungsblatt</u> would help mobilize church opinion behind the <u>Kirchenbund</u> leadership and the new rapprochement. The regulation of the Events Ordinance was designed to end strife with the churches at all levels.

These pragmatic attempts to foster "peace on the church front" were in part derivative of the Soviet foreign policy interest in détente, in particular in the ratification of the Basic Treaty by the FRG and a positive image for the impending Helsinki deliberations. The churches' stature with the state increased with their continued tactful international diplomacy. Their support of the GDR's official positions on recognition and European security, their participation in the peace movement (though "flawed" by their refusal to become members in the Moscow-dominated Christian Peace Conference), and their support on Third World issues all found resonance with the state.[13]

IV. <u>Will</u> <u>it</u> <u>play</u> <u>in</u> <u>Zeitz</u> . . . <u>or</u> <u>Wandlitz</u>?

In April 1974 the Executive Board of the <u>Kirchenbund</u> discussed with Seigewasser the possibility of building churches in the vast new urban developments throughout the GDR, against which the SED had long held a firm line. Eventually, after establishing the EKD's restoration of the East Berlin Cathedral (desired by the state for nationalistic, aesthetic, and hard currency reasons) as the quid pro quo for this <u>Neubauprogramm</u>, the churches obtained state approval for it. In November 1974 the state dissolved the Federation of Evangelical Pastors in the GDR, a small group of "progressives" that had long been a thorn in the side of the church establishments. Schönherr's positive comments regarding the GDR and socialism at the 1974 <u>Kirchenbund</u> Synod on the occasion of the twenty-fifth anniversary of the GDR seemed to herald only increasing harmony between church and state.[14]

But within the churches all was not calm, nor bright. Although most agreed that the new relationship had yielded benefits to the churches, sources of discontent surfaced. Among the church elite, differences of opinion on the proper direction of the churches' relationship with the state, based on interest, theology, and personalities, developed. Some church leaders disagreed with the private diplomatic approach of Schönherr, feeling that the churches should more openly criticize the state. At the 1972 Kirchenbund Synod, the noted theologian Heino Falcke, urging a stance of "critical solidarity" toward the state, called for greater information and personal freedom as part of "improving socialism," a position anathema to the state, which squelched the publication of his address.[15] Bishop Fränkel (Görlitz), known for exercising more criticism than solidarity, repeatedly took positions antagonistic toward the state at the synods of his Landeskirche.[16] The traditional Lutherans, in turn, tended to view the Kirchenbund initiatives as violating the separation of the two kingdoms and were skeptical of the strategy implicit in the tactful public statements on socialism or certain GDR foreign policies: accepting GDR socialism, in order to work to change it. In addition they bore an historical resentment of the "Berlin syndrome," fearing domination by church authorities in Berlin. While weakening somewhat Schönherr's internal position in the Kirchenbund, such implicit criticism of Schönherr for being too diplomatic has paradoxically worked to his, and the Kirchenbund's advantage, by giving him additional credibility with the state as the more preferable alternative.

In the same way, divergence between church leadership and grass roots has aided Schönherr with the state. This divergence was grounded in the fact that the benefits from these agreements with the state accrued primarily to the institutional church, leaving the individual Christian unaffected or worse off. Some on the grass-roots level felt sold-out; most felt the leadership should push harder for their interests, if necessary publicly.

Three problems seem to have been especially troublesome to individual Christians. Most all-encompassing, and most knotty for an ideological state, was the problem of discrimination against Christians in the schools (and also necessarily in careers). Christians often felt discriminated against, either directly or indirectly (i.e., due to social class quotas, which disproportionately affect the generally higher social class Christians). Second, youth work and outreach work were made difficult for pastors. Any "unusual" approaches (e.g., canvassing, jazz worship, etc.) were problematic. Finally, those who chose the legally guaranteed status of conscientious objector and worked in unarmed military units were subject to discrimination in education and career. All of these issues affected largely the level of the individual Christian and were often raised more aggressively by the delegates to the synods in the 1970s than by the leadership in its annual reports.

They were raised most dramatically by the suicide burning of Pastor Brüsewitz in Zeitz in August 1976. It shattered the apparent peace and sent shock waves through both the churches and the state. Despite the SED's provocative dismissal of it as the act of a lunatic, it must be taken seriously as a manifestation of this gap between church hierarchy and grass roots, between the state's official line and the social reality.[17] Realizing this, the church leadership, as well as numerous SED comrades, rejected the SED's interpretation of the event and it has since sought greater communication with the grass roots, particularly with the pastors. The state, too, has learned; the March 6, 1978 initiative must in part be understood as the state's attempt to avoid such problems in the future by reducing this differential between its propagated line and social reality.

As the Brüsewitz affair indicates, the state is in reality also less than monolithic, although one seldom detects this. The CDU was not totally in agreement with its change in role after Febru-

ary 1971 (from antagonist of the church leadership
to mobilizer of economic/political support on the
local level and international representative of
the GDR). Major personnel changes were necessary
to accomplish it. Also, the cadre of academic
ideologues and researchers of scientific atheism,
most notably Olof Klohr from Jena, lost visibility.
However, bureaucratic and party ideologues were
not subject to this displacement. Segments of the
apparat concerned with education (i.e., the Ministry of Education and the FDJ), political stability
(i.e., the Ministry of the Interior and, needless
to say, the State Security Service), and defense
(i.e., the National People's Army) are more ideological and have been less amenable to rapprochement with the churches. Hard evidence of these
divisions remains missing, although indications
of schisms do sometimes appear (e.g., the divergence between Neues Deutschland and the regional
SED papers in their reporting of the March 6, 1978
meeting: the regional papers ignored some of Schönherr's more critical comments in their versions).

V. A Neo-Constantinian Church?

Political developments in 1975-78 weakened
the state and increased the recognition of the
need for greater compromise with the church.
First and foremost, the massive influx of West Germans after 1972 led, in the context of the economic slowdown after 1975 and the previous rising economic expectations, to feelings of relative depriv-
ation in the populace. In the context of Helsinki, these were bound to lead to political discontent. Second, the economic need of the state for
hard currency from western churches became more
acute with the world inflation-conditioned rise in
import prices, arguing for minimizing tensions
with the churches at all levels. Relatedly, given
the greater dedication and honesty of many Christian workers, the state's economic interest in
higher productivity counseled pragmatism rather
than ideologically based discrimination. Finally,
despite the great attention lavished on them, the
state had simply lost many of the youth. Social

problems common to capitalism, such as criminality and alcoholism, were not uncommon among the youth, sometimes spilling over into political protest (e.g., the riots on Alexanderplatz in October 1977). Augmenting this was the increasing vocalness of certain dissidents (e.g., Bahro, Havemann, Heym). Although this political instability was in great measure an effect of Helsinki and thus foreign policy-related, I would argue that the state's policy of rapprochement with the churches has increasingly shifted from one determined by foreign policy in the first half of the 1970s to one determined by domestic policy in the latter half of the decade.

In the context of this internal weakness, Honecker met on March 6, 1978 with the Executive Board of the Kirchenbund. This meeting brought tangible improvement for the grass-roots level, as well as further institutional benefits.[18] Yet, for the church the knotty problem remains: how to reconcile the dictates of its theology and history with the interests of the organization and those of the laity. Foreign policy positions taken on the basis of conscience may build credibility with the state, but weaken it with the grass roots (e.g., the Anti-Racism Program or Bishop Gienke's support of Vietnam in the recent war with China); or vice versa (e.g., the Kirchenbund's opposition to the "Zionism is racism" resolution in the U.N. in 1975 or its protest against the expansion of military instruction in 1978). Either way, the interests of the organization may be jeopardized. In either case, however, the church leadership can often limit the damage to its credibility by invoking decisions of ecumenical organizations. Similarly, the questions of human rights (e.g., what role should the churches play vis-à-vis those applying for exit visas, or dissidents without a public forum?) pose hard tests for the churches. The dilemma facing the churches is common to both foreign policy and human rights issues: given the rejection of a retreat into apolitical isolation, how do the churches retain the integrity of their decisions without losing credibility with either

90

the state or the laity?

Many diagnosed the status of church-state relations in the GDR after March 6, 1978 as developing neo-constantinianism. While it may exhibit some features of this, this development is unlikely for three reasons. First, the churches realize that the state's policy could change, given changes in the international and/or domestic climate, and are thus, at most, only cautiously optimistic. Second, the church, however tactful and diplomatic, is no "mass organization"; as a large organization not controlled by the state, it will remain politically suspect. Third, even if the state's policy remains constant and the church remains diplomatic, inherently conflictual issues will likely arise (perhaps from the lower-level party apparatchiki or the church grass roots), bubble to the top, and disturb the Burgfrieden.

Despite these factors inhibiting a church-state duopoly, both sides have a vested interest in keeping the "peace." Both realize the costs of a new Kirchenkampf. For the churches, a probable further decline in church adherents and pastors, potential problems in communicating the Gospel publicly (a key Lutheran principle), and attenuation of the international and ecumenical ties carefully fostered and expanded since 1969. For the state, perhaps increasing alienation of the youth and the economically-dissatisfied, a potential dissident-church alliance, pressure from the FRG churches and human rights organizations, and perhaps a loss of hard currency from western churches. All in all, it is not a pleasant scenario for either side, leading one to predict a continuation of the current state of "troubled peace" as it has developed over the ten-year span of the Kirchenbund.

Harvard University

91

[1] See "Brief evangelischer Bischöfe zum Verfassungsentwurf" and "Landesbischof Mitzenheim auf einer Bürgervertreterkonferenz . . .," in Bund der Evangelischen Kirchen in der DDR, ed. Reinhard Henkys (Witten and Berlin: Eckart, 1970), pp. 112-118.

[2] This is based on discussion with informed church leaders.

[3] Hans Seigewasser, "Aus dem Referat . . . am 10. Februar 1969" and "Aus einer Rede am 19. August 1969," in Bund der Evangelischen Kirchen in der DDR, pp. 135-44, 159-62; Hermann Matern, Unser gemeinsamer Weg zur sozialistischen Menschengemeinschaft (E. Berlin: Union, 1969), pp. 12-13.

[4] Paul Verner, "Gemeinsam auf dem guten Weg des Friedens und des Sozialismus," in Paul Verner and Gerald Götting, Christen und Marxisten in gemeinsamer Verantwortung (E. Berlin: Union, 1971).

[5] Seigewasser met with the Executive Board of the Kirchenbund on 24 February 1971 and Speaker Braecklein on 25 February 1971 (Neue Zeit, 25 February 1971 and 26 February 1971, respectively); Götting met with the Executive Board only later on 30 March 1971 (Neue Zeit, 31 March 1971).

[6] On the EKU Synod in May 1970, see Neue Zeit, 6 June 1970 and Evangelische Nachrichtenagentur, 23, No. 21 (27 May 1970). On the changes in Berlin-Brandenburg (East), see Kirchliches Jahrbuch für die EKD 1970 (Gutersloher Verlagshaus Gerd Mohn, 1972), pp. 256-60. The Kirchenbund's defense of Article 4,4 appears in "Aus dem Schlußwort . . ." and "Aus dem ersten Jahresbericht . . ." and "Beschluß der Synode . . . ," in Bund der Evangelischen Kirchen in der DDR, pp. 167-68, 210, and 212.

[7] "DDR-Kirchenbund unterstützt einstimmig das Anti-Rassismus Programm," epd Dokumentation, No. 10

(15 February 1971), pp. 19-20.

[8] Braecklein's support of the Kirchenbund and departure from Mitzenheim's line is revealed in epd Dokumentation, No. 30 (23 July 1973), p. 8, and epd Dokumentation, No. 49 (15 October 1971), p. 20.

[9] See "Beschluß der Synode des DDR-Kirchenbundes vom 29. Juni 1970," in Bund der Evangelischen Kirchen in der DDR, p. 211. The "church within socialism" formula is found in "Bericht der KKL . . . ," epd Dokumentation, No. 34 (19 July 1971), p. 14.

[10] Schönherr endorsed international recognition of the GDR and membership in the U.N. and condemned U.S. aggression in Vietnam and Israeli aggression in the Middle East, as reported in Neues Deutschland, 25, No. 14 (14 January 1970), p. 2. Diverging from Schönherr's diplomatic approach were Bishop Fränkel (Görlitz) and Bishop Krusche (Saxony-Magdeburg). The Krusche controversy is found in "Kirchlicher Dienst . . ." and "DDR fordert . . . ," epd Dokumentation, No. 10 (15 February 1971), pp. 1-15.

[11] For example, in Rostock in 1971-72, school teachers warned children against confirmation class attendance, which resulted in a 90% withdrawal from these classes, according to the Lutheran World Federation Information, No. 34 (28 July 1971), p. 3.

[12] "Bericht der KKL . . . ," epd Dokumentation, No. 25 (12 June 1973), pp. 10-11.

[13] For example, the Kirchenbund's endorsement of CSCE and U.N. membership for the GDR in "Bericht der KKL . . . ," epd Dokumentation, No. 34 (19 July 1971), p. 14; Schönherr's endorsement, on behalf of the Kirchenbund, of the FRG's treaties with Moscow and Warsaw and the Berlin Agreement in Geneva in "Gespräch des epd . . . ," epd Dokumentation, No. 12 (20 March 1972), pp. 2-3; Kirchen-

93

bund participation in the Moscow Conference of
Peace Forces in 1973, in "Pressemitteilung des
Bundes . . . , " epd Dokumentation, No. 2 (21
January 1974), p. 56; support for the Anti-Racism
Program, Vietnam, and post-coup Chile, in "Bericht
der KKL . . . ," epd Dokumentation, No. 45 (19
November 1973), p. 6.

[14] "Many Christians see in socialism the possibility of realizing a better justice." Quoted
from "Bericht der KKL . . . ," epd Dokumentation,
No. 52 (11 November 1974), p. 29.

[15] Dr. Heino Falcke, "Christus befreit--darum
Kirche für andere," epd Dokumentation, No. 30
(17 July 1972).

[16] Fränkel's attacks on the Events Ordinance
are found in Kirchliches Jahrbuch für die EKD
1972, pp. 231-33. His demand for increased inter-
German communication is found in Kirchliches Jahrbuch für die EKD 1973, pp. 181-90.

[17] "Kommentare," Neues Deutschland, 31, No.
207 (31 August 1976), p. 2, and "Stellungnahme
der Kirchenleitung der Evangelischen Kirche der
Kirchenprovinz Sachsen vom 2. September 1976,"
epd Dokumentation, No. 41a (13 September 1976),
pp. 12, 15-16.

[18] Reinhard Henkys provides a review of the
March 6, 1978 meeting in "State and Church in the
GDR," Kirche im Sozialismus, Special English Issue
(June 1979), pp. 9-10.

The GDR Churches after 30 Years--
Notes of an Interested Observer

Nancy Lukens

During the planning sessions for the 1980 GDR
Symposium it was suggested that we focus our study
of various facets and institutions of the GDR on
their own respective self-perceptions as they cele-
brated 30 years of existence as a state and looked
ahead to the next decades. We realized that the
churches had not yet been the subject of a symposium seminar, and that this would be a timely study to complement others focusing on the arts, literature and social sciences.

A number of self-descriptive and evaluative
statements made during and after the 1979 anniversary period by members of both church and state
can help us gain an impression of how the churches'
role is seen within GDR society today. I myself
do not pretend to have expertise as a theologian
or church historian; I am a Germanist by training
and a layperson. Nevertheless I would like to
convey some personal observations gathered since
October 1977 when I first visited the GDR for an
extended period of time. My comments are based on
materials published in both the GDR and the FRG,
on conversations with individuals and groups, and
on public events I have attended in church circles
in the GDR while living in West Berlin from August
1979 to the present.

The first dilemma, of course, in gathering
self-perceptions of any institution is the question of whom to ask. What individuals or groups
speak for 'the Church', or 'the churches', in the

GDR? In the case of the Protestant churches, for example, the perspectives and facts emphasized might vary greatly depending on whether one asked the official leadership of the Federation of Protestant Churches (<u>Bund</u> <u>der</u> <u>Evangelischen</u> <u>Kirchen</u>) with its international and ecumenical concerns and connections, on the one hand, or any of the 50,000 some participants in the 1978 Leipzig Church Fair (<u>Kirchentag</u>), 44% of whom were under thirty.[1] Just as representative, but with an entirely different scope of reference, might be church employees engaged in managing the vast network of homes for the aged and handicapped or other social service facilities, including kindergartens and a number of private educational institutions with theological focus.

The diversity of perceptions and opinions about what 'the Church' in the GDR has been over the 30 years since 1949 and what it is today would likewise be reflected if one went to spokespeople of any of the ten independent churches (<u>Freikirchen</u>) not part of the Protestant Federation--which consists of eight regional member churches, 3 Lutheran and 5 United--or the ten additional recognized religious groups and sects. The independent churches include Methodists, Baptists, Herrnhut Brethern, Mennonites, Quakers; the smaller groups, Neo-Apostolics, Seventh-Day Adventists, Mormons, and a half a dozen others.[2]

Then again, there is the question whether one asks theological educators and students--there are protestant theological faculties or "sections" at major universities as well as three theological seminaries in the GDR--or whether one prefers to go to the grass roots and see how house church circles and worshipping congregations see themselves and their church. Among pastors, one might get different views depending on whether they are men or women, whether they serve rural parishes, or a large city one, or are hospital chaplains.

Diversity, then, is just as great in the GDR as it is in any advanced technological society.

96

However, I see a major difference between the self-perception of Christians and churches in the GDR and in the West: on the whole, the Christians mentioned in the categories above would identify themselves (with a certain positive self-consciousness) as belonging to a "Kirche im Sozialismus."[3] Of course there is a wide range of interpretations as to what that means politically. It certainly does not connote total agreement between Marxism and Christianity or with the totality of present-day GDR socialism. I have, however, repeatedly been struck by a certain parallelism in statements made by non-Christian socialists and church members in the GDR about their conscious decision to either come to the GDR after the war or to stay there when many began to leave for "greener pastures." The theological basis of the Christians' commitment to staying and working within socialism is very simply the sense of being called to live God's presence in that place.

Before I summarize aspects of the churches' self-image gathered from most of these diverse areas of church life and add some observations of my own, I would like to make two points which serve to indicate my biases. First: the Church consists of people, of personalities in relationship with God, with each other and with the world in which they try to live out their faith. And statements of church doctrine or institutional policy, any analysis of church-state functions, in the GDR or elsewhere, should be understood against the background of this brightly colored fabric--which we regrettably cannot know well from a distance. Second: what we can know better from a distance-- but usually do not make the effort to find out-- is how the GDR churches, as well as individual theologians and laypersons, represent themselves in print. Periodicals like Zeichen der Zeit, an independent Protestant monthly published for church workers, or Standpunkt, a politically oriented Protestant monthly published in the Union Verlag, present a wide spectrum of issues and theological reflections as well as practical realities of church life. All told, there are 31 theological and church periodicals in the GDR--out of a total of 519 periodicals. In 1978 the two Protestant publishing houses (Union Verlag and Evangelische Verlagsanstalt) and the Roman Catholic St. Benno Verlag together produced 338 titles with a combined total of 45.4 million copies. The total GDR book production in 1978 was 5,906 titles.[4]

This is by no means to suggest that the churches' self-understanding can only be expressed in specifically Christian contexts, but simply that there are available sources of literature that can be obtained from within the GDR. Conversely, I might add, there is no need for well-meaning Christians to send Bibles to the GDR; Christian bookstores there, in contrast to some other eastern bloc countries, are amply supplied with all commonly used translations. I offer these two comments in admittedly defensive response to the frequent query, "Oh, IS there a church in the GDR? Isn't that a communist country?" There is indeed, and it is not an underground church, but one recognized by the state, of course with mutual open admissions of differences in world view. The Church has constitutional rights as the largest private corporation in the GDR and, as such, has its own statutes, owns property, runs its own degree-granting institutions, and organizes public events.

Now I should like to summarize, in three major areas, statements made by church people during and following the anniversary year of 1979 on issues which both inform and reflect their ongoing process of self-definition.

I. The Challenge of Being a Minority Church

In a synod address about the mission and course of the Lutheran church over its 30 years of GDR existence, Berlin-Brandenburg bishop Albrecht Schönherr showed his awareness of both the pitfalls of institutions with power, and the opportunity inherent in being an institution free of the ballast of power which has historically plagued the Volkskirche or national church in Germany.

In a society where church membership, baptism and confirmation, Christian marriage and burial are by no means rituals to be taken for granted, they can once again be conscious steps taken out of faith in the power of the gospel in a secularized world. Showing his debt to Dietrich Bonhoeffer's concept of "religionless Christianity," Schönherr points out: "A minority church can achieve distance more easily than a majority church can from the occidental mixture of Christian faith and cult of mammon. Perhaps a minority church can help bring the Sermon on the Mount more into view as Jesus' great help to make this world whole."[6]

Of course, the challenge comes with working out the practical forms of support community and pastoral care without the relatively immense fiscal elbow room enjoyed by the Volkskirche in the FRG. Yet where the financing of existing or previously common structures cannot be assumed, or no longer seems appropriate, there is the freedom and the responsibility to develop new forms of grass roots church life as well as new governance structures which lead away from the employee- and pastor-centered models of the past. It is not insignificant, perhaps, that frequent reference is made in church contexts to the positive experience of the Church--the ecclesia in the broadest sense-- at the grass roots level in Latin America.[7]

Schönherr undoubtedly speaks for many others in the GDR church scene when he affirms the challenge presented by being a church without majority privilege. In an earlier address to theology students at the East Berlin Sprachenkonvikt, he noted that it is precisely in this situation that Christians can learn to live out what Dietrich Bonhoeffer meant by "Christianity in a world come of age." He warned them, however, against seeing the "religionlessness" of our times as the result of atheist propaganda, but instead as a stage in humanity's way of relating to God, which needs to be reborn constantly in the real contexts of life.[8] Methodist layman Carl Ordnung agrees with Schönherr's premise that the theology of the cross, of

powerlessness and of life for others opens revolutionary doors for GDR Christians within socialism,
but his evaluation of the past 30 years' progress
in this direction falls on the negative side.
Ordnung sees in the GDR church a tendency to react
defensively to changes such as those brought about
by the advent of socialism, rather than anticipat-
ing them and speaking to them out of the perspective of the gospel. Recent openness to seeing the
proximity of socialist thought and the Christian
gospel, he points out, has come not from within
the GDR churches, but from their necessary encounter with Latin American liberation movements.[9]

On the other hand, it is not hard to understand that the realities of GDR socialism do present the churches with a challenge, given the fact
that their leadership traditionally comes from the
educated upper classes in a society oriented toward the rule of the workers and peasants. It is
hard to let go of tradition and privilege. I have
also heard many individuals, from students in a
private church high school to lay adults in a weekend workshop situation, express the tensions that
arise in everyday situations in which they find
their opportunities to serve constructively limited as a result of their participation in church
programs or their having studied at Christian institutions.

II. The 'Social Space' of the GDR Churches

There has been much discussion, and slow but
significant changes have taken place in the everyday circumstances of the churches' life and work
since the landmark dialogue of March 6, 1978 between Erich Honecker and the Executive Council of
the Protestant Federation. Chairman Honecker lauded the churches on this occasion for their consis-
tent work toward ending the arms race, whether by
international ecumenical discussion or adult education at home. He underscored the state's respect
and support for the diaconic work of the churches,
i.e.,their social and medical care facilities,
which provide, for example, about 85% of the GDR's

services for the handicapped. He assured the church representatives that the constitutional rights to security, protection, higher education, vocational training, and development guaranteed each GDR citizen regardless of age, sex, world view, or religious conviction are secure in practice to Christians.[10] Bishop Schönherr, speaking for the Federation delegation, replied with a number of specific requests for improvements in this line, which were then worked out in discussion and summarized in the joint press communiqué published in the media in East and West.

One area emphasized by Schönherr was the need for space, both materially and in ideas, in which the church communities can work, worship, and carry on their educational programs. Since then, the 'social space' for worship and church public relations includes increased radio broadcast time and, for the first time, major slots in GDR television's second channel for documentary programs or televised worship services. Permission was granted to hold worship in prisons as well as to increase counseling personnel and religious library facilities there. Approval was given for tenured church employees to join the state pension program, and for the expansion of the import from the West of literature needed for the churches' ecumenical work. Quite apart from the March 6 agreements, there is also a program of church building construction in many new housing developments.

In summary, Schönherr noted in the March 6 statement that the situation of Christians throughout the GDR could be measured by that of individuals in their particular location and circumstances. Since then, changes have been implemented, and instances of apparent discrimination against church members have been brought in good faith to the appropriate channels for action. The fact that the churches' voice is heard and taken seriously by the state was underscored in another context when Bishop Schönherr noted, in the April 1979 synod address cited above, the state's reaction to critical questions from the churches on the sub-

101

ject of military instruction in the schools.[11]

Aside from the provisions specified in the March 6 church-state dialogue, other aspects of the 'social space' of the GDR churches should be mentioned. They include an extensive network of adult education programs, such as those of the Evangelische Akademie. Recent weekend conference topics in the Berlin academy have included, for example, the legacy of Bonhoeffer in the socialist and third world countries today; feminism in the church; and Christian language and the Tower of Babel, a seminar featuring GDR writer Franz Füh-mann, who is a professing Christian. The church in general also provides a forum for public appearances of artists and writers on a scale incomparable to that of churches in the West.

Another area of extensive activity of the GDR churches, one which reaches beyond the official membership, is that of youth work. Although only about 3-4% of the thirteen- and fourteen-year-olds are choosing the route of church confirmation at present,[12] more like 20-30% of the youth participate in programs offered by the churches, from weekend retreats and excursions to local Bible study and discussion groups and social activities.[13] It is my impression that the churches provide a "safe" forum in which young people can openly hash out their questions and form a basis for life decisions. A 45-minute television documentary filmed in Potsdam and broadcast on GDR television on May 15, 1979 showed an unrehearsed discussion of a confirmation class in which the issue of Jugendweihe (the secular socialist youth initiation ceremony) versus Christian confirmation provoked thoughtful responses by all involved.[14] Some saw no contradiction of loyalties between affirming faith in God and pledging to be a responsible member of socialist society. Others struggled with the tension they felt between the two levels and forms of loyalty asked of them. My own response to the openness of that discussion was to wonder whether youth in West Germany or the U.S., where the churches have much more power and privi-

102

lege, are similarly challenged to think through the implications of church membership and "civic religion."

Last but not least, the GDR churches' social space includes a network of ecumenical contacts and activities both domestically and abroad. Of particular interest to Americans, perhaps, is the existence since 1977 of a full-time position for an American liaison officer sent by the National Council of Protestant Churches in the United States to work with the Federation of Protestant Churches in the GDR on both official and local parish levels. The current representative, Rev. Barbara Green, lives in West Berlin and commutes regularly to both East Berlin and each of the eight regional churches in the Bund. Delegations have been sent to the GDR and to the United States several times, with discussion focusing, for example, on the mutual concerns of disarmament and peace. The GDR churches have constituent membership in the World Council of Churches based in Geneva, and an active regional committee of the international Prague Christian Peace Conference. In third world circles, a number of churches in countries that have recently become socialist, such as Vietnam and Ethiopia, have entered into ecumenical dialogue with the GDR churches in hopes of learning something from their longer history as churches in a socialist society. Since the Helsinki accords of 1975, there has been increasing participation by GDR churches in human rights concerns, as reflected by the recent publication of the Federation of Protestant Churches entitled Menschenrechte in christlicher Verantwortung (Human Rights and Christian Responsibility).[15]

III. Women in the Church and in Socialism

Without being able to do justice to the complexity and breadth of this subject, I would like merely to relate a statement made to me by one woman pastor, Frau Annemarie Schönherr, who serves as chairperson for women's work in the GDR Federation of Churches. When I asked her what she saw

as the most important development in the thirty-
five years of postwar experience in GDR churches,
she answered without hesitation:

> To me, the most significant development
> has been brought about by changes in our
> understanding of sex roles in socialist
> society. After 1945, there were sudden
> and far-reaching changes in our social
> structures which actually presupposed a
> socialist revolution, giving women a
> much greater role in society. These
> abrupt changes made secular and church
> women alike aware of a tremendous con-
> sciousness gap, and of the need to work
> through the meaning and implications of
> equality in our GDR context. Both posi-
> tive and negative experiences in this
> process have forced changes, in turn,
> in our theological understanding of
> women. We have been challenged to look
> at women of the Bible and women's roles
> in church and society today in new ways.
> We have also begun to look critically,
> along with ecumenical partners in many
> contexts, at Christian language about
> God and our theological language in
> general, and to ask what messages we
> are conveying and want to convey about
> our Christian understanding of sexual-
> ity and sex roles.[16]

It is perhaps of special significance for the
understanding GDR churches have of their part in
the ecumenical, world-wide concern for women's
issues that in March, 1980 the American woman pastor serving as National Council of Churches liaison officer to the GDR, Barbara Green, was asked
to give the sermon at the ecumenical Women's
World Day of Prayer service written by Thai church
women and held in St. Mary's Church in East Berlin.

Finally, I would like to add personal observations on two aspects of life in the GDR that are
not specific to the churches but which represent

open questions in GDR society and therefore affect the life of the church community as well. First, the issue of Vergangenheitsbewältigung. It seems to me to be a significant factor in the early history of GDR church-state relations that the respective leaders in church and state, Christians and communists, had in many cases already discovered each other as allies in the antifascist struggle of the early to mid-1930s. Thus there was a personal basis for trust and cooperation between church and government officials in building socialist society in the GDR.

There are various indications of considerable concern on the part of both church and state to deal with the realities of the Nazi past. 1) The state has financed the renovation of the major Berlin synagogue, which was destroyed in the November, 1938 pogrom, as a historical monument. Numerous events were held in November, 1978 to commemorate this pogrom, the so-called "Kristallnacht." 2) The Protestant-sponsored organization Aktion Sühnezeichen (Action for Reconciliation), founded in West Berlin in 1958 and functioning separately in the FRG and the GDR since the building of the Wall, organizes service projects for young adults, for example, the construction of a memorial at the Theresienstadt concentration camp together with Czech and Hungarian young people. At the annual Sühnezeichen (GDR) meetings, peace issues and the history of Nazism are a major focus.[17] 3) This audience need not be reminded of the number of literary works dealing with the Nazi past and holocaust themes. Suffice it to say that in the GDR churches, too, there is an ongoing discussion, with the implicit question remaining here as elsewhere: What does it mean to be a Christian after Auschwitz?

Another open question, to this observer's eye, remains that of the legal and illegal emigration of citizens from the GDR, and the related complex of attitudes concerning Freizügigkeit, the freedom to move and travel. The very fact that church leaders and delegations have been among those granted visas to attend meetings in western countries naturally creates a barrier of envy, or at least of knowledge, vis-à-vis those less privileged. I sense that it is among the members of the older generations, who have known other places, and the well-traveled set of younger church leaders that the conviction is strongest that they would never choose to live in the West. But in many instances I have been aware of some difficulty in helping the younger generations find their own identity as Christians in the socialist context without the opportunity to compare notes freely and to define themselves culturally and theologically without concrete experience of their western counterparts. There is a certain buffer space in which the church can offer employment to people who are discriminated against on the job after having sought exit visas. The church, however, can certainly not prevent others from choosing to leave rather than to stay. It remains to be seen how the churches will deal with the problems arising from the increased East-West tensions.

In summary, the GDR churches reflect the diversity of their structures and their membership on all levels of their involvement in local, regional, national, and international work, and they continue in an ongoing process of dealing with unanswered questions. Lest it be overlooked, I hasten to emphasize that the churches are by no means only institutions of social service, of church-state dialogue or ecumenical cooperation, but primarily local bodies of Christians worshipping and working through all the everyday struggles and moments of celebration which their unique situation generates. The prognosis for the next thirty years undoubtedly involves much uncertainty, and depends not only on how the churches understand themselves in the GDR, but how willing we all are to go out of our way to understand the delicate balance of world peace.

The College of Wooster

Notes

[1] Hendrik Bussiek, "Leben mit Luther und Lenin--Die Kirche in der DDR," in his Notizen aus der DDR (Frankfurt/M.: Fischer, 1979), pp. 207-17.

[2] For further information and membership statistics, see Hans-Jürgen Roeder, "Churches and Religious Groups in the GDR: An Overview with Figures," Kirche im Sozialismus, Special English Issue (June, 1979), pp. 32-38. (KiS is a journal published quarterly by the [West] Berliner Arbeitsgemeinschaft für kirchliche Publizistik.) Roeder points out, for example, that the Roman Catholic Church in the GDR, despite its location in an area that has historically been predominately Lutheran, and despite the general tendency of churches to lose membership with increasing secularization, showed a membership of almost 1.3 million in 1974, and some 3800 nuns and priests working in parishes, counseling facilities, and retreat houses. On the Protestant side, the figures were ca. 8 million in 1978, with ca. 4000 pastors and 51 diaconical (service) institutions.

[3] For more differentiated discussion, see Peter Fischer, "Kirche in der ideologischen Diaspora," in his Kirche und Christen in der DDR (W. Berlin: Gebr. Holzapfel, 1978), pp. 98ff.

[4] Statistisches Jahrbuch der DDR 1979 (E. Berlin: Staatsverlag der DDR, 1979), p. 308.

[5] Ibid., p. 309.

[6] "On the Mission and Course of the Church of Jesus Christ in the Socialist Society of the GDR," Kirche im Sozialismus, Special English Issue (June, 1979), p. 16. The article is based on an April 1979 address to the Synod of the Evangelische Kirche in Berlin-Brandenburg, Berlin-Weißensee (GDR).

[7] See Note 9.

[8] Albrecht Schönherr, "Impulse aus der Theologie Bonhoeffers für den Weg der Christen in der sozialistischen Gesellschaft der DDR," in the collection of his essays and talks, Horizont und Mitte (E. Berlin: Evangelische Verlagsanstalt, 1979), pp. 119ff. The talk was held before the Sprachenkonvikt on April 13, 1973.

[9] Carl Ordnung, "Protestantismus und Sozialismus," in Richte unsere Füße auf den Weg des Friedens. Festschrift für Helmut Gollwitzer, ed. Andreas Baudis (Munich: Kaiser, 1979), pp. 185-192.

[10] This and the following statements are paraphrased from the National Council of Churches/USA version of the joint press communiqué issued March 6, 1978 by GDR church and state parties to the dialogue. For complete texts, see the documentary newsbriefs of the Evangelischer Pressedienst (epd), "Texte aus der DDR," published daily by the Gemeinschaft der Ev. Publizistik, Frankfurt/M.

[11] See "On the Mission and Course of the Church," p. 28. Also, the statement on this issue by Bishop Krusche of Magdeburg at the June 1978 Kirchentag in Erfurt, and the letter, dated June 14, 1978, from the Konferenz der Evangelischen Kirchenleitungen in der DDR to the church membership, both cited by Fischer, Kirche und Christen in der DDR, pp. 157f.

[12] According to the Kirchliches Jahrbuch, in the GDR there were just over 5,000 confirmations in 1974, and only 4,243 in 1975.

[13] This estimate was reported by Max Stackhouse of Andover-Newton Seminary during this Symposium session; it was based on findings gathered during his 1980 tour of GDR churches.

[14] The broadcast was entitled Kirchen in der DDR. See "Chronik," Kirche im Sozialismus, 3/1979, p. 6.

[15] Menschenrechte in christlicher Verantwor-

tung (E. Berlin: Evangelischer Verlagsanstalt, 1980).

[16] My English paraphrase is based on notes from a conversation in Berlin-Weißensee from Nov. 15, 1979. The statement was approved by Rev. Schönherr.

[17] Conversation with Dr. Franz Hammerstein, former General Secretary of Aktion Sühnezeichen, West Berlin.

Recent Developments in GDR Literature

Christiane Zehl Romero

> Wenn eine neue Runde eingeläutet wird,
> stehen neue Kämpfer im Ring, oder die
> alten, die sich wieder aufgerichtet
> haben.

Thus Christa Wolf in a conversation with the
younger writer Elke Erb in May 1977.[1] Although
this dialogue, which is appended to a collection
of Erb's writings, Der Faden der Geduld (1978),
does not refer to Wolf Biermann and the chain of
events started by his expatriation in November,
1976, one tends to read it in the context of these
events and to interpret the remark not so much as
a declaration of defiance as rather one of belief
or hope--in the need for and the existence of re-
silience among writers and in the literary life of
the GDR.

On the level of "Planung und Leitung," efforts
were made to present an even more positive picture
of the future and furtherance of literature in the
GDR. At the beginning of March, 1978, for example,
Erich Honecker received the writers Hermann Kant,
Max Walter Schulz, Erwin Strittmatter, Helmut Sakowski, and Günter Görlich, an occasion used to
underline the good rapport between writers and the
SED.[2]

For both the committed writer and the maker
of cultural policy the important role of literature in the GDR remains uncontested, an importance
which was merely highlighted by the recent events:
the expatriation of Wolf Biermann, the subsequent
letter of protest (originally signed by Sarah

Kirsch, Christa and Gerhard Wolf, Franz Fühmann, Volker Braun, Stefan Heym, Günter Kunert, Heiner Müller, Jurek Becker, Erich Arendt, Rolf Schneider, and Stephan Hermlin), the expulsion from the Writer's Union on June 7, 1979 of Stefan Heym, Kurt Bartsch, Adolf Endler, Karl-Heinz Jakobs, Klaus Poche, Klaus Schlesinger, Rolf Schneider, Dieter Schubert, Joachim Seyppel, and the expulsion, emigration, or long-term permission to live abroad of Thomas Brasch, Bernd Jentzsch, Jürgen Fuchs, Gerulf Pannach, Frank Schöne, Sarah Kirsch, Jurek Becker, Klaus Poche, and Günter Kunert. But do these events, does November, 1976 represent a new round, so to speak, in GDR literature, and does or will quality not suffer as a consequence? I do not think that the answer to either question will be yes, although the toll on individual lives is something left out of such summary considerations. Nor can we predict what effects the revisions of the penal code, which went into effect in August, 1979 will have, particularly on younger, unknown writers. Still, so far at least, 1976 does not appear to mark a major cut-off point in the development of GDR literature.

For my present purpose however, 1976 shall serve as a not altogether arbitrary beginning. First of all, it raises the issue of an old and not at all venerable tradition in German literature, that of emigration and exile. "Jeder für sich, und Deutschland gegen alle" is the bitter formula Heiner Müller used for the new/old situation.[3] Wolf Biermann and those who followed him were by no means the first writers to take up or have to take up residence outside the GDR. (Uwe Johnson, Gerhard Zwerenz, Horst Bienek, Christa Reinig are but a few names.) Do the definitions used for emigration and exile under fascism--our most recent and inevitable points of reference-- really apply to either or both groups? I would argue that they do not.

First of all, the Federal Republic and West Berlin (where many of the writers from the GDR tend to stay) are in close proximity, geographi-

cally and culturally. There is a common language--
in spite of small differences--and a common cultural heritage, including Marx and Engels. There is
also, for the time being at least, easy access to
publishers and a reading public, even though new
kinds of political pressure combined with marketing manipulations make the situation anything but
easy for the individual.

Secondly, the need to leave, the danger to a
writer's personal and professional well-being, is
in many cases much more a matter of interpretation
than it was in past instances of emigration and
exile. Jurek Becker points this out defensively
and correctly in an interview given to Der Spiegel
in 1980, on the occasion of his receiving a ten-
year visa:

> Was unerträglich ist, ist ja eine sub-
> jektive Sache. Es gibt keine Norm . . .
> Ich schätze die dortigen Zustände so
> ein, daß ich nur unter erschwerten,
> extremen Bedingungen arbeiten könnte,
> und dem entziehe ich mich. Aber ich
> kann Ihnen doch keine Unterschrift un-
> ter die Erklärung geben, daß ein
> Schriftsteller in der DDR nicht arbei-
> ten kann. Viele tun es, und auf eine
> rasante Art, wie ich meine.[4]

Becker's defensiveness, or for that matter Reiner
Kunze's in his conversations with Karl Corinno,[5]
and Günter Kunert's public statement "Jetzt ist es
endgültig genug" in Die Zeit[6] reflect--among other
things to be sure--this aspect of individual interpretation. They are responses to the sometimes
implicit and sometimes explicit question: "Did you
really have to leave?" The tenor of this question
will vary according to the political orientation
of the West German interviewer. A "yes" will either be expected as a matter of course and seen as
an indictment of the GDR, or it will be read as a
faltering of courage and, potentially at least, a
betrayal of the cause of dissent in a society
which had at least started out on the right track

and now needs dissent in order to redirect itself.

Only people like Wolf Biermann oder Bernd
Jentzsch, who were not allowed back into the GDR,
or those like Jürgen Fuchs and Gerulf Pannach, for
whom it was either prison or leave, are free from
such questions. In fact, his "good conscience"
sometimes gives Wolf Biermann's public pronouncements a slightly self-righteous tone.

But should journalists or we for that matter
even make such a clear-cut division between "Ceux
qui restent et ceux qui partent," as the title of
an essay in the French journal Allemagnes d'Aujourdhui provocatively does,[7] and then distribute
praise, blame, and maybe excuses according to our
own political convictions? Those on the left would
like a little more staying power and dissent within; on the right, every new departure is considered
further proof of the repressive and untenable conditions in the GDR and the superiority of the West.

This kind of division, also of writers still
living in the GDR, into dissidents and non-dissi-
dents simply supports the ideologizing of literature of which writers from the GDR often complain.
As Thomas Brasch said in an interview in Alternative:

> In der DDR wird alles, was man tut,
> ideologisch. Selbst wenn man in
> einer Geschichte schreibt, daß ein
> Dreher Selbstmord macht, dann kom-
> men die einen und sagen: Bravo,
> jetzt hast du endlich mal geschrie-
> ben, daß der Arbeiter in der DDR
> doppelt entfremdet ist, und die an-
> deren sagen: Pfui, jetzt hast du
> geschrieben, daß der Arbeiter in der
> DDR doppelt entfremdet ist. Das
> heißt, die Geschichte wird eigent-
> lich gar nicht mehr gelesen. . . .[8]

Bettina Wegner, the singer, expressed a similar complaint in one of her texts:

Komm ich wohin mit meiner
Klampfe, um zu singen da sitzen
sie gespalten schon in zwei
Parteien. Die erste will von
mir, ich soll was Scharfes
bringen die zweite fordert, ich
soll optimistisch sein.

Für die mit ihrem Schreibblock
bin ich ein Zerstörer die
anderen sehen in mir ein Opfer
der Partei. . . .[9]

Ideology is obviously an extremely important
aspect of GDR literature. It is after all the
basic justification for the state and the basic
tool for its self-interpretation, including its
culture and literary production. But literature
is not ideology and, no matter what role one plays
for the other, must be seen historically and critically. There is a great temptation in GDR studies
to reintroduce eastern "Ideologisierung" with
"westlichen Vorzeichen."[10] Because of this danger
and because in German literary history the term is
still too closely associated with the period from
1933 to 1945 and invites too quick an analogy--
which as we saw is neither quite correct nor particularly useful--"exile" is to my mind not a useful designation for those GDR writers who now live
in the West. Besides, the group is very diverse
in civil status (from expulsion to ten-year visa)
and in self-perception (Biermann considers himself
an exile, Kunze refuses the term).

And finally, it must be pointed out that what
united the notoriously disparate exiles from the
Third Reich, i.e., a common enemy, does not exist
for the writers from the GDR. Although attitudes
vary, criticism of the GDR is on the whole toned-
down rather than stepped-up once a writer has left.
There is no hatred towards the country or its basic system of government. Instead, the critical
eye is turned upon the West, and what it often
perceives then is "Ähnlichkeit im Häßlichen," as
Jurek Becker has called this negative German unity:

> Zum Beispiel sehe ich Ähnlichkeiten
> im Anspruch des Staates, sich selbst
> zum höchsten schützenswerten Gut zu
> erklären und auf immer arrogantere
> und rücksichtslosere Art und Weise
> diesem Ziel alles unterzuordnen.
> Andrerseits sehe ich die fatale Be-
> reitschaft so vieler Leute, sich
> diesem Anspruch zu fügen. Es ist
> böse ausgedrückt, auch eine Ähnlich-
> keit in der Unterwürfigkeit.[11]

It will be interesting to see whether Becker's
new volume of stories, <u>Nach der ersten Zukunft</u>,
which will be published by Suhrkamp and--minus one
story--probably by Hinstorff in Rostock, already
draws on these perceptions.

But now, if we wish to avoid the term exile,
how do we group those writers from the GDR who
live in the West? I would suggest that for the
time being we still consider them in the context
of GDR studies. At present, their personal and
artistic responses to the experiences in the West
can only be understood and appreciated against
this background. What happens in the future will
probably depend on the individual writers. Some
will no doubt become integrated into the cultural
life of the FRG. Others, and there are already
indications of this, will see themselves as the
truly German writers, spokesmen and victims of
Germany's new and old <u>Misere</u>.

There is one great danger facing many of the
GDR writers living in the West: that of oblivion.
When the sensation value of their situation has
worn off, the media will forget them. And students of literature may neglect them, simply because they do not have a pigeon-hole into which to
fit them for discussion in the classroom or in
scholarly papers--a further reason, I believe, to
continue considering them in the context of GDR
studies as long as possible.

Passing from these theoretical and somewhat

pedantic considerations, I will now attempt to identify what appear to be the most significant developments in recent GDR literature. One is above all struck, but not really surprised, by the large number of works that deal with the man or woman of the word, the writer, the teacher, the historian. There are: Werner Heiduczek's Tod am Meer (1977, about a writer), Jurek Becker's Schlaflose Tage (1978, about a teacher), Günter Görlich's Eine Anzeige in der Zeitung (1978, about a teacher), Klaus Poche's Atemnot (1978, about a writer), Günter de Bruyn's Märkische Forschungen (1979, about a teacher and a historian), Stefan Heym's Collin (1979, about a writer), Rolf Schneider's November (1979, about a writer), Christa Wolf's Kein Ort. Nirgends (1979, about two writers). Not only novels, also poems, short stories, and sketches (such as Hans Joachim Schädlich's "Satzsuche" in Versuchte Nähe, 1977), and plays, such as Uwe Saeger's Das Vorkommnis (performed 1978), Thomas Brasch's Lieber Georg (performed 1980), or even Heiner Müller's Leben Grundlings Friedrich von Preußen Lessings Schlaf Traum Schrei (1979),[12] and Hamletmaschine (performed 1980) deal with the writer or, as in the last instance, the intellectual.

Although it is impossible to generalize about all of these works there are, I think, two major themes which emerge. One is--to put it simply-- the difficulty of saying the truth. This involves questions of social and political repression and individual courage, as well as questions of perception and expression.

The other theme is harder to put into an easy formula, very generally it is the man or woman of the word in his or her relationship to revolution, the vital and spontaneous need of the creative individual--creative in the widest sense--to do more than echo past revolutions and affirm present realities, the wish to be involved in something new, expressed in German, the wish "ein Revolutionär zu sein und kein Erbe." This theme, where it is evoked, is mostly associated with failure; the

117

need cannot be realized.

Most immediately, one would tend to associate this preoccupation with the writer/teacher/intellectual and his role in GDR society with events around Biermann's expulsion. And these were certainly an inspiration for some, most obviously for Rolf Schneider. The phenomenon however goes back farther into the seventies and is connected with a general trend towards introspection, Rückschau, and a more probing look at the possibilities for self-realization for the demanding, individualistic, reflective and/or creative person. Christa Wolf's Nachdenken über Christa T. comes to mind as an early example, if not a beginning.

Of all the works I named, Rolf Schneider's November is in many ways the most symptomatic.[13] On the one hand, it is what we call in German "unmittelbare Zeitgeschichte"--the author was intimately familiar and involved with what happened after Biermann's expulsion; on the other, Schneider, a very sensitive connoisseur and lover of literature, puts the dilemma of the writer into a larger perspective.

The central problem facing the writer in November is the threat of Sprachlosigkeit, loss of language, falling silent. The heroine, Natascha Roth, is threatened by it, both if she leaves the GDR and if she stays. About emigration she says:

> Ich habe Angst, daß ich plötzlich
> keine Sprache mehr habe. . . . Die
> Sprache, weißt du, ist nicht belie-
> big mitnehmbar. Du gehst fort und
> hast deine Sprache, und wenn du dich
> zwischen anderen Leuten bewegst, die
> eine andere Sprache reden, wirst du
> deine eigene Sprache allmählich ver-
> lieren. Wir glauben bloß, daß Men-
> schen sprechen, in Wahrheit sind es
> vielmehr die Länder. . . . Unser
> Land hier redet nämlich unverwechsel-
> bar, weißt du. Jenseits der Grenzen

118

ist immer eine andere Sprache. Sie
ist unserer im Äußeren vielleicht
austauschbar ähnlich, aber sie ist
ganz anders. (p. 177)

Schneider, perhaps sensitized by his love for the
Austro-Hungarian tradition where <u>Sprachlosigkeit</u>
has been a major theme since the turn of the century, brings up what I think is a real threat to
those of the GDR writers in the West whose literary identities were most intimately tied up with
the GDR, particularly in their criticism.

The second aspect of the threat of becoming
sterile as a writer is treated much less explicitly, although it is, I believe, a major concern in
Schneider's novel. As often in GDR literature it
is expressed through a literary figure from the
past, in this case the French poet Arthur Rimbaud.
Natascha Roth is trying to write a fictional bio-
graphy of him, but cannot really get started. Towards the end of the novel, she composes a letter
from the dying Rimbaud to his friend and fellow-
poet Verlaine. Schneider brings this as his sec-
ond-to-last chapter. In it Rimbaud answers the
question that has plagued literary historians for
a century, namely why he fell silent after compos-
ing some of the most beautiful poetry the French
language has to offer. He was still a young man
at the time and became a shabby/shady adventurer/
businessman.

Rimbaud/Roth/Schneider write:

. . . die beiden Leidenschaften meines
Lebens sind die Revolution und die Po-
esie gewesen. Als ich die eine auf-
gab, mußte ich auch die andere aufgeb-
en. Ich wurde ein Strolch, ein Land-
streicher, ein Haschischesser, ein Be-
trüger, ein Händler, ein Bauer, ein
Wrack. (p. 254)

And he continues: "Als ich begriff, daß meine Poe-
sie bloß der Nachhall der längst gescheiterten

119

Commune war [he is referring to the Commune of 1871], schrieb ich Une Saison en Enfer und dann nichts mehr" (p. 255). The revolution had inspired Rimbaud as a sixteen-year-old on his first visit to Paris. But when he realizes that after its failure all he can write about is an echo ("Nach-hall") he must fall silent. Schneider leaves it to the reader to draw analogies between the stif-ling situation in which he shows his heroine, her elation at one small gesture of solidarity, the signing of a letter protesting the expatriation of a fellow writer by the name of Bodakov, and Rim-baud's explanation.

November, with an epitaph by Joseph Roth de-scribing All Saints' Day, the first of November, is steeped in melancholy and intimations of death. So is Christa Wolf's Kein Ort. Nirgends, although the setting is May.14 "Einfach weitergehen, den-ken sie. Wir wissen, was kommt" are the last words of this "story" about an imagined meeting between the poets Caroline von Günderrode and Heinrich von Kleist. Both committed suicide-- the book's cover tells those who might not know-- she in 1806, he in 1811. The meeting takes place in 1804--"zwischen den Zeiten." What this means in historical and political terms, Christa Wolf explains in her essay on Günderrode, "Der Schatten eines Traumes," in Fortgesetzter Versuch (1979):

Die Revolution erleben sie als Fremd-herrschaft. Sie . . . haben die Wahl zwischen den verkrüppelnden Unterdrük-kungspraktiken deutscher Duodezfürsten und der Überwältigung durch Napoleon; zwischen dem anachronistischen Feuda-lismus der deutschen Kleinstaaten und der zwangsweisen Einführung überfälli-ger verwaltungs- und handelstechnischer Reformen durch den Usurpator, der den Geist der Revolution natürlich strikt niederhält: Wenn dies eine Wahl ge-nannt werden kann, so ist es eine, die das Handeln an seiner Wurzel, schon im Gedanken erstickt.15

Although her presentation invites the reader to draw parallels, Christa Wolf the essayist and interviewee also insists on the differences in the historical situation between then and now. The imaginative writer and "moralist," in the French sense, of Kein Ort. Nirgends existentializes the plight of the gifted creative individuals who ask "[t]ätig zu werden und dabei wir selber zu bleiben," "[ein] Anspruch, den auf Erden keiner je erfüllen kann" (pp. 143-44). There is no place for either the man or the woman.

It is significant, both for Christa Wolf's own development and for GDR writing by women on women, that Kein Ort. Nirgends shows a man and a woman in the same hopeless situation "zwischen den Zeiten" and yet emphasizes the differences in the cause and nature of their despair. It expresses, I believe, a new kind of feminism, a feminism, which--without wanting to give up the economic and social equality that has been won--will return to traditional modes of femininity and reassess their potential for a renewal of society. The dialogue between Kleist and Günderrode implies a need for the man to free himself from male role models and their demand "zu handeln," without reflection on and consideration of the possible consequences of these actions. In an interview which appeared in the Süddeutsche Zeitung in 1979, Christa Wolf suggests that in the future GDR society women might help men to make such changes:

> Es kann eine Periode eintreten, in der Frauen den Männern in diesem mit Zahlen nicht zu messenden Bereich - nämlich bei der Frage, wie man miteinander lebt - helfen könnte.[16]

This idea, that the traditionally feminine qualities associated with nurturing and the private sphere might be needed in modern GDR society and would help improve it, is quite widespread in recent writing. In spite of Christa Wolf's and others' beliefs, however, there is some danger in this emphasis on the traditional female roles of helper and supporter, namely that of losing rather than gaining ground in the area of women's equality, not legally perhaps, but socially.

For lack of time I would like now to mention, rather than discuss, two additional aspects of recent GDR literature. One is thematic, namely an ever more pervasive treatment of newly emerged but already ossified barriers between high and low. "Die Welt wird was sie war, eine Heimat für Herren und Sklaven," a character in Heiner Müller's play Der Auftrag says.[17] And again: "was die Menschen eint, sind die Geschäfte. Die Revolution hat keine Heimat mehr" (p. 1260). Although Müller's voice is the most vociferous in complaining about a betrayed, unfinished, fettered revolution, it is by no means the only one.

The other recent tendency is formal and particularly significant: an increasing use of short sketches, scenes, observations. "Moleküle als Indiz," Elke Erb calls her short texts in Faden der Geduld.[18] Other examples--they vary widely in structure, length, content, style--are Reiner Kunze's Wunderbare Jahre, Hans Joachim Schädlich's Versuchte Nähe (1977), texts in Jürgen Fuchs' Gedächtnisprotokolle (1977), Günter Kunert's Camera Obscura (1978). These texts do not make any claims to totality and representativeness. They carefully and precisely collect or reflect concrete facets of everyday reality and exemplify most strikingly a general turning towards the everyday and its details, which is apparent everywhere in GDR literature, particularly in the new drama.[19]

Some of the most interesting and exciting writing from the GDR occurs in these short pieces. One example, "Die Gestalt des Wolfs," by Elke Erb:

> Effeff hatte so schön die Gestalten
> der alten Großmutter und des kleinen
> Rotkäppchens gefressen, als die Ge-
> stalt des Jägers mit dem Messer kam
> und sie befreite. Die Gestalten

122

füllten Effeff mit "Steinen" anstatt
dessen, tanzten fort. Alles nagt,
was nagen kann in Effeff, an den un-
gestalten "Steinen" nunmehr, sie ver-
wittern! (p. 19)

In the conversation with Christa Wolf to which I
alluded earlier, Elke Erb gives the following
interpretation:

Ich weise darauf hin, daß Wirklichkeit nicht unvermittelt uns entgegen-
tritt, sondern interpretiert, zu Mär-
chengestalten, Kunstgestalten, Denk-
gestalten umgeformt ist, bis das Ei-
gentliche hinter ihnen verschwindet.
. . . Effeff, "befreit" von den Gestalten, die er "gefressen" hatte,
ist an den Rand geführt. Da wird es
ganz schwierig. Die Gestalten hinter-
lassen Ungestaltes in Effeff . . .
Er muß den Mut finden, mit Ungestaltem
umzugehen. Effeff muß selbst gestalten, sich selbst gestalten, sonst ver-
wittern die Steine, machen ihn unpro-
duktiv. Er muß das schaffen. (pp. 124f.)

To me this short and difficult text is a sign of
the vitality of GDR literature. It deals with the
individual's need for creative change both thematically and structurally, and it includes an element of sobriety in the notion of change, namely
pain.

Writing such as this seems to indicate new
beginnings in GDR literature and to show that it
is successfully freeing itself from the heavy burden of a narrow definition of socialist realism
and of Erbe. There are many signs, I think, which
point to a continuing opening of literary horizons,
e.g., Robert Weimann's further attempts to broaden
the concept of Erbe to include other cultures and
their traditions, such as the magic realism of
South America. Even Dieter Schlenstedt in his article "DDR Literatur und ihre Literaturgeschichte,"

123

which tries to distinguish between "Literatur im Sozialismus" and "sozialistischer Literatur" appears to me to be an attempt in this direction.[20] The political events, expulsions, exclusions, and moves may very well be symptoms of long-range changes and may represent only the most obvious and negative reactions to these changes. They may highlight but also obscure efforts on the part of many writers and critics within the GDR to expand the possibilities of literature formally and thematically.

Tufts University

Notes

[1] Elke Erb, Der Faden der Geduld (Weimar/ Berlin: Aufbau, 1978), p. 126.

[2] For a more detailed account compare Jérome Vaillant, "Ceux qui restent et ceux qui partent . . . ," Allemagnes d'Aujourdhui, No. 63 (May/ June 1978), p. 3.

[3] Heiner Müller, "Wie es bleibt, ist es nicht," Der Spiegel, 12 Sept. 1977, p. 212.

[4] Der Spiegel, 3 March 1980, p. 207.

[5] Appended to Reiner Kunze, Die Wunderbaren Jahre (Frankfurt/M.: Fischer, 1978).

[6] Die Zeit, 9 Nov. 1979, p. 11.

[7] Jérome Vaillant, pp. 3-7. This article, the introduction to a volume devoted to GDR literature at this juncture, does not suggest that we should make a distinction.

[8] Alternative, 20, No. 113 (April 1977), 97.

[9] Quoted from Sonja Schwar-Arendt, "Trouba-

124

doura mit Löwenherz," Die Zeit, 1 Feb. 1980, p. 16.

[10] Cf. Frank Trommler, "Ideologische und ästhetische Aspekte beim Interpretieren von DDR-Literatur," Der Deutschunterreicht, 30, No. 2 (April 1978), 5ff.

[11] With Ulrich Schwarz and Rolf Becker, "Ja, wenn Stalin ein großer Mann war . . . ," Der Spiegel, 3 March 1980, p. 212.

[12] Published in Theater heute, 20, No. 3 (1979), 26ff.

[13] Rolf Schneider, November (Hamburg: Knaus, 1979).

[14] Christa Wolf, Kein Ort. Nirgends (Weimar/Berlin: Aufbau, 1979).

[15] Christa Wolf, Fortgesetzter Versuch. Aufsätze, Gespräche, Essays (Leipzig: Ph. Reclam jun., 1980), p. 297.

[16] Interview with Wilfried F. Schoeller, Süddeutsche Zeitung, 10/11 March 1979, p. 129f.

[17] Printed in Sinn und Form, 30, No. 6 (1979), 1258.

[18] Elke Erb, p. 118.

[19] For example, Jürgen Groß' Match, Uwe Saeger's Das Vorkommnis, Rudi Strahl's Die Flüsterparty; but also ostensibly more removed plays like Stefan Schütz' Heloise und Abelard and Christoph Hein's Cromwell.

[20] Dieter Schlenstedt, "DDR-Literatur und ihre Literaturgeschichte," Weimarer Beiträge, 26, No. 2 (1980), 39.

Von Aufenthalten, Hosenknöpfen und Kindheitsmustern: Das Dritte Reich in der jüngsten Prosa der DDR

Alexander Stephan

> Wir haben allzufrüh der un-
> mittelbaren Vergangenheit
> den Rücken zugekehrt, begie-
> rig, uns der Zukunft zuzuwen-
> den. Die Zukunft wird aber
> abhängen von der Erledigung
> der Vergangenheit.
>
> Bertolt Brecht[1]
> 13. August 1953

Die Auseinandersetzung mit Nationalsozialismus und zweitem Weltkrieg lief in der DDR früher
und intensiver an als andernorts. Daran ist kaum
zu rütteln und darauf ist oft genug hingewiesen
worden. Kaum jemand zwischen Stralsund und Zwickau
hat Entnazifierung mit der Unterschrift unter einen
Fragebogen verwechselt; alte Nazis und Kriegsver-
brecher wurden in der DDR seltener als in der Bundesrepublik in die Spitzen des öffentlichen Lebens
hochgespült. Statt sich hinter apologetischen My-
then wie Nullpunkt und Kahlschlag zu verstecken,
knüpfte die kommunistische Nachkriegskulturpolitik
unmittelbar an das Exil und an den innerdeutschen
Widerstand an.[2] Und an Stelle der Bücher von Ed-
win Erich Dwinger und Hans Hellmut Kirst, ganz
zu schweigen von kollektiv zusammengeschmierten
Landserheftchen, druckten Verlage in der sowje-
tisch besetzten Zone seit 1945 die Exil- und KZ-
Literatur von Bruno Apitz, Heinrich Mann, Anna

127

Seghers und Arnold Zweig. Widerstand und Unter-
grund gehörten zu den Standardthemen der 50er Jahre, Wandlungs- und Bildungsgeschichten bevölkerten
die kulturelle DDR-Landschaft der 60er Jahre.[3]

   Trotzdem ist der literarische Bewältigungs-
prozeß auch in der DDR nie recht zu einem Abschluß
gebracht worden--sofern ein Thema wie der Nationalsozialismus der Jahre 1933 bis 1945 überhaupt abzu-
schließen ist. Dazu hatte man sich allzu stark
auf die Behandlung der vorbildlichen, aber durch-
aus untypischen Geschichte der Widerstandsbewegung
konzentriert; und dazu hatte man allzu früh den
Themen aus der unmittelbaren Vergangenheit die Mär
vom sozialistischen Aufbau und von der Ankunft im
DDR-Alltag vorgeordnet.[4] "Viele unserer Schriftsteller," klagte der Altexilant Walter Ulbricht im
Gründungsjahr der DDR, ". . . beschäftigen sich .
. . mit den Fragen der Emigration. . . . Wozu ist
das notwendig? Das war einmal und ist jetzt vorbei. Wenn sie das Privatbedürfnis danach haben,
kann man sie nicht hindern, aber sie können von
uns nicht verlangen, daß wir ihnen Papier dazu ge-
ben."[5]

   Die Folge dieser partiellen Verdrängung der
Vergangenheit war, daß die Masse der DDR-Bücher
zum Dritten Reich jahrelang im Traktathaften und
in der Weltanschauungsdiskussion steckenblieb.
Die Fixierung auf den positiven Helden und auf zu-
kunftsweisende Happy-Ends verhinderte eine Auseinandersetzung mit dem täglichen Faschismus; und die
enge Auslegung des Begriffs Typik machte eine Ver-
mittlung des Bewältigungsprozesses durch Hinter-
fragen des eigenen, subjektiven Entwicklungswegs
unmöglich. Völlig undenkbar war es schließlich,
auf dem Umweg über die Faschismusanalyse zum Ab-
bau von falschen Denk- und Verhaltensweisen in der
DDR beizutragen. "Ein wenig stört mich," meinte
Christa Wolf dazu 1975 im Zusammenhang einer Le-
sung aus dem Manuskript ihres Romans Kindheitsmuster in der Ostberliner Akademie der Künste,
"daß viele unserer Bücher über diese Zeit enden
mit Helden, die sich schnell wandeln, mit Helden,
die eigentlich schon während des Faschismus zu

ziemlich bedeutenden und richtigen Einsichten kommen, politisch, menschlich. Ich will keinem Autor sein Erlebnis bestreiten. Aber mein Erlebnis war anders."[6]

Neuland ist so bei der Auseinandersetzung mit dem Nationalsozialismus auch heute, dreieinhalb Jahrzehnte nach Zerschlagung des 12jährigen Reiches, noch genug zu pflügen. Mit gutem Grund findet deshalb seit einiger Zeit in der DDR, parallel zur westdeutschen Hitler-Welle, aber ohne deren kommerzielle Manipulationen, eine Wiederbelebung des Themas Faschismus statt, die--qualitativ zumindest--alles bisher dortzulande Geleistete in den Schatten stellt. Filme wie Ich war neunzehn (1967) und Mama, ich lebe (1976) füllen die Kinos; auf Schriftstellerkongressen streiten sich die 40- und 50jährigen über das Verhältnis zu ihren Vätern;[7] und in den Buchhandlungen steht man Schlange nach den neuesten antifaschistischen Romanen und Erzählungen von Christa Wolf, Hermann Kant, Alfred Wellm, Franz Fühmann, Helga Schütz, Wolfgang Kohlhaase, Erich Loest und anderen.

Darum soll es im folgenden gehen: die jüngste Prosa der DDR zum Thema Drittes Reich, ihre Voraussetzungen, ihre Ziele und ihre Grenzen. Drei Romane mögen dabei für drei Ansätze stehen, die sich abzuzeichnen beginnen: Hermann Kants Der Aufenthalt (1977) für das Fortschreiben der sozialistischen Bildungsbücher der 60er Jahre; Alfred Wellms Pugowitza oder Die silberne Schlüsseluhr (1975) für die scheinbar apolitischen Darstellungen des täglichen Faschismus; und Christa Wolfs Kindheitsmuster (1976) für die vorsichtigen Versuche, durch die Bewältigung von Vergangenheit zur Gegenwartsbewältigung beizutragen.

Gemein sind allen drei Strömungen die Voraussetzungen: auf dem Sektor Politik die relative Stabilisierung der DDR seit Anfang der 70er Jahre, in deren Gefolge neben sozialistisch-realistischen Erfolgsgeschichten immer mehr auch Erzählungen mit unglücklichem Ausgang, mit negativen Helden und mit gesellschaftlichen Außenseitern treten; sozio-

129

logisch der Versuch der mittleren Generation, der
zwischen 1925 und 1935 Geborenen also, ihrer mehr
oder weniger vom Faschismus geprägten Kindheit
nachzuspüren und sich der problematischen Neuan-
fänge nach 1945 zu erinnern; und literaturge-
schichtlich die Auflockerung des präskriptiven
Systems des sozialistischen Realismus, in deren
Gefolge Realismus nicht mehr mit Vorbildlichkeit
und Typik nicht mehr mit der Abbildung des "Vor-
wärtsdrängenden, Herausragenden im Sinne des his-
torischen Fortschritts" verwechselt wird.[8] Dazu
noch einmal Christa Wolf:

> Ich glaube nicht, daß wir die Zeit
> des Faschismus in diesem Sinne "be-
> wältigt" haben, auch wenn es in un-
> serem Staat in unvergleichbar ande-
> rer und gründlicherer Weise gesche-
> hen ist als zum Beispiel in der
> Bundesrepublik. Ich spreche jetzt
> von einer anderen Art der Bewälti-
> gung: die Auseinandersetzung des
> einzelnen mit seiner ganz persön-
> lichen Vergangenheit, mit dem, was
> er persönlich getan und gedacht hat
> . . . es ist, glaube ich, . . .
> Aufgabe von Literatur, etwas Bewe-
> gung hineinzubringen in die inneren
> Schichten, mit deren Unbeweglichkeit
> man sich gern beruhigt, indem man
> Erstarrung mit wirklicher Ruhe ver-
> wechselt. . . .[9]

Nun müssen freilich gemeinsame Voraussetzungen nicht auch gemeinsame Zielsetzungen nach sich
ziehen. Das gilt besonders, wenn jene potentielle
oder tatsächliche Existenz von faschistoiden Denk-
mustern in der DDR diskutiert wird, auf die Günter
Kunert 1975/76 im Zusammenhang einer Debatte um
Kleist, Goethe und die deutsche Romantik hingewiesen hat,[10] und die jüngst vom Akademiepräsidenten
Konrad Wolf im Rahmen einer Tagung zu "Kunst im
Kampf gegen Faschismus--heute und gestern" auf dem
Umweg über die Negation offiziell bestätigt wurde.[11]

Hermann Kant etwa drückt sich nämlich einfach
vor derart heiklen Themen. <u>Aufenthalt</u> nennt er
seinen Roman und das nicht nur, um die Erlebnisse
jenes 19jährigen Mark Niebuhr einzugrenzen, der
1945/46, nichtbegangener Kriegsverbrechen ange-
klagt, in einem Warschauer Gefängnis verbringt;
"Aufenthalt" spielt auch auf die Entwicklung von
Niebuhr an, auf seinen Weg von einem Mitläufer der
Faschisten zu einem standhaften Sozialisten. Nur
schreibt man freilich inzwischen das Jahr 1977,
gibt sich modern und möchte keinesfalls mit Willi
Bredel oder Dieter Noll verwechselt werden. Widerständler und Kommunisten treten bei Kant deshalb keine auf. Ebensowenig führt der Weg des
Mark Niebuhr auf den bekannten und ausgetretenen
Pfaden in die Arme eines sowjetischen Politinstruk-
teurs oder eines Mitglieds des Nationalkomitees
Freies Deutschland. Erziehung und weltanschau-
liche Gewißheiten werden vielmehr, ein wenig scham-
haft, in der Erzählstruktur des Romans verborgen:
in der robusten ideologischen Standhaftigkeit des
alles wissenden Autors und, daraus folgend, in dem
besserwisserischen Verhältnis des Erziehers zu
Jung-Niebuhr. Die "geringe Spanne an Bildung,"[12]
mit der Kant seinen Helden am Ende des Buches ent-
läßt, wird so mehr als wettgemacht, der vorzeitig
abgebrochene Bildungsprozeß des Kriegsgefangenen
Mark Niebuhr zu einem positiven Ende geführt, das
den vielbelächelten Wandlungsromanen der DDR-Früh-
zeit alle Ehre gemacht hätte. Auf die Frage "Wie
lange haben Sie für den 'Aufenthalt' gebraucht?"
gibt Kant sich in einem Selbstinterview, das nach
Christa Wolfs vorsichtig-tastendem Selbstgespräch
zu <u>Nachdenken über Christa T.</u> in seiner Simplizi-
tät recht peinlich berührt, die logische Antwort:
"Zweiunddreißig oder fünfzig Jahre."[13]

Abhilfe bringt da auch nicht, daß der Erzähler allerlei Schnurren, Anekdoten und Witzchen in
die Handlung einbaut. Im Gegenteil. Denn gerade
dort, wo seine Fabulierkunst tatsächlich einmal
sinnvoll eingesetzt ist und an die Groteske oder
an das Absurde heranreicht, wird besonders deutlich, daß es ihm immer nur um die Brüche in der
Welt von Mark Niebuhr, dem Soldaten geht, und nie

131

um die Ungereimtheiten in der Welt von Hermann
Kant, dem Funktionär des DDR-Schriftstellerver-
bands. Die Chance, durch die Augen eines naiven
jugendlichen Helden einen frischen Blick auf die
letzten Kriegsjahre zu werfen, wird so vergeben;
das Nachdenken über die komplexe Beziehung zwischen Wissen und Erinnern des Erwachsenen auf der
einen Seite und den Jugenderfahrungen, die diesem
Erinnern zugrundeliegen und es färben, auf der
anderen Seite, bleibt aus. Kants Aufenthalt reiht
sich beinahe nahtlos in die Ränge jener DDR-Bücher
ein, bei denen nichts herauskommt, weil in ihnen
"nichts schiefgehen" kann.[14]

Ähnliches scheint auch auf das zweite Buch
zuzutreffen, um das es hier gehen soll: Alfred
Wellms Pugowitza oder Die silberne Schlüsseluhr.
Ja, schlimmer noch: die Ereignisse der Jahre 1945/
46 scheinen diesmal zur Idylle verniedlicht, wäh-
rend die Konfrontation zwischen Faschismus und
Kommunismus zu den Privatgeschichtchen eines alten
ostpreußischen Fischers namens Komarek und eines
elternlosen zwölfjährigen Jungen verkommt, der
Heinrich heißt und Pugowitza genannt wird. Ein
Kinderbuch also, aus dem der Lektor vergessen hat,
Sätze zu streichen wie: "Vom Gemüt her ist der
russische Mensch gutmütig . . . , und ihm ist die
Gastfreundschaft zu eigen"?[15] Eine Fibel für FDJ-
Bibliotheken, in der der Kommunismus mit einem
großen, "reich" "mit zarten Hühnerkeulen . . . ,
mit . . . Götterspeise und mit süßer Limonade"
(S. 124) gedeckten Tisch verwechselt wird?

Ich glaube nicht, obwohl dieses Buch sicher-
lich auch für jugendliche Leser geschrieben wurde.
Was Wellm versucht, ist vielmehr, einen überaus
komplexen und problematischen Abschnitt deutscher
Geschichte dadurch erzählbar zu machen, daß er ihn
auf einfachste menschliche Erfahrungen reduziert:
auf die erste Begegnung mit den sowjetischen Be-
setzern zum Beispiel, die vor allem deshalb glimpf-
lich verläuft, weil sich Komarek aus dem ersten
Krieg zufällig ein russisches Wort gemerkt hat,
pugowitza, zu deutsch Hosenknopf; auf die Versu-
chung, durch den Schwarzmarkt zu schnellem Reich-

132

tum zu kommen; und, kaum angedeutet durch einen
legendären Spätheimkehrer aus dem Spanienkrieg,
auf den zähen, mühevollen Aufbau der neuen, sozialistischen Gesellschaftsordnung.

Naivität also, gewiß, aber nicht jene Naivität, die unreflektiert drauflosschwafelt und verwaschene Emotionen an die Stelle von Erkennen und
Wissen setzt, sondern Naivität, wie sie Anna Seghers meinte, als sie mit Tolstoi und gegen Lukács
für eine "bewußte" Unmittelbarkeit beim Schreiben
plädierte.[16] Bilder von Landschaften mit Seen,
Wäldern und Äckern, die damals, 1946, gerade ihre
Besitzer zu wechseln begannen; das alte Lehrer-
Schüler Verhältnis, bei dem sich die Beziehung
zwischen Gebendem und Nehmendem unmerklich ändert
und das dadurch nie in die Nähe jenes Stafetten-
prinzips gerät, das Willi Bredel schon im Titel
seiner Trilogie Die Väter (1943), Die Söhne (1949/
1952/1960), Die Enkel (1953) plakativ aushängt.
Und immer wieder simple, an Bobrowski oder auch
an die zeitgenössische russische Dorfliteratur von
Valentin Rasputin und Tschingis Aitmatov erinnern-
de Sätze wie: "Es hängen Erinnerungen an den Lie-
dern. Versteckenspiele an den Sommerabenden. Der
Himmel, unter dem die Krähenschwärme zogen. . . .
Er konnte lange nicht verstehen, daß die Lieder
ihn belogen hatten. Er nahm sich vor, die Melo-
dien und die Jahre zu vergessen. Aber es gelang
ihm nicht."[17]

Legt man Wellms Buch trotzdem mit einem etwas
unguten Gefühl aus der Hand, dann also gewiß nicht,
weil Komarek, zu alt, um am Aufbau der neuen Ordnung teilzunehmen, am Schluß in seine heimatlichen
masurischen Wälder zurückkehrt. Unwohl fühlt man
sich eher, weil Wellm konsequent die Frage umgeht,
was denn nun nach dreißig Jahren in Groß-Pelzkuh-
len und Umgebung aus jenem kindlich-utopischen
Traum vom Gleichheitskommunismus geworden ist,
weil er dort, wo Hermann Kant unverrückbare Gewißheiten zu besitzen scheint, eine Leerstelle hin-
terläßt. Was durch die naive Perspektive des
Zwölfjährigen auf der menschlichen, Franz Fühmann
würde sagen: mythischen, Ebene gewonnen wurde,

droht so auf der gesellschaftlich-historischen Ebene wieder verlorenzugehen. <u>Pugowitza</u> ist somit nicht weniger, aber auch nicht mehr als ein gelungener historischer Roman über die Frühzeit der DDR.

Genau an dieser Stelle kommt unser dritter Beispieltext, Christa Wolfs <u>Kindheitsmuster</u>, ins Spiel. Dessen "Stoff" ist nämlich nach Christa Wolfs eigener Aussage nicht mehr allein der "Faschismus (seine sozialökonomischen Wurzeln, die Eigentumsverhältnisse, aus denen er entstehen konnte usw.), sondern: die Struktur der Vergangenheitsbeziehungen meiner Generation, das heißt: . . . die historisch konkrete Behandlung der Vergangenheit soll mir einen Zugang zur Gegenwart eröffnen."[18] Deshalb der Titel: <u>Kindheitsmuster</u>; und deshalb die recht komplizierte Struktur des Romans, die sich aus drei Erzählschichten zusammensetzt: einer Vergangenheitsebene, auf der die Jahre 1933 bis 1946 behandelt werden, und zwei Gegenwartsebenen mit der Beschreibung eines Besuchs der Erzählerin in ihrer heute polnischen Heimatstadt Landsberg an der Warthe bzw. mit der Aufzeichnung von Erfahrungen und Gedanken bei der Niederschrift des Manuskripts zwischen 1972 und 1975. Das Ergebnis ist, daß die Gegenwart der Erzählerin (und, das sei hinzugefügt: auch die der Autorin und die des Lesers) weder, wie bei Kant, der Vergangenheit als Kontrollmechanismus übergeordnet ist, noch, wie bei Wellm, ausgespart bleibt. Gegenwart wird vielmehr durch den Prozeß der gesellschaftlichen, psychologischen und moralischen Selbstbefragung der Schreibenden teils direkt, teils vermittelt durch autobiographisches Nachdenken über den Provinzfaschismus im Landsberg der Jahre 1933ff. zum eigentlichen Thema des Buches. Vor die Frage: "Wie konnte das geschehen?" tritt die wichtigere Frage: "Wie sind wir so geworden, wie wir sind?"[19] und damit implizit das alles entscheidende Thema: "Kann sich so etwas hier und heute wiederholen?"

Die Antwort, kann man sich vorstellen, fällt bei Christa Wolf nicht so sicher aus, wie bei

Kant: "Ja, ich denke," heißt es da in jener bereits mehrfach zitierten Leserdiskussion in der Akademie der Künste, "das kann hier nicht wieder passieren. Doch wie man sieht, ist die Welt als Ganzes ungeheuer gefährdet in bezug auf faschistische und faschistoide Einflüsse . . . Da gibt es im Manuskript auch verschiedene Hinweise darauf . . . Gedankenlosigkeit, Unwissen, ungelebtes Leben. Da treten plötzlich Züge in den Leuten hervor, die einen erschrecken lassen, auch bei uns."[20]

Nun macht das Niederschreiben von Hinweisen noch keinen Roman aus und mit Zügen von Gefährdungen läßt sich Gestaltung nicht ersetzen. Will sagen: Christa Wolf hat sich ein Thema vorgenommen, das allem Anschein nach in der DDR heute noch nicht voll ausdiskutierbar ist. So kommt es, daß die Warnung vor einem "täglichen Faschismus im Land des realen Sozialismus"[21] auf einige wenige, unscheinbare Episoden beschränkt bleibt: Die Frage, ob sich die Verfolgung von Juden in der DDR wiederholen könnte, springt auf und wird in einem Halbsatz abgetan, noch bevor dem Leser die Situation in der Sowjetunion in den Sinn kommen könnte; Lenka, die halbwüchsige Tochter der Erzählerin, die bezeichnenderweise für ihre Umwelt selbst nur noch eine Phrase wie "pseudo"[22] findet, weiß von DDR-Jugendlichen zu berichten, die ausgerechnet in Prag Nazilieder singen; und ein befreundeter Lehrer, der aus recht dunklen Gründen unfähig ist, das Leben länger zu ertragen, streicht kurz vor seinem Selbstmord in Musils Der Mann ohne Eigenschaften die Sätze an: "Man hat nur die Wahl, diese niederträchtige Zeit mitzumachen (mit den Wölfen zu heulen) oder Neurotiker zu werden. Ulrich geht den zweiten Weg" (S. 114).

Trotzdem gilt es festzuhalten: Christa Wolfs Roman leistet, obschon auch er das Klassenziel nicht erreicht, mehr als die einschlägigen Bücher von Hermann Kant und von Alfred Wellm, von Erik Neutsch und von Helga Schütz, von Benito Wogatzki und auch von Wolfgang Kohlhaase.[23] Weltanschauungsdiskussionen und Wandlungsthemen haben in

Kindheitsmuster nämlich einer subjektiven Authentizität des Erzählens Platz gemacht und damit die Voraussetzung geschaffen für das von Kurt Batt für die sozialistische Literatur geforderte "Messen der heutigen Existenz an den moralischen Forderungen gegenüber den Taten von gestern."[24] Ideologische Sicherheit ist gekoppelt worden mit mahnendem und selbstkritischem Aufzeigen von falschen Denk- und Verhaltensmustern in der eigenen Gesellschaft. Das Verhältnis zwischen der Schuld der Väter und Mütter und der moralischen Integrität der Söhne und Töchter wird durch eine Figur wie Lenka zumindest angerissen; und die Aktivierung des Lesers wird durch die Problematisierung des Verhältnisses von ich, du und sie beim Schreiben befördert. Kurz: wo Hermann Kant und, auf andere Art, auch Alfred Wellm das Thema Nationalsozialismus möglichst weit auf Distanz bringen, wird der Leser von Kindheitsmuster durch den exemplarischen Selbstverständigungsversuch eines einzelnen Menschen angehalten, über die permanente Präsenz von faschistoiden Verhaltensmustern nachzudenken.

Geschichte wäre, so gesehen, in der Tat immer auch Vorgeschichte der eigenen Gegenwart und Erinnerung wäre die "Vorwegnahme von Noch-Nicht-Gewordenem."[25]

University of California

Anweisungen

[1] Bertolt Brecht, "Kulturpolitik und Akademie der Künste," in B.B., Gesammelte Werke (Frankfurt/M.: Suhrkamp, 1967), XIX, 543.

[2] Alexander Stephan, "Pläne für ein neues Deutschland. Die Kulturpolitik der Exil-KPD vor 1945," Basis. Jahrbuch für deutsche Gegenwartsliteratur, 7 (1977), 54-74.

[3] Leonore Krenzlin, "Rückblick aus dem Heu-

te," <u>Sonntag</u>, 14. 9. 1975, S. 3; u. <u>Sonntag</u>, 21. 9. 1975, S. 3; Karl-Heinz Hartmann, "Das Dritte Reich in der DDR-Literatur. Stationen erzählter Vergangenheit," in <u>Gegenwartsliteratur und Drittes Reich. Deutsche Autoren in der Auseinandersetzung mit der Vergangenheit</u>, hrsg. von Hans Wagener (Stuttgart: Reclam, 1977), S. 307-28; Manfred Behn, "Neuere antifaschistische Prosa der DDR," <u>Sammlung. Jahrbuch für antifaschistische Literatur und Kunst</u>, 1 (1978), 61-70; Therese Hörnigk, "Das Thema Krieg und Faschismus in der Geschichte der DDR-Literatur," <u>Weimarer Beiträge</u>, 24, No. 5 (1978), 73-105.

[4] Vgl. zum Beispiel Erich Loest, "Pistole mit sechzehn," <u>Sinn und Form</u>, 29, No. 1 (1977), 75: "Es scheint obenhin betrachtet denkbar, der Schriftsteller E. L. hätte sich um das Jahr 1955 herum einem Roman über die HJ zugewendet. . . . Denn nie ging er selbstsicherer an das Montieren von Fabeln heran . . . , nie war er überzeugter, genau zu wissen, wie ein Roman beschaffen sein mußte . . .; flink war er mit dem Urteilen und Verurteilen bei der Hand, . . . denn er wußte <u>alles</u> über den Sozialistischen Realismus und sein Kern- und Glanzstück, den Positiven Helden. . . . Also könnte, meinte er, niemals ein Hitlerjugendführer der Held eines Romans sein, sondern . . . immer nur ein Widerständler, ein kommunistischer am besten. Nein, es gab nichts in der Theorie und Praxis der fünfziger Jahre, das ermuntert hätte, sich am HJ-Stoff zu versuchen. . . ."

[5] Walter Ulbricht, "Zweijahrplan und Kulturarbeit. Aus der Rede auf der Arbeitstagung der Kulturarbeiter der SED (7.9.1948)," in W. U., <u>Zur Geschichte der deutschen Arbeiterbewegung. Aus Reden und Aufsätzen</u> (Berlin-Ost: Dietz, 1971), III, 576.

[6] "Diskussion mit Christa Wolf," <u>Sinn und Form</u>, 28, No. 4 (1976), 861.

[7] Vg. die Debatte zwischen Volker Braun, Hermann Kant, Christa Wolf, Alexander Abusch und ande-

ren im Rahmen der Arbeitsgruppe "Literatur und Geschichtsbewußtsein" auf dem VII. Schriftstellerkongreß der DDR, VII. Schriftstellerkongreß der Deutschen Demokratischen Republik. Protokoll (Arbeitsgruppen) (Berlin-Ost: Aufbau, o.J.), S. 76-166.

[8] Loest, "Pistole mit sechzehn," S. 75.

[9] "Diskussion mit Christa Wolf," S. 865.

[10] Günter Kunert wirft hier dem DDR-eigenen Lexikon deutschsprachiger Schriftsteller (Leipzig: Bibliographisches Institut, 1972) vor, "Goethes Urteil über die Kleistsche Dichtung als Zeichen von Krankheit, von Hypochondrie" ungeprüft zu übernehmen: ". . . wohingegen eine Welt, die sich als 'gesund' deklariert . . . , soweit selbst der Normalität enträt, daß sie ihre eigenen Leiden verkennt. . . . Wir wissen: es war dies die Welt des Faschismus und ist es heute immer noch dort, wo der Faschismus zur Macht gelangt . . ." "Pamphlet für K.," Sinn und Form, 27, No. 5 (1975), 1093.

[11] Konrad Wolf, "Kunst im Kampf gegen Faschismus--heute und gestern," Sonntag, 20. 5. 1959, S. 9: ". . . unsinnig ist es, bei jungen Menschen unseres Landes einen unterschwelligen Trend zu faschistoiden Verhaltensweisen anzunehmen."

[12] Silvia u. Dieter Schlenstedt, "Sehen Wissen Erinnern," Neue deutsche Literatur, 21, No. 6 (1973), 108.

[13] Hermann Kant, Der Aufenthalt (Berlin-Ost: Rütten & Loening, 1977), Klappentext.

[14] Wolfgang Werth, "Ein Mann ohne Gegenwart," Süddeutsche Zeitung, 12. 10. 1977.

[15] Alfred Wellm, Pugowitza oder Die silberne Schlüsseluhr (Berlin-Ost: Aufbau, 1975), S. 56.

[16] Anna Seghers, "Brief an Georg Lukács v. 28.

6. 1938," in: <u>Marxismus</u> <u>und</u> <u>Literatur</u>, hrsg. v. Fritz J. Raddatz (Reinbek: Rowohlt, 1969), II, 112.

[17] Wellm, <u>Pugowitza</u>, S. 100.

[18] Hans Kaufmann, "Gespräch mit Christa Wolf," <u>Weimarer</u> <u>Beiträge</u>, 20, No. 6 (1974), 103.

[19] "Diskussion mit Christa Wolf," S. 876.

[20] A. a. O., S. 876f.

[21] Andreas Lindner, "Nachtrag zum Fall Biermann," <u>Zeit</u> (nordamerikanische Ausg.), 3. 6. 1977.

[22] Christa Wolf, <u>Kindheitsmuster</u> (Berlin-Ost: Aufbau, 1976), S. 292 passim.

[23] Erik Neutsch, <u>Der</u> <u>Friede</u> <u>im</u> <u>Osten</u> (Halle: Mitteldeutscher Verlag, 1974). Helga Schütz, <u>Vorgeschichten</u> <u>oder</u> <u>Schöne</u> <u>Gegend</u> <u>Probstein</u> (Berlin-Ost: Aufbau, 1971); dies.: <u>Das</u> <u>Erdbeben</u> bei <u>Sangerhausen</u> <u>und</u> <u>andere</u> <u>Geschichten</u> (Berlin-Ost: Aufbau, 1972); dies.: <u>Festbeleuchtung</u> (Berlin-Ost: Aufbau, 1974); dies.: <u>Jette</u> <u>in</u> <u>Dresden</u> (Berlin-Ost: Aufbau, 1977). Benito Wogatzki, <u>Romanze</u> <u>mit</u> <u>Amélie</u> (Berlin-Ost: Neues Leben, 1977). Wolfgang Kohlhaase, <u>Silvester</u> <u>mit</u> <u>Balzac</u> <u>und</u> <u>andere</u> <u>Erzählungen</u> (Berlin-Ost: Aufbau, 1977).

[24] Kurt Batt, "Realität und Phantasie. Tendenzen in der Erzählliteratur der DDR," <u>Neue</u> <u>deutsche</u> <u>Literatur</u>, 24, No. 2 (1976), 14.

[25] Ernst Bloch, <u>Das</u> <u>Prinzip</u> <u>Hoffnung</u> (Frankfurt/M.: Suhrkamp, 1959), S. 10.

The Treatment of Holocaust Themes in GDR Fiction from the Late 1960s to the Mid-1970s: A Survey

Nancy A. Lauckner

Now that the emotionalism over the NBC-TV series Holocaust has subsided somewhat, it is appropriate to recall that holocaust themes have been presented frequently in both GDR and FRG literature since 1945. At first, this resulted from shame over the Nazi treatment of the Jews and from the desire of postwar authors to portray the Jews' fate in order to re-educate the German people. Interestingly, this trend has not quickly abated as the years have passed, nor have the nature and focus of the themes changed much, as I hope to show here by offering a survey of holocaust themes in GDR fiction from the late 1960s to the mid-1970s, starting almost twenty-five years after the war's end. With the exception of one long story, Fred Wander's Der siebente Brunnen (1971), I will focus on novels and treat Jurek Becker's Jakob der Lügner (1969) and Der Boxer (1976), Hermann Kant's Das Impressum (1972) and Der Aufenthalt (1977), and Christa Wolf's Kindheitsmuster (1976). While these are not the only GDR works which treat holocaust themes during the chosen time period, they are among the best and well represent the themes used at this time.

Three of the works selected focus directly on the holocaust: Becker's Jakob der Lügner and Der Boxer and Wander's Der siebente Brunnen, but each treats a different aspect of the holocaust in its own way. Becker's Jakob der Lügner depicts the early stage of ghetto life and deportation to the extermination camps. In theme, characters, and style, it represents a prelude to Der siebente Brunnen. Becker's self-effacing Jakob unintentionally becomes a hero when he passes along some good news he has accidentally learned about the Red Army's progress and then is forced to invent more reports from his imaginary radio when he sees that his "news" brings life and hope to the despairing ghetto, enabling many to live who would otherwise have committed suicide. Using the ingenious technique of the imaginary radio and its miraculous effects on the ghetto, Becker expresses the power of hope to lift spirits and help people retain their humanity and survive even in the most dreadful circumstances. The character of Jakob, however, represents an even greater tribute to the strength and endurance of the human spirit, for he alone knows that his news items are false and bears the burden of having to create them anyway because the entire ghetto depends on this lifeline. Thus, except for one lapse which costs the life of his closest friend, he continues his "lies" despite his own desperate loneliness and the awareness that there may be no hope.

Often a holocaust theme casts an irremediable pall of gloom over a work, yet this novel escapes that fate in a way unique in holocaust literature. Remarkably, Jakob der Lügner treats its theme with a gentle, charming, yet dignified humor that provides an unforgettable, delightful atmosphere without detracting from the suffering of the characters. This humor derives from several sources, among them Becker's ingenious fable of Jakob's difficulties because of his imaginary radio[1] and the author's skillful use of a reluctant hero with this plot. Most important, however, is Becker's modern adaptation of the Yiddish tradition[2] of treating melancholy and tragic events from a humorous perspective.[3] The warmth of this tradition infuses the "unbekümmerten und ostentativ gemächlichen Plauderton" used to recount the daily horrors[4] and appears in the three major types of humor which Becker employs—situational, narrative, and dialogue.[5] Becker's facile invention

of hilarious situations and his use of expressive
narrative language and felicitous dialogue worthy
of a Sholem Aleichem[6] create "die einzelnen Humo-
resken und Miniaturen" of which the novel consists,
as Reich-Ranicki points out.[7] Characterization,
too, contributes to the humor, as Becker skill-
fully sketches typical, average characters with
all the usual human weaknesses, whose interactions
in the ghetto reveal human comedy as well as those
of the traditional shtetl characters. Even the
narrator's capricious invention of two endings and
his use of fairy-tale elements and special effects
like Jakob's imitation of a radio are consonant
with humor in the Yiddish tradition. All the humor here is used successfully to provide just
enough distance and relief from the horrors to enable the reader to confront the holocaust theme.
Thanks to Becker's humorous approach, Jakob der
Lügner is an optimistic work despite the death of
most of its characters.[8] One reads it with plea-
sure tinged with sadness and remembers it with
gratitude.

Fred Wander's Der siebente Brunnen takes up
where Becker's work ends, in a sense, because it
treats the next stage of the holocaust: the concentration camp experience, the forced marches,
and liberation.[9] This long story might also be
considered a short novel as it contains twelve
chapters which use the same first person narrator
and many repeated characters. In theme, characters, and style, it often resembles the work of
Jurek Becker, Isaac B. Singer, and Elie Wiesel,
and occasionally that of Bruno Apitz and Anna Seghers. The central theme uniting all of Wander's
stories is a psychological and philosophical one,
reminiscent of Victor Frankl's Man's Search for
Meaning: What enables certain individuals to
retain their humanity and survive even in the most
degrading and life-threatening circumstances?
Pointing out the tenuous line between exerting the
will to live and yielding to the longing for
death's peace (p. 109), Wander focuses on characters who develop good survival and coping tactics
and shows that survival depends on the individu-

al's determination to taste life to its depths no
matter what it brings (p. 29) and to hold fast to
the dream "von seinem verlorenen schönen Leben,
von der Freiheit und von der Reinheit des Herzens"
(p. 17). He enumerates many ways of accomplishing
this: protection of children; discussion of beautiful memories; comradeship with others; religious
faith and prayer; self-sacrifice for friends; practice of previous special interests like literature, mathematics, and music; determination to get
revenge; political associations for resistance,
often organized by communists; and finally, the
power of love. Like Jakob, one of Wander's characters also finds the strength to tell encouraging
lies to keep others' hope alive, although he knows
the dreadful truth (p. 83). Repeatedly the narrator asks why the inmates attempt to prolong life
even in the face of torture and imminent, inevitable death, and finally recognizes: "Wenn der
Mensch sterben soll, entdeckt er den Zauber des
Daseins" (p. 121).

Although the influence of the Yiddish story-
telling tradition is evident in many of Wander's
tales, he seldom uses the humorous aspects as
Becker does. Rather he tells his story realistically and straightforwardly, heightening the human
drama by providing glimpses into his characters'
happy past and describing their varied efforts to
survive their present plight. His work is remarkable for its sympathetic psychological insights,
not only into the victims but into the persecutors
as well, for he repeatedly shows the Jews seeking
reasons for the cruelty of the guards (p. 24) and
pitying them for not realizing their guilt (p. 13).
Like Christa Wolf, he portrays the ordinary citizen's indifference to their suffering as self-pre-
servation (p. 64) and even recalls the generosity
of a few helpers (pp. 99f.).

Wander relieves the stark realism of his work
and provides a more universal context by using
techniques typical of the Yiddish tradition. Thus,
he uses Biblical quotations, letting the words of
Jeremiah and Ezekiel about ancient persecutions

symbolize this one as well, and he also places the holocaust in the context of other persecutions by quoting the wisdom of later Jewish sages (pp. 69f., 105f., 109, et passim). His frequent symbols complement the work well, for some, like the forest motif (p. 110) reminiscent of the tree symbolism in Jakob der Lügner,[10] derive from the experiences of his characters, while others stem from the wisdom of the sages, like the title symbol of "der siebente Brunnen," which Wander uses to express purification through suffering and hope for the future (p. 48). Despite its setting, his book, too, is an optimistic work, for it ends with the joy of liberation and the rebirth of life.[11] Symbolically it has a mass hero because the individuals who survive represent the survival of the Jewish people itself and of human dignity (p. 136).

Becker's Der Boxer, the third work which focuses on a holocaust theme, is a major literary portrayal of the psychological adjustment problems of Jewish survivors, a topic seldom treated in detail.[12] Here Becker develops a holocaust theme in a postwar setting to show the continuing effects of the past on survivors. After six years in concentration camps, his protagonist, Aron Blank, can not adjust satisfactorily to postwar life and demonstrates symptoms common to many survivors: he suffers from insomnia and nightmares about the camps; distrusts and spies on outsiders; fears fascism, and becomes paranoid about non-existent anti-Semitic outbreaks and pogroms; lapses into reclusiveness intensified by introversion, loneliness, tiredness and boredom; cannot get used to having possessions and money; takes up drinking to dull his melancholy; and maintains an ambivalent relationship with other survivors. One of his few positive characteristics is exaggerated in a manner common among survivors: he is obsessed with his "son" and determined to ensure survival and a good life for him. Existing as an "Opfer des Faschismus und nichts anderes" (p. 249), Aron vividly demonstrates the power of the past over the present for many survivors.

This theme accounts for the sombre mood of Der Boxer, which contrasts so sharply with the intimate warmth of Jakob der Lügner, even though Aron survives and Jakob perishes. Essentially Der Boxer is a literary version of a clinical study, a psychological portrait of a survivor unable to shake off the past, so Becker necessarily develops his theme and character realistically. Although Aron represents an extreme case, his depiction is accurate, for many survivors share some of his reactions. In contrast to the previous two works, Der Boxer is depressingly pessimistic, because Aron's total passivity and mere existence in the postwar world are far harder to bear than the valiant struggle of the characters in the other works to live with dignity despite their degrading circumstances. The human spirit triumphs in them, while it capitulates in Aron. Both the victory and the defeat are historically accurate, although the latter probably occurred more frequently. By placing Aron's resignation in the postwar era, Becker portrays the devastating long-term psychological effects of the holocaust especially well.

He also adapts some of the techniques used in Jakob der Lügner to the special needs of Der Boxer. Again the influence of Yiddish tradition is evident in the conversational flavor[13] achieved here by the exchanges between the first person narrator and Aron as the latter tells his story, and in the characterization of Aron, who shares with Jakob such traditional characteristics as "List, Umsicht, Geduld und menschlich[e] Güte."[14] Some distance is created by the device of the two narrators and by subdued humor and irony. However, the distance is far less pronounced than in Jakob der Lügner, and the humor is necessarily much less frequent, less lighthearted, and more acrid.

The three remaining novels do not focus on the holocaust, yet each work contains Jewish characters and provides insight into holocaust-related themes from the different perspectives of the effect the holocaust had on the protagonist and other Germans. This perspective is found less often

146

in earlier postwar works, and we will probably witness an increase in the use of it now that greater temporal distance from the holocaust enables more Germans to examine their attitudes and actions in that period.

Thus Kant's <u>Das Impressum</u> primarily concerns David Groth's taking stock of his life when the Party calls him to ministerial rank, but the holocaust, though a minor theme in the novel, deeply affects him and his future as a good Party member.[15] Because he is named for his father's Jewish employer, David Blumenthal, and enjoys his patronage, David is linked with the Jews from his birth. Blumenthal becomes one of the earliest victims of the holocaust because his public derision of a nationalistic speech by the councillor Wolter in February, 1933 results in his being drowned by Wolter. When David's father, Wilhelm Groth, goes to court to accuse Wolter of the crime, he is sentenced to hard labor at Dachau for daring to defend a Jew's reputation against a German. David himself suffers persecution in school because a fascist teacher, Kasten, repeatedly derides him for his "Jewish" name, his connection with Blumenthal, and his father's fate; he is refused admission to the <u>Mittelschule</u> and <u>Gymnasium</u> because of his father's record. Kasten is also responsible for the death of the second Jewish character, Ascher, who returns to his destroyed warehouse after <u>Kristallnacht</u>, only to be forced to stand in a crucifixion pose while Kasten's SA men fire chamber pots at him. Untreated for his wounds, Ascher dies at Neugamme.

Although the fate of these two Jews and Wilhelm Groth's suicide are only incidental to the main plot, Kant's narrator explicitly justifies recounting them in great detail because "David [wäre] am Ende nicht . . . , was er ist, wären in seinen Anfängen nicht so viele blutrünstige Schäbigkeiten gewesen" (p. 48). Thus, his exposure to the holocaust and his own persecution give him an anti-fascist, humanitarian viewpoint that prepares him to become a good Party member.

His father teaches him to avoid attracting attention without compromising the family's antifascist stance (p. 60) and imbues him with the humanitarian principles of standing up for truth and concern for others (pp. 62-63) that David later sees represented by the Party. These early experiences repeatedly affect David's subsequent attitudes: thus, he always believes he is engaged in a struggle (p. 135); he condemns all forms of prejudice (pp. 207-208); and he has great difficulty in maintaining a civil relationship when he discovers the fascist past of a fellow employee (pp. 235-36).

Kant treats his holocaust theme, like his main plot, with the realism and humor characteristic of all his works. The chamber pot incident and Blumenthal's characterization of Wolter's speech as "so tief und so mitreißend wie der Küchenbach" (p. 35), however, demonstrate well that Kant's humor ridicules the Nazis, rather than disparaging the suffering of the Jews. Like the humor used by previously mentioned authors, Kant's holocaust-related humor also serves as a distancing device.

Again in <u>Der Aufenthalt</u>, Kant's holocaust theme is only secondary, and he uses it from the perspective of the effect of the holocaust on his protagonist Mark Niebuhr and other Germans, specifically addressing the issue of guilt.[16] In this novel, too, Kant employs the techniques of realism and humor, but the latter occurs very seldom with the holocaust theme. When it is used in this connection, it tends to be a satirical, even bitter humor directed against the war criminals rather than the Jewish victims. Little distance is achieved by this humor because of its bitterness and scarcity.

Kant focuses on Mark's experiences as a prisoner of war and his gradual political reeducation about German war crimes. The holocaust theme plays a part in this reeducation and appears in several ways. One of Mark's fellow prisoners, who constantly makes vulgar anti-Semitic remarks, offends the others because they prefer to leave this aspect of the outside world behind them and to forget that they once shared these views (p. 125). However, contact with three Jews precludes forgetting, gradually teaches Mark about war crimes, and prepares him to realize his own guilt.

The first of these is the Russian Jewish woman doctor who treats Mark's frostbitten feet and concussion and converses with him about Roman history and Barthold Niebuhr. While she serves as a living corrective to the propaganda he has heard about Jews and "das kommunistische Flintenweib" (p. 97), he resists her calling him a fascist (p. 93) until he catches a first glimmer of understanding as he watches her expression run the gamut of emotions as she practices the many ways one can say the word "Deutscher" (p. 90). Although he never sees her again, her influence already modifies some of his false political ideas during his time in her tutelage and certainly prepares him to be receptive to the corrective political teachings of others later. This influence lingers even after his release, always forcing him to re-examine his opinion (p. 103) and to consider opposing views (p. 104).

The next Jewish character, Herzog, has much less effect on Mark's political reeducation yet contributes significantly to his release. A prisoner himself, Herzog serves as interpreter for "der Chef," who interrogates Mark on behalf of the Polish prisoners about his alleged participation in war crimes. Despite spitting at Mark on command, Herzog clearly suffers from the anti-Semitism of the Polish prisoners even though they side with him against the Germans (pp. 195, 207). Yet it is Herzog's letter to the authorities certifying Mark's innocence which aids greatly in effecting his release. By that time Mark has learned enough to recognize the irony and perhaps also the touching decency of a Jew's speaking out for a German wrongfully accused of war crimes (p. 596).

149

The third Jewish character is long since dead by the time her name appears in the story, yet her fate prompts Mark to learn about Nazi crimes and decisively affects his growing awareness of guilt. On a demolition detail, he finds a pencil box cover bearing the name Jadwiga Sierp and the date 1934. Correctly interpreting a fellow prisoner's drastic symbolic hint that the owner was Jewish and that she was murdered by the Germans (p. 284), he finally starts to think of something besides his own plight and to realize that others have suffered even greater injustice (p. 286). He tries to imagine what Jadwiga's life was like in order to see her as another human being. Recognizing his lack of detailed knowledge about the fate of the Warsaw Jews but knowing the Germans are responsible for it, he still denies any personal guilt because he did not participate in these crimes (pp. 292-93). Thus he is ready for the graphic lessons he learns on his visit with the Polish lieutenant to the former Warsaw ghetto, where the enormity of the German war crimes finally becomes a reality to him (pp. 409-32).

These contacts with the holocaust lead him to question others and to learn all he can about these crimes until he realizes that, despite having no direct personal responsibility for war crimes, he shares in the guilt because his role as a common soldier facilitated others' commission of unhumane acts (pp. 484, 509). Thus he finally understands his situation and his responsibility to the Poles (p. 491).

Wolf's Kindheitsmuster, too, does not focus on its holocaust theme, but rather on the narrator's process of reunification with her childhood self through conscientiously recalling the past.[17] As in Der Aufenthalt, the holocaust theme here is only part of the larger theme of the unbewältigte Vergangenheit, which is treated from the perspective of its effect on the protagonist and other Germans and specifically focuses on the issue of guilt and the need to come to terms with the past. Although several Jewish characters appear in the work, they play such a minor role that they cannot be discussed separately here. Their stories, however, are part of the considerable information on the persecution of the Jews presented in connection with Nelly's story and portrayed as general knowledge among the German populace at the time they were happening: the persecution for participation in Rassenschande, the boycott of Jewish businesses and the expulsion of Jews from certain professions, the loss of Jewish businesses to Aryans, emigration to escape worse consequences, various kinds of anti-Semitic propaganda, persecution of Jewish school children, Kristallnacht, genealogical research to establish one's race, the Endlösung, the concentration camps, and the death marches.[18] Such memories vividly corroborate Wolf's depiction of a childhood "in den Schatten der Öfen von Auschwitz" (p. 326).

Because she focuses her holocaust theme on the protagonist and other Germans, Wolf concerns herself with the memory process and portrays German forgetfulness as a defense mechanism to avoid the pain of recognizing one's complicity in Nazi crimes (p. 303). Clearly, she espouses Kant's view that most Germans who were adults in the Nazi era share in this guilt, even if they did not participate directly, because their conforming and non-intervention permitted these crimes (p. 227). However, she takes the issue of guilt and the need to come to terms with the past one step farther than Kant by describing the current attitudes of GDR citizens toward the past and particularly towards the holocaust. Thus, she shows that the sympathies of GDR youth, as represented by Lenka, are entirely with the Jews and the other victims, although their rather inexact knowledge about the past prevents a strong emotional reaction to it (p. 309). Surely Wolf intends Kindheitsmuster to correct this deficiency.[19] The reactions of contemporaries of her own age are more varied, among them indifference to the Nazi era as so distant and unrelated to them as the Tertiary (p. 200), the unthinking disrespect evinced by visitors to Buchenwald (p. 310), the view that Soviet offenses against German civilians more than outweigh any German crimes (pp. 465-66), and a consciousness of guilt and embarrassment in dealings with Jews (p. 181). Certainly Wolf hopes that Kindheitsmuster will facilitate her contemporaries' access to their own memories of the past,[20] an appropriate recognition of guilt, and the subsequent building of an improved postwar relationship between Germans and Jews.

Thus, this brief survey shows that the early postwar interest in holocaust themes continues unabated in GDR literature in the late 1960s to the mid-1970's. Little change has occurred in the treatment of these themes since the early period. The frequency and extent of their use remain essentially the same. However, the proportion of superior authors treating these themes is somewhat greater now, and there also seems to be a growing interest in portraying the postwar effect of the holocaust on Germans as they confront the guilt issue and try to come to terms with their past, while previously the focus has been largely on the Jews. It will be interesting to observe whether the future will bring increased use of holocaust themes and any important changes in their treatment.

The University of Tennessee, Knoxville

Notes

[1] Melvin Kornfeld, "Preface," in Jacob the Liar, trans. by Melvin Kornfeld (New York/London: Harcourt Brace Jovanovich, 1975), p. vii.

[2] Fritz J. Raddatz, "Eine neue sozialistische Literatur entsteht," in his Traditionen und Tendenzen: Materialien zur Literatur der DDR (Frankfurt/M.: Suhrkamp, 1972, p. 372.

[3] Marcel Reich-Ranicki, "Roman vom Getto: Jurek Becker, Jakob der Lügner," in his Zur Literatur der DDR (Munich: Piper, 1974), p. 148.

[4] Reich-Ranicki, p. 146.

[5] Nancy A. Lauckner, "Jurek Becker's Treatment of the Past," unpublished paper read at the Fourth GDR Symposium, Conway, N.H., June 1978, p. 17. See that paper, on which this essay is partially based, for more detailed discussion of the treatment of the holocaust themes in Becker's Jakob der Lügner and Der Boxer.

[6] See also Kornfeld's comparison of Becker's narrative techniques with those of Sholem Aleichem, pp. v-vii.

[7] Reich-Ranicki, p. 146.

[8] Raddatz points out that "die optimistische Tragödie" has a long tradition in socialist literature (p. 372).

[9] Fred Wander, Der siebente Brunnen (Berlin/Weimar: Aufbau, 1976).

[10] Jurek Becker, Jakob der Lügner (Neuwied/Berlin: Luchterhand, 1970), pp. 5-7 et passim.

[11] See preface to Wander, Der siebente Brunnen, pp. 1-2.

[12] Jurek Becker, Der Boxer (Frankfurt/M.: Suhrkamp, 1976).

[13] Cf. Klaus-Dieter Hähnel, "Jurek Becker: Der Boxer," Weimarer Beiträge, 23, No. 7 (1977), 148.

[14] Hähnel, pp. 144, 149.

[15] Hermann Kant, Das Impressum (Frankfurt/M.: Fischer, 1975).

[16] Hermann Kant, Der Aufenthalt (Berlin: Rütten

& Loening, 1977).

[17] Christa Wolf, Kindheitsmuster (Berlin/Weimar: Aufbau, 1976).

[18] For further information on this and other aspects of the holocaust theme in Kindheitsmuster mentioned here, see the two treatments on which my brief discussion in this paper is based: Nancy A. Lauckner, "The Socialist Writer as Link Between Past and Future: Christa Wolf Confronts the 'Unconquered Past,'" unpublished paper read at Third GDR Symposium, Conway, N.H., June 1977; and Nancy A. Lauckner, "Christa Wolf's Kindheitsmuster," unpublished chapter of a book in progress on the works of Christa Wolf, eds. Theodor Langenbruch and Nancy A. Lauckner.

[19] See Christa Wolf, in "Diskussion mit Christa Wolf," Sinn und Form, 28, No. 4 (1976), 869-70.

[20] Christa Wolf, in "Diskussion mit Christa Wolf," 864-65. See also Heinz Plavius, "Gewissensforschung," rev. of Kindheitsmuster, Neue deutsche Literatur, 25, No. 1 (Jan. 1977), 144.

Satire and Societal Criticism
in the GDR Picaresque Novel

William Walker

R.C. Andrews observed that "the comic novel is not a natural growth in the GDR. Socialist realism, one might suppose is far too serious an ideal to be entrusted to humorists."[1] If one were to accept this assumption as valid, one might feel equally disinclined from believing that the picaresque rogue, society's non-partisan, alienated rascal par excellence, could occupy a significant place in the GDR literary tradition, which promotes, at least theoretically, the socialist world view of collective, non-alienated human existence. These introductory assumptions about literature in the GDR are at best partial truths, as indicated by the fact that at least two GDR writers have found the caustic, critical satire of the picaresque novel eminently suited for their respective novels: Erwin Strittmatter's Der Wundertäter (Vol. I, 1957), and Manfred Bieler's Bonifaz oder Der Matrose in der Flasche (1963).[2] The following investigation will focus on the surprisingly different ways in which Strittmatter and Bieler use satire as a means of effecting societal criticism within the potentially constraining framework of GDR socialist realism. The analysis will take into account the degree to which the nature and object of their satire is conditioned by the ideological position of each writer, with Strittmatter as an example of the committed socialist and Bieler as a dissident voice.

In the first volume of Der Wundertäter, Strittmatter describes in an episodic fashion the tribu-

155

lations of a naive simpleton from the rural German working class, Stanislaus Büdner, as he seeks moral and physical survival in a debased, exploitative society between the years 1909-1945. Beginning with the ejection of Stanislaus from his impoverished village, Strittmatter creates a vast panorama of perilous stations for his hero which ends seventy-six episodes later in the desertion of Stanislaus from the German army during World War II. In a manner reminiscent of Grimmelshausen's *Simplicius Simplicissimus*, the concluding pages of the novel trace the hero's flight into exile on a small Greek island, where he elects the life of a solitary monk.

Strittmatter establishes a socialist perspective for the examination of the novel's stations by creating what Ulrich Wicks has called the essential picaresque situation: an oppressive social climate which is "chaotic beyond ordinary human tolerance."[3] The initial ejection of Stanislaus from his native village has its origin in the perverse behavior of an exploitative, oppressive bourgeois class. Stanislaus must not only undertake a journey away from home in order to support his father, an unemployed labor agitator; he must also escape the wrath of a count who seeks revenge for Stanislaus' disclosure that the count's wife is involved in coercive, adulterous adventures with the household servants. The severity of the social climate is such that the Büdner line has evolved by necessity into a nearly indestructible organism: "Kurzum, die Büdners trotzen Tod und Verderben wie die Unkräuter am Wegrand, deren Lebenskraft der Stunde ihrer Entdeckung und Verwendung zuharrt" (p. 10).

As the arduous journey for survival begins, the primary object of Strittmatter's satire is the constellation of debased ministers, work-masters, military officers, and other representatives of the bourgeois class who conspire to use and abuse Stanislaus for their own purposes. The experiences of Stanislaus with eight different work-masters alone serve to illustrate the manner in

156

which a satirical depiction of the bourgeoisie
emerges from the juxtaposition of the oppressor
"der jeden Schläger und Aufsetzer marktfähig macht
und mit Gewinn verkauft" (p. 120) and the oppressed, "die Ochsen des Handwerks" (p. 88). Although
the author's point of view towards the bourgeoisie
is revealed through such narrative devices, Strittmatter relies heavily upon the irony inherent in
the employers' own remarks to reveal the self-
serving nature of the bourgeois value system: the
baker Klutsch requires Stanislaus to rise for work
by 5:00 a.m. and to continue laboring until mid-
night; Klutsch bases his work practices on the rationale: "ein jaches Pferd muß müde gemacht werden" (p. 133). In another episode Stanislaus is
dismissed from his job for having broken his arm:
"Ohrfeigen sollt' man dich. Auf meine Kosten den
Arm brechen! Soll man jeden Zugelaufenen bei der
Krankenversicherung melden?" (p. 201).

Michael Nerlich has observed that once the
rogue recognizes the peril, coping becomes mani-
fest in either of two comic ways: either "im gut-
mütigen Lachen" or "im spöttischen Gelächter."[4]
Stanislaus is indeed clearly cognizant of the dangers in society and recognizes that he must adopt
strategies for maintaining his physical and moral
well-being: "Er hatte entdeckt, daß man nicht nur
seine Glieder, sondern auch sein Herz vor leicht-
sinnigen Verletzungen schützen mußte" (p. 41).
Stanislaus does not elect to satirize society in a
cunning, ironic fashion; to the contrary, he opts
for indifference to society's dangers and becomes
a comic devil who allows his fantasy free play
while enjoying life's few pleasures whenever the
opportunity appears.

In his reflections on Hitler, for example,
Stanislaus reveals his total indifference to society's evils: "Es waren Nachrichten über Verhaftun-
gen von Hitlerschmähern zu ihm in die Gärten des
Geistes und der Wissenschaft gedrungen" (p. 226).
Instead of searching out the causes for societal
abuses and confronting the opponent in a satiric
fashion, Stanislaus merely places the blame on

God's shoulders: "Gott saß vielleicht auf einer
blauen Wiese und spielte mit den Menschen wie Kinder mit Marienkäfern" (p. 171). "Neben Gottes
Thron sitzt ein kleiner Teufel. Er ist der Hof-
narr des heiligen Herrn in den Wolken. . . .
'Treib ein wenig Unwesen,' sagt der Herr zum Teu-
felchen, 'sonst frißt mich die Langweile!'" (p.
97).

Stanislaus consequently indulges in countless
comic episodes, including the enactment of mock
crucifixions in the village square or magic tricks
to demonstrate that his youthful, mischievous nature cannot be corrupted or restrained by oppression. It is precisely this type of disaffiliation
from a personal engagement of society's problems
which causes Fritz J. Raddatz to state: "Stanislaus ist kein Kämpfer, eher ein Versponnener."[5]
Reich-Ranicki continues this line of thought by
noting: "Nicht der Klassenkämpfer, der Schalk hat
hier das Wort. Vielmehr handelt es sich um eine
primitive, unverblümte, gesund-kräftige Lebens-
weisheit, die bisweilen amüsant ist, meist harmlos
wirkt, und immer vordergründig bleibt."[6]

Strittmatter relies extensively on the responses and reactions of the bourgeoisie to Stanislaus'
mischievous behavior as an additional means of satire. In one episode, a pious minister responds to
the amorous intentions of Stanislaus towards his
daughter in an unseemly, grotesque fashion: "Bau-
ernlümmel! Hurer! Verführer! . . . Hungern, bis
dir die Geilheit aus dem Blute schwindet! . . .
Wenn wir nicht fromm und heilig wären, sollte dein
Arsch nicht mehr in die Hose passen, so wollt' ich
dich gerben" (p. 117).

Of equal importance for the satiric tone of
the novel is the contribution made by an aged co-
worker of Stanislaus, the baker Gustav. Gustav,
a long-time socialist, continuously attacks the
evils of fascism in his dialogues with Stanislaus;
the manner in which he presents his comments is
invariably ironic and humorous. In his remarks on
Hitler, for example: "Er wird alles umgestalten

und keinen auslassen. Jetzt hat er meine Frau von der Fabrik befreit. Alle Arbeit den Männern! Wie? Der Adolf ist, wenn ich's dialektisch betrachte, ein menschlicher Mensch" (p. 226). Even in the presence of a socialist critique of existing social conditions, Stanislaus remains indifferent and uncommitted. As Gustav observes: "Andere Jungleute sind straff und marschieren, du aber schleppst, wenn ich's dialektisch betrachte, den Kopf unterm Arm" (p. 225). "Alle Welt macht Marschmusik, und du streichst die einsame Fiedel" (p. 225).

The following question should be posed at this point: To what extent is satire in Der Wundertäter compatible with socialist realism in the GDR? In his address to the First Congress of Soviet Writers in 1934, Andrej Shdanov gave a definition of socialist realism which was to become the normative guideline for the later production and publication of literature in the GDR: "Der sozialistische Realismus . . . fordert vom Künstler wahrheitsgetreue, historisch konkrete Darstellung der Wirklichkeit in ihrer revolutionären Entwicklung. Wahrheitstreue und historische Konkretheit der künstlerischen Darstellung muß mit den Aufgaben der ideologischen Umgestaltung und Erziehung der Werktätigen im Geiste des Sozialismus verbunden werden."[7] Although the concept of a socialist realism has been subject to interpretation, especially during "freezes" and "thaws" in GDR cultural policy, it is apparent from Kurt Hager's 1971 address before the SED that socialist realism still maintains its essential function of promoting and reinforcing socialist thought among the masses: "Die sozialistische Kultur und Kunst hat die Aufgabe, die Entwicklung sozialistischer Persönlichkeiten und ihre bewußte schöpferische Tätigkeit zu fördern und zur Stärkung des sozialistischen Bewußtseins einen hohen Beitrag zu leisten."[8]

Strittmatter has clarified his understanding of socialist realism to mean a presentation of the dialectic class tensions which underline GDR social reality, especially in terms of economic and political contradictions inherent in a bourgeois ideology: "Dialektik und sozialistischer Realismus gehören zusammen. Das wird - wie mir scheint - von uns zu wenig beachtet. . . . Es ist mir einfach nicht möglich, alle Verästelungen eines Vorganges, den ich beschreiben . . . will, aufzuspüren, wenn ich mich nicht in die ökonomischen und politischen Zusammenhänge, in die ihm innewohnenden Widersprüche vertiefe."[9] The debased nature of the bourgeois class, as opposed to the naive, healthy optimism of Stanislaus, is revealed through the satire which emerges from the dialectical juxtaposition of oppressor and oppressed.

Although satire in the first volume of Der Wundertäter serves as a means of exposing and illustrating the contradictions inherent in a bourgeois ideology, it does not resolve the contradictions. The passive aloofness and comic mischievousness of Stanislaus can not be sustained in the midst of the brutality of the war, which is described in the concluding pages of the novel. Stanislaus is reduced to tragic pathos and near defeat: "Furcht und Empörung machten ein klapperndes Bündel aus ihm. . . ." (p. 347). The degree of alienation and misery which Stanislaus experiences becomes so great that he feels his only alternative to be exile. While in exile on a Greek island, he does experience an epiphany that reveals to him an apparent resolution of the conflict; the revelation, however, is not that of participating in a new socialist order where alienation and oppression will be eliminated. To the contrary, his vision of the future is that of a utopian reintegration with nature: "Es braucht nicht viel, sich zu verstehen, wenn die alten, verläßlichen Dinge da sind: die Berge, der Himmel, die Quelle, das Feuer, das Tier, und die Frucht; wenn die verwirrende Vielfalt der Welt die Menschen nicht bestürmt. . . ." (p. 448).

The conclusion of the first volume of Der Wundertäter, when considered in connection with the non-aligned stance of Stanislaus throughout the novel, indicates clearly the degree to which a

160

fully realized socialist perspective is absent in the consciousness of Stanislaus, even in spite of Strittmatter's use of satire to reveal the incongruities and contradictions inherent in bourgeois ideology. It comes as no surprise that Strittmatter elected to continue the novel. The second volume of Der Wundertäter, which appeared in 1972, traces the return of Stanislaus to the Soviet Zone after the end of World War II, where he actively participates in the construction of a new socialist order as a journalist and aspiring novelist. The absence of satire and roguish behavior in this volume would seem to indicate that Strittmatter considers the type of societal criticism found in the first volume to be no longer necessary in a society without bourgeois abuses.

The nature and object of satire within the context of the GDR picaresque novel may be understood even more clearly when comparing the first volume of Der Wundertäter with the strikingly different picaresque novel by Manfred Bieler, Bonifaz oder Der Matrose in der Flasche (1963). The hero of Bieler's novel, the adventurer and sailor Bonifaz, returns to Germany during the final days of World War II after having been interned as a prisoner of war for four years. The release of Bonifaz is contingent upon his oath of strict neutrality upon his return to Germany. During the sixty-seven episodes of the novel, Bonifaz struggles to survive the perilous final days of the Nazi regime, the subsequent Russian occupation, and a series of absurd, potentially life-threatening stations during his journey through postwar Germany.

While Strittmatter's satire is directed at the bourgeois class exploitation of the worker, Bieler concentrates a major part of his satire on the relativity and changeability of man's allegiances and "virtues" in light of self-interest. The chaotic, uncertain nature of the situation becomes a study in paradox: "Morgen war Unrecht Recht und Recht Verbrechen!" (p. 14).

The degree to which individuals' values can

be changed to suit changing circumstances is developed satirically in each of the novel's three
primary stations. During the first station, the
final days of the Nazi resistance in Bonifaz' home
town, Tesch, the local sculptor Professor Wollgast
busily reconstructs the statue of Freia into that
of Roosevelt and Stalin. In a similar vein, the
friar Lewerenz decides to let his hair grow longer.

The second station of the novel, commencing
with the ejection of Bonifaz from the Soviet Zone,
where he served as acting mayor of the town of
Roßbach, and continuing with Bonifaz' journey to
the West, focuses on patriotism and economic self-
interest. The rationale for perverse behavior is
given by a swindler: "Die Zeiten sind schlecht.
Warum sollten die Leute besser sein?" (p. 115).
While the industrialist Mr. Radau confines his
business rivals to their cells for having promoted
the nationalization of big business, two milita-
rist madmen, Vieth and Dierk, recruit human beings
for the testing of experimental rockets. The per-
versity of their scientific method is exposed by
Vieth's grotesque statement: "Man muß Opfer bringen können für die Forschung" (p. 148).

In the final station of the novel, Bonifaz
once again finds himself in the city of Tesch. In
a manner reminiscent of Bertolt Brecht's Die Rund-
köpfe und die Spitzköpfe, Bonifaz confronts a society of frenzied, anti-communist reactionaries who
all sport "eingedrückte Nasen" as a sign of their
affiliation with the ultra-conservative "Neue-
Form-Nasen-Anhänger der Regierung." The leader of
the organization is made to resemble Hitler, and
the members have license to humiliate and inter-
rogate individuals who do not join the organization.

The satiric tone of the novel, however, is
not restricted to the picaresque situation, but
is extended to conscious, clever manipulation of
language on the part of Bonifaz. Bonifaz remarks
candidly: "Die Natur hat dem Menschen nicht die

162

Sprache gegeben, damit er den Mund hält" (p. 126).
Indeed, as Bonifaz recognizes, it is not one's
"bark" alone but one's "bite" that makes the cru-
cial difference in dealing with society: "Denn
wenn Sie nicht richtig beißen können, kommt der
beste Rindsbraten so raus, wie Sie ihn reinge-
steckt haben. . . . Wer gut tut beißen, der kann
gut verdauen" (p. 12).

In a manner clearly reminiscent of Jaroslav
Hašek's clever dialectician and passive resister
Schwejk, Bonifaz engages his dreaded foes satirically through his mastery of dialectical humor.
Dialectical humor, as it is practiced by Bonifaz,
involves irony as the standard device for appearing to affirm an aspect of society when in fact
one is negating it. Bonifaz is adept, for example, at linking a situation with an anecdote as a
means of satirizing society without directly jeo-
pardizing his own safety. In his remarks on the
Nazis, Bonifaz states: "Meinem Freund Maiko hatte
mal im Laufen geträumt, daß die großen Verbrecher,
wenn die Nazis werden ausgewirtschaftet haben, wieder an die Macht gehen, aber in Zivil, nicht mit
den alten Orden. Daran erkennt man, was für einen
Blödsinn man im Marschieren träumen kann" (p. 24).
Bonifaz also employs the play on words and the
simile as characteristic devices for his dialectical satire. In acknowledging the primacy of sex
over any other concerns, he ridicules the notion
of social equality in a classless society: "Der
Mensch aber ist ein Gesellschaftstier, und zur
Gesellschaft gehören Frauen. Fressen, Saufen und
die christliche Demokratie können auch ein Leben
ausfüllen, aber erst in der Geschlechterliebe, sage ich dir, erhebst du dich über deinen Nächsten"
(p. 121). Bonifaz uses the simile in one instance
to ridicule the legal codes by linking his remark
with a sexist remark about women: "Aber jedes Ge-
setz hat eine schwache Stelle. Das ist wie bei
den Mädchen" (p. 33). Finally, Bonifaz is adept
at carrying statements to their absurd conclusion.
In one episode he ridicules the fanaticism of the
Hitler cult: "Der Führer kann nicht sterben, weil
er in allem lebt. Sehen Sie, streng genommen

163

würde das bedeuten, daß er nicht nur in den Wäldern und in den Wolken und in den Kanonen lebt, was sowieso bekannt ist, sondern zum Beispiel auch in meiner Marmeladenstulle . . ."(p. 32).

In Bieler's novel, as in the first volume of Der Wundertäter, a clear ideological endorsement of socialism is missing. Indeed, certain remarks by Bonifaz indicate that a communist may suffer from the same changeability as any other person. When asked if he is a communist, Bonifaz responds with a satiric anecdote about the hotel owner Moser, who joined ranks with the Nazis after leaving the Communist party (p. 36). In this manner Bonifaz talks around issues without directly answering the questions posed to him. Bonifaz also ridicules the socialist reorganization in the Soviet Zone when he issues a series of proclamations as acting mayor of Roßbach: he abolishes the upper and middle classes, money, compulsory labor, the national anthem, and marriage; and substitutes the word "Mensch" for "comrade."

The concluding episode of the novel reveals the degree to which Bieler declines to endorse socialism as the answer to the little man's plight. As Bonifaz crosses over into the Soviet Zone after escaping from Tesch, a sly innuendo to a border guard makes Bonifaz' partisanship suspect: "Eigentlich hab' ich jetzt überhaupt nichts mehr. Nur noch meine Nase" (p. 201). The reference to his nose refers obviously to his experiences with the "Neue-Form-Nasen" reactionaries and reveals an unwillingness to affiliate himself with collective ideologies. Indeed, it is this very quality which motivated Wilfried van der Will to label Bonifaz a "Verneiner der organisierten Gesellschaft,"[10] a potential counter-revolutionary element in the development of a socialist order.

As in the first part of Strittmatter's Der Wundertäter, Bieler employs satire as a didactic tool for exposing and criticizing the failings of society; however, unlike Strittmatter, Bieler goes beyond criticism of bourgeois ideology alone and extends his indictment to any ideology which represses individuality and freedom or promotes fanaticism and militarism. This is most graphically illustrated in one of the final episodes of <u>Bonifaz</u>, where it becomes apparent to Bonifaz that he must show the citizens of Tesch the dangers of militarism; he ignites a bomb exhibition, yet saves the viewers from burning to death in the conflagration. Bonifaz remarks to the audience: "Ihr sollt nicht verbrennen. . . . Ihr sollt am Leben bleiben! Aber ihr sollt wissen, wie euer Krieg aussieht. Da ist niemand, der euch hilft, ihr Plattnasen!" (p. 200).

In light of Bonifaz' objection to the excesses of organized society, it should come as no surprise that Bieler defected to the FRG immediately after the Soviet invasion of Czechoslovakia in 1968. Bieler's rationale for leaving the GDR was motivated by the same principles that directed Bonifaz' actions: "Solange es nicht wenigstens zehntausend in einem Volke gibt, die den Wert des Lebens nicht ausschließend an seiner Dauer messen, so lange wird sich nichts ändern."[11]

From an analysis of two GDR picaresque novels, it is clear that both humor and satire can play an effective role in GDR literature, specifically as devices for criticizing bourgeois ideology and for promoting a more humane, compassionate social order. From an analysis of these two works alone, however, it is clear that neither work attempts to resolve the tension between oppressor and oppressed in a closed fashion, nor does the reader witness the transformation of the alienated, non-partisan rogue into a collectively minded individual with a clear socialist orientation. The possibility for that realization is left open, however; the picaresque novel does not inherently limit the possibilities for that realization to occur. The problem would seem to be more one of the author's own relationship to the socialist concept and to the recurring problems which arise from the fluctuating GDR cultural policy.

Bradley University

Notes

[1] R.C. Andrews, "A Comic Novel from East Germany," German Life and Letters, 20, No. 2 (January 1967), 104.

[2] Erwin Strittmatter, Der Wundertäter (Berlin/Weimar: Aufbau, 1957). Manfred Bieler, Bonifaz oder Der Matrose in der Flasche (Berlin/Weimar: Aufbau, 1963; Berlin/Neuwied: Luchterhand, 1963). Page references for Bonifaz are to the West German paperback edition, Munich: dtv, 1974.

[3] Ulrich Wicks, "The Nature of Picaresque Narrative: A Modal Approach," PMLA, 89 (March 1974), 241.

[4] Michael Nerlich, Kunst, Politik und Schelmerei (Frankfurt/M.: Suhrkamp, 1969), p. 192.

[5] Fritz J. Raddatz, Traditionen und Tendenzen (Frankfurt/M.: Suhrkamp, 1976), I, 57.

[6] Marcel Reich-Ranicki, Deutsche Literatur in West und Ost (Munich: Piper, 1963), p. 420.

[7] Cited in Wolfgang Powroslo, Literatur der DDR im Unterricht (Düsseldorf: Schwann, 1977), p. 30.

[8] Powroslo, p. 33.

[9] Erwin Strittmatter, "Vom Werden unserer sozialistischen Nationalliteratur," Neue deutsche Literatur, 6, No. 8 (1958), 87-88.

[10] Wilfried van der Will, Pikaro heute (Stuttgart: Klett, 1967), p. 29.

[11] Cited in Raddatz, I, 57.

"Der Wunsch nach Welt":
The Travel Motif in the Poetry of Sarah Kirsch

Susan G. Figge

Invitations to travel, descriptions of air-
plane trips and train rides, visits to the Soviet
Union, Italy, the Black Sea, and excursions to
Potsdam and Wiepersdorf--the motif of travel is
central to the poetry of Sarah Kirsch. Kirsch
herself acknowledges the importance of travel in
her life and her writing:

> . . . [der] Wunsch nach Welt, das
> Überall-zuhause-sein-Wollen, ist
> nicht ohne weiteres Substanzlosig-
> keit. Ich lebe von der Entdeckung,
> von der Eroberung immer neuer Land-
> schaften; ich erobere sie mir dann
> auch schreibend. . . . Insofern
> wage ich es, den Umzug in andere
> Gegenden, auch den letzten Umzug,
> immer als eine Erleichterung und
> eine Bereicherung für mich persön-
> lich zu empfinden. Ich komme zu
> Dingen, die ich vorher weder kannte
> noch konnte--es ist eine Leichtig-
> keit und Lockerheit, die ich brau-
> che.[1]

If we examine Kirsch's four collections of
poetry, Landaufenthalt (1967), Zaubersprüche
(1973), Rückenwind (1976), and Drachensteigen
(1979), we find a close relationship between the
use of the travel motif and Kirsch's understanding of the requirements and uses of her art. Crisis periods arising from personal or political

167

circumstances find particular expression in poetic descriptions of travel, such as the "Lichtbilder" poems of <u>Zaubersprüche</u> or the "Wiepersdorf" cycle in <u>Rückenwind</u>. Travel experiences, real and fanciful, supply the structure of many of the poems, provide a central source of imagery, and serve as a context in which Kirsch as traveler-poet explores, escapes, and finally accepts the clash between freedom and its limitations which is a central theme of her poetry.

<u>Landaufenthalt</u>, Kirsch's first major collection, contains her least ambivalent celebration of the GDR and socialist reality as they are revealed to her anew through the experience of travel.[2] On an airplane trip she describes the lakes below as mirrors forming a pattern of connections through reflection: "das ist meine Erde" ("Der Wels ein Fisch der am Grund lebt," p. 5). The tone is personal and affectionate in her recollections of fellow citizens demonstrating against injustice, of children swimming on rubber swans, of old people napping on park benches. This loving attention to homely detail is repeated in "Fahrt II" in the careful reproduction of images hurled through the train windows:

> Aber am liebsten fahre ich Eisenbahn
> durch mein kleines wärmendes Land
> in allen Jahreszeiten: der Winter
> wirft Hasenspuren vergessne Kohlplantagen
> durchs Fenster, ich seh die Säume der
> kahlen Bäume
> zarte Linie ums Geäst sie fahren heran
> drehn sich verlassen mich wieder (p. 6)

This poetry, with its enthusiasm about travel, its closely observed details of nature, and its concentration on movement-related optical effects, expresses Kirsch's wish for active and direct experience of her own country and the world, a wish which the GDR critic and poet Adolf Endler describes as a common characteristic, indeed a program, of Volker Braun, Karl Mickel, Bernd Jentzsch, and other poets of this generation.[3]

168

But Kirsch's awareness of the impossibility of fulfilling this program is also reflected in the poetry of Landaufenthalt. "Fahrt II," for example,
concludes with a strong sense of geographical and
political limitations imposed on human connected-
ness and communication. On all sides there are
barriers to further travel--the sea or the moun-
tains or the barbed wire border--cutting her off
from people who share the same culture and speak
the same language. Kirsch's celebration of the
GDR becomes a lament over borders and the loss of
human contact.

Sometimes these limitations can be overcome
by feats of the poetic imagination, and many of
the travel poems in Landaufenthalt suggest poetic
strategies for satisfying the "Wunsch nach Welt."
An imaginary journey, "Lange Reise," involves a
fleeting and almost simultaneous presence in geo-
graphically and politically widely separated places, using a montage technique to establish moral
connections between places as far apart as Cologne
and Vietnam, as the perfume capital is invaded by
the smell of seared flesh. In "Meine vielgereist-
en Freunde berichten mir" a series of apparently
unconnected travel reports suggests "wie es in der
Welt zugeht," creating a picture dominated by human frailty, cruelty, and forgetfulness. In their
rapid changes of location and breathless style
these poems suggest a striving for totality and
simultaneity of experience which is in part a protest against stringent travel restrictions but
which also represents an existential need to overcome all limitations of time and space.

This need for freedom of movement and experience is described in many of the travel poems of
Landaufenthalt as an essential precondition for
poetic creativity. "Ich soll in einem Flugzeug"
belongs to a group of poems dealing with a trip to
the Black Sea. Reflecting on Ovid's banishment to
these shores, Kirsch realizes that for her the
trip will mean release, new impressions, and new
sources for her work. For Ovid it meant isolation,
imprisonment, and the loss of genius, forcing him

169

to write fawning poetry in a vain attempt to re-
gain his liberty. The need for freedom involves
not only the yearnings of a restless spirit but
also a battle for artistic survival. In "Hirten-
lied" this struggle assumes new complexities as
the poet confronts her urgent need to escape the
personal and creative winter in the GDR with her
own sense of poetic commitment.4 The poet as
shepherd, keeping watch at the border of the country, must overcome the urge to flee, must remain
in spite of wind, fire, and ice. She ties herself
to trees, lies under rocks. She must stay awake
to protect her herd, packing ice in her shirt,
cutting off her eyelids. The commitment to stay
and the wish to escape are distilled into images
of violence and danger which contrast starkly with
the traditional version of the piping shepherd and
his sheep.

Clearly these poems reflect the particularly
complex and sometimes discouraging artistic climate in the GDR during the sixties.5 But the necessity of freedom for continuing creative activity has personal and domestic as well as social
and political dimensions. In "Rückkunft" the
poet, resting from her travels, visits a friend
in an idyllic country setting:

Meine Freundin lebt auf dem Land da zieht
zweimal am Tag die eine Schafherde am Fenster
                                      vorbei
einmal am Abend die zweite, die Wohnung ist
                                    freundlich
der Mann klug gütig fast schön die
Kinder gesund alles in Ordnung. . . . (p. 65)

But the flatness of the language reveals a life of
paralyzing monotony, and the poet enjoys making
her friend restless and greedy for adventure:
"ich schlafe sehr gut dort am Rande der Welt /
nachdem / ich sie gierig machte auf Schiffe und
Meere" (p. 65).

Travel means exploration, new encounters with
the past and present, active participation. The

alternative in "Rückkunft" is rest and contentment, placidity and routine, and all the appealing
but painfully limiting domestic virtues. Both
modes are necessary to life and to the life of the
poet, however much they appear to be in conflict.
"Zwischenlandung" offers a beautifully whimsical
statement about the dialectic of creativity: the
need for change and freedom and new experience on
the one hand, and the necessity of routine, roots,
and the orderly life in familiar surroundings on
the other. In "Zwischenlandung" the poets wander
throughout the year, exploring, adventuring, and
plunging into experience for its own sake. They
return to their own firesides when the yearning
for the joys of domestic life overwhelms them.
The poets in their wanderings lack substance--
their coats are too thin against the cold, they
yearn for a bowl of real soup. But they grow
restless in turn at the domestic fireside, and
armed with warm mittens from under the Christmas
tree, they sally forth again. The poets must
somehow manage to keep a foothold in both worlds.
The tension between creativity and routine, like
the tension between the need for freedom of movement and the necessity of political commitment,
is constant, unavoidable, and necessary.6

In the opening poems of Zaubersprüche routine
has reached the level of suffocation.7 But the
travel poetry, rather than offering release and
new experience of the world, only confirms the
personal loneliness and pessimism that give the
volume in general the urgency of a crisis of confidence in self, human nature, and society. The
travel poetry is characterized by the perspective
of the lone and lonely traveler, increasingly
aware of both personal and artistic isolation.8
In the "Lichtbilder" poems travels in the Soviet
Union and in Czechoslovakia, together with fantasy
excursions to places long ago and far away, are
the occasions for a self-conscious exploration of
loneliness and separation, of human greed, exploitation and cruelty, and finally of the dangers to
art and the artist in contemporary society.

171

In "Georgien, Fotografien," the opening of
the "Lichtbilder" sequence, straightforward syn-
tax, spare language and imagery imitate the supposedly objective and random arrangement of detail
in a snapshot, revealing in spite of the deceptively simple style the pattern of human distraction
and indifference:

> Das Fußballspiel. Die Akazien blühn
> die Stadt ist voller Duft die Straßen
> sind leer, Fußball in Radio und Fern-
> sehen ich hörs aus den Fenstern. Die
> Taxifahrer rufen sich zu: Nr. 4 ein
> Mann aus Tbilissi schoß das Tor. Sie
> überfuhren einen Hund. Zwei Stunden
> schrie er im Park. (p. 24)

Other "photographs" contrast the elemental beauty
of the Georgian landscape with the harsh realities
of life for those who dwell in it ("Haustiere im
Gebirge") or reveal the present pleasant tourist
attractions as shot through with reminders of past
agonies ("Kachetien"). The recording camera style
not only emphasizes the primacy, for Kirsch, of
the initial visual impression, but also reveals
her lack of emotional participation in what is
seen and observed. Many of the subsequent poems,
however more complex in imagery and style, maintain this sense of life observed from the outside,
the awareness of personal isolation, of inner cold-
ness and indifference:

> Ich kannte nur mich und das war zu wenig. Saß da
> Mit mir auf der Bank ich in der Mitte ich rechts
> von mir
> Und links auch noch alles war frei und besetzt
> da beschloß ich
> Mit mir nicht zu reden. Mir tat nichts weh ich
> wünschte
> dich nicht ich
> Saß lediglich und die Sonne
> Beschien mich wie eine x-beliebige Stadt Wiese
> Platane. (p. 28)

The fusion of social critique and personal

isolation in the "Lichtbilder" travel sketches focuses on the enduring power of art and the dangers that beset its practitioners. The figure of the isolated and endangered poet predominates: the poet Tschawchawadse, shot in 1907 by counterrevolutionaries ("Das Landhaus"); the painter Ebert, out on a drunk, lost in a maze of Berlin bars ("Der Maler Ebert"); Annette von Droste-Hülshoff, for whom Kirsch feels a particular affinity, lost in her hopeless love for Levin, in her isolation in the country ("Der Droste würde ich gern Wasser reichen"). In "Kirche in Mzcheta" Kirsch turns a deceptively simple anecdote into a complicated statement about the dangers to the artist whose uniqueness finds official acceptance:

Kirche in Mzcheta. Sie ist asymmetrisch; die
Ornamente gleichen sich nicht. Wo ein Pferd
springen müßte, weidet ein Stier; hier Wein-
laub, da Rosen. Ein Bogen ist breiter und
niedriger als der vorige; das Dach nicht
grün und nicht braun:
Abnahme durch den Bischof. Diese Schönheit!
Soll bleiben: unwiederholbar: sagte er
Und ließ dem Meister abhaun sie, die Hand
Ist sichtbar, nachgebildet in Stein. (p. 23)

Ostensibly about the inhumanity of the Czarist church, the poem can also be read as a parable of the unorthodox artist in any totalitarian system. The work is exciting and is accepted because of its very uniqueness. But the artist is destroyed --his hand is cut off--whether to preserve the very uniqueness of the work or to prevent further irregularities which might prove too dangerous in the maintenance of order and tradition.

These fellow artists stand throughout the "Lichtbilder" as warning signposts along the poet-traveler's way as Kirsch visits the standard tourist attractions and reflects not only on dangers to the artist, but also on dangers to art itself-- its degradation into deceptive and exploitative artifice. For example the "Klosterruine Dshwari," no longer inhabited, is brought back to an artificial life by tape recorded chants of the old monks:

> Sie sind sehr alt, nur ihre Stimmen
> Sind kunstvoll auf ein Band gebracht
> Sie psalmodieren, ein Knopfdruck macht sie
> stille. (p. 26)

The artificial re-creation of the onetime real
life of the place still inspires pious pilgrims
and brings profit to those in authority:

> Bis Abend kommt, die Zeit des Weins
> Sie schlafen in der vollen Spule
> Der Abt auf seinem hohen Stuhle
> Zählt die Kopeken in der Höhlung eines Steins.

A hundred years ago the art of the chanting monks
brought comfort to the peasants and money to the
monastery. Today the life behind the art is dead,
but the artifice continues as a lucrative tourist
attraction.[9]

Questions of art and artifice in society are
central in the poem "Playboy and Cowboy," where
Kirsch analyzes a painting which captures for her
the essence of America. This imaginary travel
picture portrays two men, perhaps brothers, who
meet in front of a forest of maple trees. One
wears jeans and jacket fancifully decorated, a
travesty of the worn work clothes of the other.
The two men are caught in a symbiosis of hatred
and exploitation, a kind of fraud--the cowboy
earning a hard living in a dying way of life, the
playboy exploiting the adventurous and romantic
cowboy image:

> Des einen Arbeit ist des andern Müßiggang!
> So hörte ich im Traum mich fragen: ob vielleicht
> Die Welt des Geldes sie gespalten hat, die beide
> hassen
> Und nicht mehr tauschen läßt
> Pferd gegen Ford . . . (p. 39)

Art as artifice, the clever and richly decorated
imitation of the cowboy's simple clothing, sup-

ports the parasitic existence of the playboy.

Not all dangers to art and the artist come
from without. The achievement of genuine poetic
statement requires a sometimes painful receptive-
ness to past and present experiences. In "Litho-
graphie" an ordinary sightseeing excursion becomes
the occasion for a complex reflection on the assimilation of the past as a necessary precondition
for living and writing in the present. On a visit
to the Jewish cemetery in Prague the poet sees the
gravestones as the teeth of the great whale that
swallowed Jonah. Just as this cemetery has swallowed up the Jews, so it threatens, with the re-
buke of its tragic history, to overwhelm the poet's
attempt to live meaningfully in the present:

Wir laufen Zickzack durch die schwarzen Male
Damit wir draußen gegenwärtig sind
Dies ist kein Ort, wir waren auf Papier
Vorher, auf Stein, gezeichnet und geätzt. (p. 35)

A relic of the past, the cemetery like all historical monuments is no place in itself. The poet's
obligation is to live and create in the present in
spite of and because of the past. The concluding
conceit establishes the necessary connection. As
in the process of lithography, where stone is
etched and pressed against paper, so in the creation of poetry the printed words, the poems, are
the product of "etching," of the personal and historical experience of the poet. "Gezeichnet und
geätzt"--the assimilation of the past is painful
and difficult, but without it the paper remains
blank; there is no poetry.

The experiences which have marked the poet
and found their expression in the "Lichtbilder"
travel poems are given a whimsical concluding analysis in "Besinnung":

Was bin ich für ein vollkommener weißgesichtiger
                                        Clown
Am Anfang war meine Natur sorglos und fröhlich
Aber was ich gesehen habe zog mir den Mund

175

In Richtung der Füße   (p. 43)

The summary impression is a negative one, but it increases receptivity and sensitivity:

Nun schneide ich mein Haar nicht mehr und horche
Wie dir und mir die Nägel wachsen, Hühnchen
Die Daunen ausgehn, sie Fett gewinnen   (p. 43)

Ordinary people misunderstand the clown's sad and comic tales. It is the fellow travelers, the sailors and chauffeurs, who nod in agreement, whose knowledge and experience of the world and of human nature match that of the poet-clown:

Die in den blauen Jacken können mit Bei-
                         spielen belegen
Haben die Koordination im Kopf, und
Was man trank vorher und nachher und dann
Schweigen sie   (p. 43)

In the course of the "Lichtbilder" poems the traveler emerges as a basic metaphor for the artist: they share rootlessness and restlessness, the need for freedom and access to limitless opportunities for new experience. Both are always in some sense outsiders looking in. But the poet, unlike her fellow travelers, and in spite of attendant dangers to herself and to her art, does not keep silent.

Kirsch's third collection of poetry, <u>Rücken-wind</u>, extends the range of her symbolic geography.10 Full of spatial imagery, the poems are again preoccupied with overcoming limitations of space and time: "Wenn mein Leib / Meine nicht berechenbare Seele sich aus den Stäben / Der Längen- und Breitengrade endlich befreit hat" ("Ende Mai," p. 41). Although Kirsch leaves behind much of the loneliness and bitterness of the <u>Zaubersprüche</u> and makes halting progress toward new possibilities for intimacy, her affirmation of oneness and sharing are held in constant tension with images of separation and distance.11

176

Travel poems at the beginning of the volume
describe occasions which promise escape from loneliness, routine, and responsibility, only to confront the escapee with the same set of difficulties in a new context. In "Der Ausflug" an excursion to Potsdam promises the poet a change from
beer to whisky, from the humdrum routine to a Bac-
chanalian celebration of the summer solstice, complete with bonfires, lanterns, and a thunderstorm.
An artists' commune, inhabiting an old villa, is
throwing a party. The poet wanders into the
house:

> Es sahen uns Bilder an, Augen-
> Blicke, die festgehaltene Freundin
> Vorm Fenster, flogen vom Weinlaub, Jelänger-
> > jelieber die
> > Ranken.
> Wildlockige Mädchen, Maler-Frauen, schwammen
> > heran.
> > Auftrag:
> Die Schönheit. Abgefallene Blüten
> Rosen Jasmin arrangiert im Verhältnis
> Eins zu zwei. (p. 16)

The flow of images, the languid metamorphosis of
paintings into vines and finally into real women,
signals a threat. The women in the paintings are
"festgehalten," the objects of "Augen-Blicke," as
necessary to the mood of the place as the vines
curling around the windows and used in the same
way--as objects for paintings: "Auftrag: die Schönheit." Both the women and the flowers are "Abge-
fallene Blüten," carefully arranged for the purposes of art and effect. But the atmosphere,
beauty,and luxury of the house are enticing, and
the poet is tempted by these apparently perfect
conditions for creative activity:

> > Minutenlang
> War ich überzeugt, zog ein, ich spannte
> Ne Hängematte von Rose zu Rose, rauchte benga-
> > lische
> > Ringe, setzte

Die Schreibmaschine auf den Marmorsockel, in
                                    Zukunft
    Idyllen! (p. 17)

But it occurs to her that in this setting, while
spilled wine may seem appropriate, children crum-
bling cake would be out of place: ". . . doch als
die Musik vorbei war, der Regen im See, ging ich
weg von Jean zu Bier und Kuchenkrümeln" (p. 17).
This "Ausflug" can be only temporary diversion.
The beer and cake crumbs, the routine, the daily
bread, must be held in tension with the need for
change, freedom, excitement. Indeed the escape
might have cost her the very freedom she seeks;
she might have been "objectified" like the "Maler-
Frauen" or have lost touch with the messiness of
daily life: there are no idylls.

    Following "Der Ausflug," the Wiepersdorf
poems describe a similar promise of escape and
the resulting confronation. Although the trip to
Wiepersdorf, one-time country estate of the Arnims,
now a vacation center for GDR artists, suggests a
flight into the past--"Hier ist das Versmaß ele-
gisch / Das Tempus Praeteritum" ("Wiepersdorf 1,"
p. 18), the present intrudes into the idyllic
setting--the old house, the park, the woods--on
every level:

                        . . . Ich staunte
    Vor Stunden noch enge im Hochhaus
    In der verletzenden viereckigen Gegend, nun
    Das--ich dachte bloß noch: Bettina! Hier
    Hast du mit sieben Kindern gesessen, und wenn
    Landregen abging
    Muß es genauso geklappert haben Ende Mai
    Auf die frisch aufgespannten Blätter--ich sollte
    Mal an den König schreiben
                        ("Wiepersdorf 2," pp. 19-20)

The identification with Bettina von Arnim and her
appeal for justice, <u>Dies Buch gehört dem König</u>,
prompts thoughts of the king, an image which for
Kirsch evokes the whole complex of private and political engagement, affection, and duty, and which

178

confronts her with the very problems she had
sought to escape. Again and again the pleasures
of the Wiepersdorf holiday are undercut by the
intrusion of present relationships and responsibilities. The poems of the cycle alternate between moods of resolution and of vulnerability,
between comfort and protection in nature, "[e]ine
Bannmeile schöner, frischer Wald" (p. 21), and
her loneliness in the old house, "in diesem /
Volkseignen Schloß wo private / Unken mir Kummer
vorschrein" (p. 25). Even the state invades this
peaceful bit of countryside as tanks on maneuvers
kill two men and destroy a house ("Wiepersdorf 6,"
p. 24).

The "Wiepersdorf" cycle is shaped by the need
to escape and the inability to do so, the necessity of freedom and the call of responsibilities,
memories, and relationships that await the city
dweller, the artist, and the woman alone. Kirsch
is able to accept this contradiction and create
from it. In the final two poems she runs away
from all that is frightening her--here embodied in
the hermaphrodite walking in the park--and she
finds a hiding place behind the statue of a clown.
Taking on his mode, she puts a bemused assessment
of herself into the mouth of a man confused by the
restless goings-on of the modern woman:

> Leider leider werden die Damen
> Immer schnurriger. Was die nicht mehr
> Können und alles vermögen! Die trennen sich
> Dreimal im Leben von Diesem und Jenem, die
>   schleppen
> Nur das Nötige mit die Kinder, die Arbeit
> O wie mir graut!   ("Männliches Steinbild im
>   Park," p. 29)

Through this act of self-parody the poet gains a
humorous distance and is able to identify the necessities of her life: her child and her work.

In the "Wiepersdorf" cycle, travel emerges as
escape and discovery, forcing the poet to confrpnt
and affirm the very difficulties she has sought to

flee. This acceptance makes possible in the rest
of Rückenwind a kind of reverse travel poetry, in
which Kirsch concentrates on distilling comfort
from images of separation and distance. In the
magnificent poem "Der Meropsvogel" she turns an
image of parting into one of reunion: "Er fliegt
doch er sieht fliegend zurück, er entfernt sich,
nähert sich trotzdem" (p. 37).

In Drachensteigen,[12] published after Kirsch's
1977 departure from the GDR, the poems from East
and West Berlin, "Allerleirauh," continue the images of spatial imprisonment and yearning for freedom of movement that dominate the geography of the
earlier volumes.[13] In "Krähenbaum" the apartment
building, whose heating system swallows up the
leaves of a nearby tree--a solitary piece of nature in the urban landscape--becomes a symbolic
prison and a metaphor for the destructive forces
at the heart of the city. A house figures again
as a kind of prison in "Trennung":

Wenn ich in einem Haus bin, das keine Tür hat
Geh ich aus dem Fenster.
Mauern, Mauern, und nichts als Gardinen
Wo bin ich denn, daß   (p. 15)

Even the travel and freedom of others, the medi-
ated contact with distant places, brings comfort.
The poet hopes for "Briefe von Dick und Doof"
("Post," p. 7); she celebrates the freedom of the
kite and the fact "daß wir dich kannten" ("Der
Rest des Fadens," p. 16). But she sees her greatest happiness and chance for creativity in the
life of a carefree wanderer:

Aber am schönsten: mit dir
Oder ohne dich
Über die Boulevards laufen nichts im Gepäck
Als Rosinenbrot, Wein und Tabak
Die Leute der Länder festhalten
Im Auge und später
Sprechen davon, den Himmel beschreiben den
                                    Schnee
                  ("Allerleirauh," p. 14)

180

Again travel, being underway, is more than escape
from a city, from a lover, from an uncomfortable
political situation. It means the freedom to
leave people and things behind ("nichts im Gepäck"), to explore, to experience, and to create
out of that experience.

This understanding of poet and traveler
reaches its highpoint in the love poetry of "Ita-
lienische Amseln." Whether it is the departure
from the GDR and from months of worry and harassment, the blossoming of a new love affair, the
leisure to write as she wishes: in these poems
from Italy Kirsch balances the images of dedication and belonging with those of freedom, flight,
and creativity. The old tensions have resolved
themselves at least temporarily amid the plenty,
generosity, and warmth of the Italian countryside.
Barriers between herself and nature have disappeared. "Der Scirocco bewirft mich mit Ästen und
Zapfen, Kröten springen mir ins Hemd" ("Die Wiese," p. 25). For once her art is perfectly in
harmony with her surroundings:

> Jeder Baum am richtigen Fleck.
> Man könnte sagen Felder gibts
> die mein Herz sind: blauer Weizen
> und Mohnblumen reingeworfen eins
> zu zwei. Kunst oder Welt fliegt
> davon. ("Die Toscana," p. 30)

The landscape serves as the perfect background and
continuation of a new found intimacy. Images of
confinement have become those of contentment. The
police, "die ganz scharfen Carabinieri," are no
longer a threat, "halten Wache mit Federhüten und
rauchen" (p. 26). Even domestic activities no
longer smack of the imprisonment of dull routine:
cooking and writing belong together:

>   . . . ich brate
> Den Hasen im Topf und er kriegt
> Einen Whisky am Schluß und ich auch ich hab
> Das Schreibzeug aufm Küchentisch und lebe und
>   lebe

181

und lebe immer noch. . . ("Brief," p. 47)

A happy constellation of circumstances brings
Kirsch to exactly that state she has always looked
to travel to provide. For now at least the spiritual resting place for the weary traveler is the
freedom and flightiness, the warmth and welcoming
of the southern landscape. But the clash between
restlessness and the need for roots, between freedom and commitment, in however many guises it may
appear, is essential to Kirsch as traveler-poet.
Even in the midst of the Italian contentment she
sees the future in terms of further travels:

> Ich sage dir ich sehe manchmal
> Jedes Blatt einzeln am Baum oder
> Aufm Kies kleine Sicheln oder wie das
> Weitergeht mit mir: kurze Aufenthalte
> Alles wieder zusammenpacken und fort
> ("Jedes Blatt," p. 28)

The College of Wooster

Notes

[1] Hans Ester, "Gespräch mit Sarah Kirsch,"
Deutsche Bücher, 9, No. 2 (1979), 108-109.

[2] Landaufenthalt (Berlin/Weimar: Aufbau, 1967;
Ebenhausen bei München: Langewiesche-Brandt, 1977).
Quotations are taken from the Langewiesche-Brandt
edition.

[3] Adolf Endler, "Sarah Kirsch und ihre Kritiker," Sinn und Form, 27 (1975), 163-164.

[4] For a discussion of the winter poems in
Landaufenthalt, see Christina Cosentino, "Die
Lyrikerin Sarah Kirsch im Spiegel ihrer Bilder,"
Neophilologus, 63, No. 3 (1979), 422.

[5] Manfred Behn-Liebherz, "Sarah Kirsch," in

Neue Literatur der Frauen, ed. Heinz Puknus
(Munich: Beck, 1980), pp. 159-162.

[6]"Sarah Kirschs Gedichte sprechen alle von
Freiheit. Sie hat einen heftigen, unideologischen
Freiheitsbegriff, der sich gewiß auch an den Grenzen der eigenen Psyche und Physis reibt." Urs
Widmer, "Sarah Kirsch ist eine Hexe," *Petrarca-
Preis 1975-1979*, ed. Joachim Heimannsberg (n.p.,
1980), p. 146. The concept of freedom in Kirsch's
poetry is many sided and reflects the political
and cultural climate within the GDR as well as
events in Kirsch's private life. Her poems have
an open-endedness which permits neither a strictly
political nor a purely biographical interpretation.

[7]*Zaubersprüche* (Berlin/Weimar: Aufbau, 1973;
Ebenhausen bei München: Langewiesche-Brandt, 1974).
Quotations are taken from the Langewiesche-Brandt
edition.

[8]Cosentino sees this mood as the result of a
personal crisis, the origins of which are not revealed in the poetry itself, p. 423. Adolf Endler
cautiously mentions an "eloquente Gleichgültigkeit"
on the part of critics and public which accounts
in part for the mood of isolation in the poems, p.
159.

[9]For another interpretation of art and artifice in this poem see Eberhard Lämmert, "Stimmen-
zauber," in *Frankfurter Anthologie 2: Gedichte und
Interpretationen*, ed. Marcel Reich-Ranicki (Frank-
furt/M.: Insel, 1977), pp. 246-248.

[10]*Rückenwind* (Berlin/Weimar: Aufbau, 1976;
Ebenhausen bei München: Langewiesche-Brandt, 1977).
Quotations are taken from the Langewiesche-Brandt
edition.

[11]For some biographical background to *Rückenwind*, see Jürgen Serke, *Frauen schreiben: Ein neues Kapitel deutschsprachiger Literatur* (Hamburg:
Gruner & Jahr, 1979), p. 196.

[12] *Drachensteigen* (Ebenhausen bei München: Langewiesche-Brandt, 1979).

[13] The return to this complex of imagery no doubt reflects the isolation and harassment Kirsch experienced following her public support of Biermann in 1976.

Imagery of Alienation and Integration
in Volker Braun's Poetry

Christine Cosentino

Volker Braun, an ardent admirer of Friedrich
Hölderlin, is undoubtedly familiar with Jürgen
Kuczynski's study "Hölderlin - Die Tragödie des
revolutionären Idealisten."[1] In this essay, published in 1969, the GDR sociologist ponders the
dichotomy of the ideal and reality ("das Ausein-
anderklaffen von Ideal und Wirklichkeit") in revolutionary transitional times--a problem which the
protagonist Hyperion perceives as a painfully alienating experience. Making a historical general-
ization, Kuczynski views this phenomenon as characteristic of any revolution, including socialist
revolutions; he refers back to Lenin, who once
warned "daß die neue Gesellschaft nicht in einem
Glashaus aufgebaut wird" (pp. 98-99).

It seems to me that no GDR author is more in-
tensely preoccupied with this dichotomy than Braun.
It is the basic theme of his aesthetic writings,
his poetry, his plays, and his prose as well. As
Kuczynski points out in his Hölderlin essay, ide-
alistic revolutionaries like Hyperion, Schiller,
Hölderlin, Gorki, and so many others of yesterday
and today were shocked by this contradiction, and
in bewilderment and consternation turned their
backs on the revolution. Braun too is not unaffected by the problem of alienation but he does
not feel crushed by it. The cleft between revolutionary ideal and objective reality evolves in his
works as a cleft between the individual and the
group, the "I" and the "We"--a cleft that is often
imagined and often very real, but always to be

185

overcome.

The interrelationship between the individual and society is reflected in the imagery of the various volumes of Braun's poetry. The theme is dealt with in a broad spectrum of emotional shades: joy, enthusiasm, idealism, hope, expectations, scepticism, disillusionment, disappointment, frustration, and--deeply rooted in Braun's Marxist Weltanschauung--fresh starts, new alternatives, new impetus. "Früher einmal," says Braun, referring to his poetry volume Provokation für mich (published in 1965), "gab es bei mir einen privaten, irgendwie rücksichtslosen Ton, der nur sich selbst aussprach, dann"--and this refers to the volume Wir und nicht sie (published in 1970)--"habe ich mich bewußt in ein Kollektiv zurückgenommen, sowohl was die Sprechweise anging als auch das Adressieren der Dinge. Das muß jetzt aus der abstrakten Öffentlichkeit wieder heraus."[2] The new emergence and self-assertion of the individual against the backdrop of an abstract, rather theoretical collective manifests itself in a volume of poetry published in 1974, Gegen die symmetrische Welt. Braun's political development through these three decisive stages, and the multifaceted, often alienated relationship of the individual and society is reflected in his imagery, which merits investigation.

Braun's early poems are "Provokationen," rebellious provocations, delivered with impatience, vehemence and often irreverence. With boundless enthusiasm he envisions a new socialist society, which he optimistically perceives as a state of harmonious interplay, a total integration of the individual into the group, but without the loss of the individual's identity: "bewegliche Einheit--/ Jeder spielt sein Bestes aus zum gemeinsamen Thema. / Das ist die Musik der Zukunft: jeder ist ein Schöpfer! / Du hast das Recht, du zu sein, und ich bin ich: / Und mit keinem verbinden wir uns, der nicht er selber ist."[3] This unwavering belief of the young Kraftmensch that the group, i.e., society, the "We," can provide total happiness ("to-

186

tales Glück") in a state of total integration is
reflected in a series of images reminiscent of two
earlier literary movements, Storm and Stress in
the eighteenth century and Expressionism in the
twentieth century. These images emanate vigor,
intensity, vitality, and unrestrained emotions.
"Water" and the "sky" are preferred motifs to suggest vastness and the unlimited possibilities for
growth in a productive interaction between the individual and the group as a unit. "Hier wird täg-
lich das alte Leben abgeblasen," the reader is
told in the poem "Kommt uns nicht mit Fertigem":
"Unsere Schultern tragen einen Himmel voll Ster-
ne. / ---an alle Ufer / Trommelt die Flut eurer
Erwartungen!" (P., p. 10). In the poem "Anmerkungen für Bürger der Deutschen Demokratischen
Republik" Braun points impatiently to the abun-
dance of opportunities for all, which the new society offers: "Laßt kein Stück Himmel blaß und
nackt westwärts treiben. / Helft den Himmel mit
Regenbogenfarben / Anfüllen" (P., p. 44). And
with youthful righteousness, in a utopian outcry
for totality, he informs the "more mature" Staatsbürger in "Mitteilung an die reifere Jugend":
"Unser Glück ist total: es läßt sich nicht aus-
rechnen. / Unsere Vorsicht vor uns ist vergeblich:
wir sind maßlos. /. . . . / Laßt die Zweige den
Himmel ausspähn: dann ist der Baum jung!" (P., p.
19). Still, Braun's optimism can hardly be called
blind. Although he himself is at this point still
untouched by the shadow of alienation, he does not
fail to notice that there is a sharp political gap
between certain admired individuals and the society that promises a common cause. Alluding to his
writer-colleague, the ideological non-conformist
Reiner Kunze, Braun asks a pointed, provocative
question in his poem "R.": "Darf auch nur ein
Mensch / Allein treiben im Schiff seiner Lust? /
Darf auch nur ein Mensch / Fliegen am Mast seiner
Ungeduld? / Darf auch nur ein Mensch / Verloren-
gehn? / Hier?" (P., p. 50).
    At the end of his volume Provokation für mich
Braun takes up a theme that is to prevail in his
writings during the next years: stagnation, oppression, apathy, listlessness--a negative spirit

which pervades both society and the individual.
The poem "Mitteilung an meine bedrückten Freunde,"
for example, contains a warning to spineless lack-
eys who do not have the courage to speak up against
Party pressure (P., p. 51). The volume ends on a
sober note, namely with the realization that parallel to the desired utopia of "total happiness"
there exists a gray reality of opportunism and indifference: "Ich bin der Soundso, den ihr kriti-
siert / Weil er Worte wie MÜDIGKEIT, TRÄGHEIT /
Erwähnt, die schon / Ungewohnt sind" ("Gebrauchs-
anweisung zu einem Protokoll," P., p. 73).

In his first volume of poetry, Braun per-
ceived himself primarily as an individual, but as
an individual within a group; his poetry manifests
a firm belief that an eventual state of total integration is feasible--without serious obstacles
or hazards. Only a few years later, in his next
collection of poetry, Wir und nicht Sie (1970),[4]
the poet appears de-individualized, as an abstract
Staatsbürger whose identity is indiscernible in an
abstract community; as a Staatsbürger he subjects
the collective to a critical investigation. In
his analysis of society's structures Braun makes
use of a Leitmotiv which abounds in his lyrical
oeuvre in multifaceted forms: he weaves into his
poetry imagery which suggests by means of association conditions of stagnation, petrification, suf-
focation, restriction--modes of confinement that
citizen and state have to overcome if the envisioned productive interplay of individual and society is to remain intact. Objects from the industrial world, such as steel, iron, iron bands,
metal, concrete, putty, iron barriers, and any
kind of fortification recur; they lend themselves
by their very nature to the poet's intention to
shed light on the topic of stagnation. But parallel to this particular kind of imagery is another that aims at synthesis: blasts, bursts, and
explosions suggest the idea of a breakthrough,
liberation from fossilized political forms, re-
vitalization, in short, a solution.

In the volume Wir und nicht sie, Braun intends primarily to expose crippling conditions of stagnation within the group, the state, the Party, Ideally--and here Braun refers back to his youthful "provocations" of earlier years--the collective should provide a promising and fertile foundation for the individual to unfold and develop his identity. In his poem "Schauspiel" he writes: "Jeder sagt, was er denkt - wir spielen das Stück / Unseres Lebens" (p. 19). But GDR reality looks different, is undermined by a new disturbing and threatening conflict, a split between the Party and the people or, as Braun puts it, a conflict "zwischen den politisch Führenden (die bewußt die Umgestaltung der Gesellschaft organisieren oder bewußt oder unbewußt hemmen) und den Geführten (die bewußt oder unbewußt die Pläne realisieren oder kritisieren)."[5]

Braun's intention is to provoke and force a passive, sterile, and fatigued "We" into re-entering the process of sociopolitical interaction. If the Party does not deign to ask the individual citizen for his political opinion--says Braun provocatively--the individual should not even bother to open his mouth, if his confined state is a matter of indifference to him: ". . . [Er] braucht nicht reden, wenn er nicht zugleich / Ändern will seinen beschränkten Zustand" ("Offentliche Meinung," Wir, p. 75). Blindly accepted guidelines are tantamount to recruitment, stagnation, and an infringement on personal freedom. A shallow exchange of political platitudes threatens to extinguish the revolutionary spark: "Zufriedne Helden schanzen sich in den Ebenen ein" ("Lagebericht," Wir, p. 7).

Yet despite these discrepancies, Braun never seriously doubts that Party, people, and individual serve a common cause, as rooted in the Marxist Weltanschauung. The Party, too, is ultimately interested in dealing with paralyzing apathy and stagnation: "Und vieles ist möglich / Euch ist nichts möglich / Oder, was wir brechen, unsere Schranken / In die fordert euch das Land" ("Wir und ihr," Wir, p. 18). In the poem "Das weite Feld," a discussion between frustrated collective

189

farmers exposes seemingly irreconcilable differences, deeply rooted in old traditions and norms.
The farmers are obstinate and stubborn, their
hands clutch agricultural field plans--a situation that seems to express the farmers' instinc-
tive greed in holding on to their private possessions: "Ein konkretes Bild," comments Braun, "das
die Schwierigkeiten der neuen Haltung enthält."[6]
But what initially looked like a negative attitude toward new social situations--the farmers'
verbal denunciations--is given a positive orientation toward the end: ". . . aufbrechen / Das Blick-
feld! den Finger legen / Auf das Land!" ("Das
weite Feld," Wir, p. 14). The difficulty in overcoming stifling conventions, to say "We" instead
of "I," manifests itself most penetratingly in one
of Braun's finest poems, "Prometheus." Braun comments about this poem: "wir tragen das Feuer in
den Himmel, und es wird uns nicht vom Himmel gebracht";[7] and in the poem itself, the reader is
told: "Was uns Neues gelingt, sprengt / Fast die
Adern vor Schmerz" (Wir, p. 66). And: "Was glaub
ich denn / Wenn nicht an uns?" (p. 67).

The volume Gegen die symmetrische Welt (1974)
focuses on the plight of the individual in certain social situations.[8] The individual reemerges
from an anonymous, abstract mass of people and
speaks for himself. The tone is subjective and
intimate. Yet the group or collective is not
viewed as an antagonistic force but rather as the
sum of the pain and the joy of countless individuals, with the poet's own individuality in the
foreground. We are dealing with the process of
meaningful integration, or as Braun puts it: the
question "ob wir, wenn wir uns vom Ich zum Wir
bewegen, auch vom Wir zu einem reichen, kräftigen,
verantwortlichen Ich kommen. . ."[9] If society and
Party superimpose restrictions upon the individual
that deviate sharply from an ideal revolutionary
concept, and if the individual is incapable of
mustering up the courage to voice his disillusionment openly, then feelings of alienation are bound
to well up. But Braun does not stop here. Since
the social conditions in the GDR are developing

toward equality for all, in his words, it is up
to the individual himself to decide what he does
with his life and how he deals with his disappointment about social discrepancies. "Da es aber nun
so ist, daß die Fähigkeiten und der Mut der Leute
verschieden sind, aber immer mehr von ihnen selbst
abhängt, wird das die Zeit, von der Marx sagt, daß
die wirklichen Freuden und die wirklichen Leiden
erst beginnen."[10]

Braun sees the roots of alienation in the individual himself. The rebellious, enthusiastic,
optimistic Staatsbürger of earlier years has given
way to a more sober, restrained, doubtful and suffering individual--often disillusioned and pained
by a dissatisfying relationship with Party and people because of a lack of communication. Apathy,
shyness, fear, cowardice threaten his development
within the group. Yet a similarly disturbing lack
of sincerity and openness is attributed to the Party. Braun is deeply concerned about a revitaliza-
tion of communication and productive interaction:
"ein unbedingtes Gebraucht-werden-wollen . . . im
positiven Sinne."[11] That is, the transcension of
alienation: "Ich schlag (mein Beruf) die Schalun-
gen von Beton / Von der Brust" ("Freiwillige Aussage," SW, p. 7).

Braun focuses on conventions and traditions
that paralyze the individual and on the individual's recurring inclination to isolate himself, to
resist interaction with the community: "Wieviel
Tünche, -viel Lack / Leimt mich, Kitt, fest" ("Be-
schäftigung," SW, p. 9). Fear of exposing one's
self overshadows even the very intimate, private
sector of a love relationship: "Wo ist der Gang /
In diese Tiefe, der Blick woher / In dies versie-
gelte Feld?" ("Schwierige Forschung," SW, p. 13).
Or the poet writes: "Komm, mach dich leicht,
streif von den Gliedern / Das Blei, das dich be-
schwert / Die Last, ich bin bei dir" ("Du liegst
so still," SW, p. 15).

In the poem "An Friedrich Hölderlin," the
protagonist views himself against the backdrop of

191

history in unison with an admired predecessor
who failed to bridge the gap between a utopian
ideal and reality, and who ended tragically:
Braun identifies with Hölderlin. With his deliberate, collage-like usage of metaphors from Hölderlin's odes, and with his conspicuous allusion
to Hölderlin's poem "Hälfte des Lebens," Braun
evokes associations of loneliness and isolation
which have a suffocating effect: "Aber die Früchte,
wer soll sie / Die Fässer aussaufen, nehmen /
Dieses dröhnende Feld? / Die eisernen Reifen, wie /
Fallen sie von meiner Brust / Wenn sie sich weitet?" (p. 18). Yet the iron grip of alienation
does not led to paralysis. Hölderlin's "Gott in
Stahl gehüllt"--an image from the hymn "Der Rhein"
--evolves in Braun's poem as a symbol for new integration. Breaking down the cold barrier of
steel, i.e., of alienating contradictions and subsequent isolation, the poet, the "I," reenters the
process of communication: "Nicht träge / Sind wir
geboren, Mann, dein <u>Gott in Stahl gehüllt</u> / Geht
unter den Werktätigen: / Bis doch zu eingeborenem
Brauch / Wird, was uns guttut, und / Brust an
Brust weitet sich so, daß sie aufsprengt diese /
eiserne / Scheu voreinander!" (p. 18).

In his poem "Im Ilmtal"--a poem reminiscent
of Goethe's "An den Mond"--Braun views himself in
a similar manner as an individual enveloped by
isolation: "In der gebauten Natur / Geh ich allein" (<u>SW</u>, p. 16). Looking back to earlier, happier years--probably the years of the "provocations"--the poet mourns and intimates: "Einmal
lebte ich so freudig / Mit den Genossen." But
Braun revokes the state of isolation with a new
image of reintegration, a flowing river which
mightily forces its way through the ground: "Bäume
dich, in den befestigten / Ufern, reiß dich los /
Flüßchen, gib so, gib den Gefühlen deinen Raum! /
Zu den verstreuten, tätigen / Gefährten, wer es
auch sei, muß ich kommen, und nie / Verlassen den
großen Kreis" (pp. 16-17). The image "water" is
used repeatedly to give contour to the desired
state of interaction. We hear in the poem "Die
Industrie": "Und die ganze Haut / Greift nach den

Freunden / . ./. ./Daß sich unsere Spuren / Tref-
fen (ich sehe es), ein Netzwerk / Auf das Land /
Ein Meer / Sozusagen / Das kommt" (SW, pp. 24-25).
Or: "der Erde / Aufgeschlagenes Auge / Und der
weiße, neugeborene Strand / Den wir betreten /
Zwischen uns" ("Durchgearbeitete Landschaft," SW,
p. 34).

Braun's preoccupation with symptoms of alienation, isolation, and stagnation is an ongoing
process. In 1978 the Mitteldeutscher Verlag published a collection of excerpts of his most important works, called Im Querschnitt.[12] It also contains a number of new poems, which, not surprisingly, allude to the above mentioned theme.[13] Inertia and apathy continue to weigh heavily on the
poet's mind: "Der Himmel aus massivem Blei, die
Lungen voll Filz" ("Das Verbrechen," Querschnitt,
p. 31). The "I," the poet, openly submits himself
to self-criticism, aiming to come to terms with
this fear, which he aptly calls "infertility":
"Meine schamhaften Freunde / . . . Haben mich an-
gestiftet / Zum Mord / An manchem jungen Gedanken / Eh er geboren war. / . . . Wenn ich ihnen
folge, denen es / Um einen Namen geht und nicht
um mich dich uns / Bin ich bald unfruchtbar" ("Ge-
dankenkinder-Mord," Querschnitt, p. 57).

Braun, however, never really succumbs to the
"iron grip"--"den eisernen Reifen"--of political
and creative sterility. Despite obstacles and im-
passes, the journey toward the goal of responsible
interaction goes on. But the goal, though visible,
is still far away. In a recent poem, the parable
"Vom Besteigen hoher Berge," Braun condenses the
frustration, strain, disillusionment, isolation,
and hope of the individual in an appropriate metaphor, "mountain climbing": "Warum sind wir so
müde./ Müssen wir nicht längst umkehren / . . . .
Und uns aus den Sicherungen schnüren / Denn dieser
Weg wird nicht zum Ziel führen. / Aufstieg gleich
Abstieg, heiß, kalt. / Und den Gipfel in wieder
erreichbarer Ferne zu sehn" (Querschnitt, p. 99).

Rutgers University

Notes

[1] Jürgen Kuczynski, "Hölderlin - Die Tragödie des revolutionären Idealisten," in his _Gestalten und Werke. Soziologische Studien zur deutschen Literatur_ (Berlin/Weimar: Aufbau, 1969).

[2] Volker Braun, "Interview," in his _Es genügt nicht die einfache Wahrheit. Notate_ (Frankfurt/M.: Suhrkamp, 1976), p. 120.

[3] Braun, "Jazz," in his _Provokation für mich_ (Halle: Mitteldeutscher Verlag, 1965), p. 18.

[4] Braun, _Wir und nicht sie_ (Frankfurt/M.: Suhrkamp, 1970.

[5] "Es genügt nicht die einfache Wahrheit," in _Es genügt nicht die einfache Wahrheit. Notate_, pp. 19-20.

[6] "Interview," p. 117.

[7] "Interview," p. 122.

[8] _Gegen die symmetrische Welt_ (Frankfurt/M.: Suhrkamp, 1974).

[9] "Tabus," in _Es genügt nicht_, p. 107.

[10] "Interview," p. 127.

[11] "Interview," p. 119.

[12] _Im Querschnitt. Volker Braun. Gedichte. Prosa. Stücke. Aufsätze_ (Halle: Mitteldeutscher Verlag, 1978).

[13] Most of these poems were published again in Braun's latest volume of poetry, _Training des aufrechten Gangs_ (Halle: Mitteldeutscher Verl., 1979).

Das Frauenbild im frühen DDR-Drama und in
der proletarisch-revolutionären Literatur:
Fred Reichwalds Das Wagnis der Maria Diehl

H. Jochen Hoffmann

Die zahlreichen Versuche in der DDR, schon im
Drama der Anfangsjahre neben den sich verändernden
Eigentumsverhältnissen auch die neue Rolle der
Frau künstlerisch zu gestalten, führten einige
westliche Kritiker zu der Annahme, der Kampf der
Frau um Selbstverwirklichung sei bereits "fester
Bestandteil der proletarisch-revolutionären Literatur seit ihren Anfängen in den zwanziger Jahren"
gewesen.[1] Neuere Untersuchungen weisen jedoch am
Beispiel der Roten Eine-Mark-Romane zahlreiche Ge-
meinsamkeiten zwischen dem Frauenbild der proletarisch-revolutionären Literatur und der bürgerlichen nach, die eigentlich verdrängt werden sollte:
Die stereotype Frauendarstellung bleibt unverän-
dert, im Mann/Frau Verhältnis ändert sich wenig.[2]
Erst wenn wir uns verdeutlichen, daß die sozialistische Literatur nicht unabhängig, also streng
geschieden von der bürgerlichen entstand, sind wir
weniger verwundert, die stereotype Frauendarstellung auch im frühen DDR-Drama vorzufinden. Fred
Reichwalds Das Wagnis der Maria Diehl (1958) soll
als zentrales Beispiel für diese Darstellungsweise
hier näher untersucht werden.[3]

Eine Verwandtschaft Maria Diehls zu ihren
Schwestern in der proletarisch-revolutionären Literatur wird erkennbar, wenn wir Rohrwassers For-
schungsergebnisse als Ausgangspunkt betrachten.
Rohrwasser zeigt in seiner Studie Saubere Mädel,
starke Genossen - proletarische Massenliteratur?,
daß Frauen in den Roten Eine-Mark-Romanen "als

Hemmschuh politischer Aktivitäten" (S. 96) erscheinen, denn sie sind unzuverlässig, naiv, gefühlsbetont. Der Genosse ist von seiner inneren Haltung her das Gegenteil, was durch die äußere Erscheinung möglichst unterstrichen werden sollte. So bot sich, wie Rohrwasser ausführt, ein "monoton wiederholendes Bild":

> Der Kommunist war der starke, überlegene - wenn nicht hochgewachsene, so doch ausgeglichenere Charakter, der sich durch Jugendlichkeit, innere Autorität, und eine beruhigende Stimme ausweisen konnte. (S. 100)

Mit anderen Worten: es kommt in der proletarisch-revolutionären Literatur zur Profilierung eines "männlichen Kommunismus" und zwar auf Kosten der Frauengestalt. Als Vorkämpfer für eine neue Gesellschaft qualifiziert sich dort nur der durch körperliche Kraft und geistige Überlegenheit ausgewiesene Kommunist, der "starke Genosse," wie Rohrwasser ihn im Titel seiner Studie treffend bezeichnet.

Wichtig für die vorliegende Untersuchung ist, wie Emmerich am Beispiel von Willi Bredels Erzählung "Petra Harms" (1950)[4] zeigt, "daß diese Tendenz der Frauendarstellung auch in der frühen SBZ- und DDR-Literatur anzutreffen ist, ja dominiert."[5] Das Nachwirken dieser Tendenz in der DDR läßt sich neben Maria Diehl auch an anderen Stücken nachweisen, z.B. Werner Kubsch: Die ersten Schritte (1950) oder Helmut Sakowski: Steine im Weg (1961), wobei Sakowski deutlich bemüht ist, die stereotype Darstellung seiner weiblichen und männlichen Helden zu überwinden. Es ist eine Bemühung, die die theoretische Diskussion gegen Typisierung und Schematisierung in der DDR-Literatur widerspiegelt, die nach der kulturpolitischen Wende 1956-57 auf breiter Basis geführt wurde.

Im Drama Das Wagnis der Maria Diehl benutzt der Autor die im bürgerlichen Drama bekannte Figurenkonstellation der Frau zwischen zwei Männern,

196

um die Festigung der Macht des Proletariats in der
neuen, sozialistischen Gesellschaft zu zeigen.
Hier wird jedoch die Liebe Maria Diehls - soweit
sie besteht - als hemmendes Element dargestellt,
weil sie vom fortschrittlichen Denken und gesellschaftlichen Handeln ablenkt.

Das Stück, für das der Autor den National-
preis erhielt, "entstand" zwischen 1954 und 1957.[6]
Es spielt in einer der neuen Landwirtschaftlichen
Produktionsgenossenschaften (LPG) der DDR, in der
Maria Diehl kurz zuvor zur Vorstandsvorsitzenden
gewählt worden ist, wo jedoch der Agronom Joachim
Keding, der Verlobte Marias, ihre als typisch weib-
lich dargestellten Schwächen geschickt ausnützt,
um wesentliche Leitungsentscheidungen in seinem
Sinne zu beeinflussen. Hinter ihrem Rücken sabo-
tiert er die Aufbauarbeit in der LPG. Marias Liebe macht sie blind gegenüber Kedings Stör- und
Sabotageakte, jedoch "wagt" sie es - der Titel
soll es andeuten -, sich zum ersten Mal ihrem Verlobten zu widersetzen und ein Parteimitglied, Walter Buschow, als neuen Stallbrigadier einzustel-
len. Damit ist der Weg geöffnet für die fort-
schrittliche Entwicklung der LPG, denn Buschow
durchschaut Kedings Charakter und enthüllt am Ende
des Stücks dessen nationalsozialistische Vergangenheit. Es kommt zum Kampf der Männer, worauf
Maria Keding erschießt.

Schon die vereinfachte Zusammenfassung des
Stücks zeigt, daß in Werken der fünfziger Jahre
mit Frauen ein Einfluß deutlich wird, den Rohrwasser als den der Partei und damit der Genossen
zeigt. Reichwalds Stück stellt auch insofern das
Weiterleben der proletarisch-revolutionären Tradition dar, als es eine Wirklichkeit "widerspiegelt," wie sie nach Meinung der Partei sein soll
und nicht, wie sie wirklich ist. Maria Diehl ist
zwar Titelfigur des Dramas, aber in ihren Haupt-
merkmalen entspricht sie der stereotypen Frauengestalt der proletarisch-revolutionären Literatur. Neu ist allerdings, daß sie in einem Staat
lebt, wo sie als Frau eine leitende Stelle inne-
haben kann, ohne sie sich erst erkämpfen zu müs-

197

sen. Reichwald billigt ihr jedoch keine innere
Entwicklung, kein Emanzipationsbewußtsein zu.
Stattdessen werden ihr, indem sie sich Keding
zweimal widersetzt und eigene Entscheidungen
trifft, zwei Mutproben auferlegt. Maria Diehl
besteht die Mutproben, aber ihre Emanzipations-
fähigkeit ist damit nicht erwiesen.

Marias Befangenheit in kleinbürgerlicher
Weiblichkeit läßt ihr ihre verantwortliche Position zu einer Last werden, die sie unvorbereitet
trifft und die zu befragen sie nicht lernt. So
findet Keding sie "zu gutmütig" (S. 42) im Umgang
mit den Landarbeitern, und sie erlaubt sich "Ge-
fühlsduseleien" (S. 47), wo aus Sicht der Männer
in der LPG männlich-energisches Verhalten klarere
Verhältnisse schaffen könnte. Wenn sie den Argu-
menten der entgegengesetzt planenden Männer nicht
entgegentreten kann, gibt sie ihrem Geschlecht
die Schuld: "Als Frau ist man einem Mann eben
nicht gewachsen" (S. 47).

In bezug auf Arbeit ist Maria Diehl doppelt
belastet, denn zu Hause muß sie für Keding, mit
dem sie zusammenlebt, kochen und den Haushalt
führen, obwohl sie in der LPG mehr leistet als
er. Sie wird typisch kleinbürgerlich gezeichnet
und entsprechend drängt sie ihren Verlobten aus
Sorge um ihren Leumund zur Ehe: "Wir sollten wirklich bald heiraten. Die Leute reden schon über
uns" (S. 41).

Nahezu verhängnisvoll wird für Maria ihre
politische Naivität, die sie zum manipulierbaren
Werkzeug der sie beherrschenden Kräfte werden
läßt, denn Keding wie auch Buschow benutzen Marias
Position als Vorsitzende, um ihre eigenen Pläne zu
verfolgen. Ironisch ist, daß gerade der destruk-
tiv arbeitende Keding seinem neuen Rivalen unlau-
tere Motive zutraut: "Sollte er versuchen, deine
Autorität als Vorsitzende zu untergraben, dann
kenne ich keinen Spaß" (S. 46).

Maria ist eine Figur, die politische Zusammenhänge nicht erkennt und ihre eigenen Handlungen

nicht als politische Tat werten kann. Dadurch
haben die agierenden Männer der LPG großen Einfluß auf sie. Gleichzeitig wird so jedoch auch
die Szene vorbereitet für Walter Buschow als Ver-
treter der aufsteigenden Klasse, unter dessen Führung die LPG (und damit auch Maria) aus den Klau-
en des Saboteurs gerettet werden kann. Als Keding
"väterlich, belehrend" darauf hinweist, daß die
Entscheidung der Partei, gerade Buschow in die LPG
zu schicken, politisch zu sehen ist, muß sie zuge-
ben: "Ich habe darüber noch nie nachgedacht" (S.
43). Sie überläßt sich ganz seiner ideologischen
Führung und hilft seine Dominanz zu zementieren,
wenn sie ihn dafür libidinös belohnt.

> Keding: . . . vielleicht ist es bes-
> ser, wenn wir in Zukunft öfter über
> politische Dinge reden.

> Maria: Dafür wäre ich dir sehr dank-
> bar, Achim.

> Keding: Dann gib mir einen Kuß . . .
>   (S. 46)

Hier kommt zum Ausdruck, was schon die Darstellung des Mann/Frau Verhältnisses der Literatur der zwanziger Jahre charakterisierte: Die Frau
darf in dieser Literaturtradition kein eigenstän-
diges Denken entwickeln. Daher darf auch die junge Parteigenossin Gerda, eine Freundin Marias,
Keding nur ansatzweise und verharmlosend kritisieren (S. 43). Schon bald tut es beiden leid, überhaupt "Kritik" geäußert zu haben, und sie wenden
sich dem Thema "Mode" zu (S. 43). Gelegenheit
zur eigenen Reflexion bekommen sie nicht, denn allein den Männern wird im Stück das Recht und die
Fähigkeit zuerkannt, das Bewußtsein der Frau zu
formen.

So rückständig wie bei Reichwald, dessen
Stück die höchste Aufführungszahl der Saison er-
lebte, schrieb man auch in den Anfangsjahren schon
nicht mehr. Denn es entsteht ein Bild einer durch
Liebe blind gewordenen, kleinbürgerlichen Frauen-

gestalt, die unfähig ist, in gesellschaftlichen
Zusammenhängen zu denken. Nahezu bis zum Schluß
des Stückes läßt Maria Diehl sich von ihrem Verlobten irreführen und deutet dessen Feindschaft zu
Buschow als "Eifersucht" (S. 53). Die entscheidende Aufklärung über Kedings Saboteurtätigkeit
und nationalsozialistische Vergangenheit schafft
erst Buschow.

Buschows Ähnlichkeit mit den männlichen Haupt-
gestalten der proletarisch-revolutionären Literatur reicht von seiner kritiklosen Unterordnung unter die Parteibeschlüsse (S. 44) bis in seine Pri-
vatsphäre. Die Partei schickt ihn von der Stadt
aufs Land, von der Industriearbeit in die Landar-
beit. Dabei muß das Private der Klassenaufgabe
weichen. Buschow hat kein eigenes Zuhause, und
der Parteisekretär findet es für Buschows Partei-
auftrag nützlich, daß er, der Fünfunddreißigjäh-
rige, noch alleinstehend ist (S. 44). So kann er
sich ausschließlich auf die landwirtschaftliche
Ertragssteigerung sowie die Gründe für regelmäßig
auftretende Rückschläge in der LPG-Verwaltung und
-Leitung konzentrieren.

Buschow scheint einen nahezu unfehlbaren Blick
dafür zu haben, wer für die Mißstände in der LPG
verantwortlich ist und wer nicht. Schon nach der
ersten kurzen Begegnung mit Keding erkennt er ihn
als "Inspektortyp" (S. 45), was für ihn gleichbe-
deutend ist mit Ausbeuter und Klassengegner. Er
wird "das Gefühl nicht los" (S. 54), daß Keding
und dessen Helfer das Futter vergiftet haben (S.
52, 54). Umgekehrt vermutet er sofort, daß der
Altkommunist Franz Klein nicht aus Faulheit seine
Arbeit vernachlässigt und "einen schlechten Ruf"
bekommen hat, sondern weil Keding seinen Ruf ge-
zielt untergräbt (S. 48). Die Ähnlichkeit zu
Handlungsmustern in der proletarisch-revolutionären Literatur der zwanziger Jahre ist auffal-
lend. Darüber heißt es bei Rohrwasser: "Die in-
stinktive Sicherheit, unterscheiden zu können,
wer zum eigenen Lager zählt und wer zu den Geg-
nern, ist ein notwendiges Charakteristikum der
positiven Helden der linken Romane geworden" (S. 30).

Als Buschow zusätzlich noch als der "soge-
nannte 'starke Genosse'" bezeichnet wird (S. 43),
wird er von Reichwald in mehrfacher Hinsicht als
Held im Sinne der proletarisch-revolutionären Literaturtradition legitimiert. Buschows "instink-
tive Sicherheit" und Unfehlbarkeit in der Partei-
arbeit steht im scharfen Kontrast zu der im Stück
durchgängig gezeigten Unsicherheit und Argumenta-
tionsschwäche Marias. In der - allerdings nicht
überzeugenden - Schlußszene des Stückes bietet
Reichwald jedoch eine über tradierte Handlungsmuster hinausgehende Lösung, wenn er plötzlich
eine zu einem sozialistischen Bewußtsein gewandel-
te Maria vorstellt, die ihren Verlobten mit der
Waffe an der Flucht hindert und tötet. Mit dieser
drastischen Tat sind jedoch nur auf den ersten
Blick die Voraussetzungen für den Typus des sozialistischen Wandlungsdramas erfüllt, wie sie von
Werner Mittenzwei definiert wurden, der dann von
"Wandlung" spricht, wenn eine Figur "durch ein besonders eindringliches Erlebnis schlagartig zu
neuen Erkenntnissen oder Verhaltensweisen gedrängt
wird,"[7] in denen sich ein gesteigertes gesellschaftliches Bewußtsein widerspiegelt.

Diese als Höhepunkt von Reichwalds Stück ge-
meinte drastische Tat wirkt jedoch künstlich und
dem Stück aufgepropft, weil sie szenisch ungenü-
gend vorbereitet ist und so im Mißverhältnis steht
zu der im Stück angelegten "weiblichen" Schwäche
der Frauenfigur, der die Fähigkeit zum selbst-
ständigen Denken und Handeln und damit zur Entwicklung eines eigenen Bewußtseins abgeht. Ihren
Entschluß zur Tat faßt Maria erst im Augenblick
des Handgemenges der Männer; er kommt zu unvermittelt, um als reflektierter, emanzipatorischer
Schritt einer Frau angesehen zu werden, die nun
aus einem neuen gesellschaftlichen Bewußtsein heraus selbst aktiv für die Sache der jungen sozialistischen Ordnung eintritt.

Noch überraschender wirkt im Kontext unserer
Analyse das Wandlungsbekenntnis, mit dem eine
zweite Fassung abschließt.[8] Dort verliert Keding
im Handgemenge mit Buschow seinen Revolver, den

Maria aufhebt, ihn aber nicht an ihren Verlobten zurück - sondern an Buschow weitergibt mit den Worten: "Ich liebte ihn - doch hasse ich jeden, der unsere Welt zerstören will."[9] Die klare politische Identifizierung mit der Sache Buschows klingt aus dem Mund Marias, deren politische Naivität im Stück mehrfach deutlich gemacht wird, wenig überzeugend. Die Frau assistiert lediglich bei der Festnahme, und der Parteifunktionär bleibt entsprechend tradierter Handlungsmuster bis zum Schluß agierende Person. Versucht man jedoch die Waffenübergabe an Buschow - gestützt auf Marias Bekenntnis - als Ausdruck neuen Bewußtseins und kämpferischer Solidarität mit der neuen Klasse zu deuten, müssen die Intensität des Augenblicks und Marias mangelnde Gelegenheit zur Reflexion mitberücksichtigt werden. Unter solchen Umständen scheint eine in der Handlung nicht angelegte Wandlung für eine Figur wenig glaubhaft.

Marias Tat ist nicht allein aus den gesellschaftlichen Vorgängen herzuleiten, denn sie reagiert auch als Frau auf die um sie werbenden Männer, von denen ihr Geliebter als Klassengegner und ehemaliger Nazi entlarvt wird. Da Keding sie belogen hat, kann er nicht mehr ihr Liebhaber sein. So gesehen wirkt ihre Tat auch als Affekthandlung einer sich hintergangen fühlenden Frau.

Wenn wir also die zweite Schlußfassung als Teil des ganzen Stückes sehen, wo doch die traditionsgebundene Figurenzeichnung auch durch ähnlich gestaltete Nebenfiguren (z.B. Gerda) ergänzt wird, erweist sich, daß Reichwald den in der sozialistischen Literaturtradition etablierten Typus eines idealen Parteiarbeiters als Garant des sozialistischen Fortschritts zeichnet. Dadurch wird die Rolle Maria Diehls, immerhin seine Titelfigur, abgewertet, und sie bleibt Objekt der Geschichte.

Wenn nun der stereotypen Darstellungsweise eine Vorstellung der Frau als Objekt der Geschichte zugrunde liegt, so bahnt sich ebenfalls in den fünfziger Jahren - besonders in der nach 1956-57 beginnenden Phase in der Kulturpolitik der DDR -

eine Entwicklung an, nach der die Frau jetzt eher als Subjekt der Geschichte erscheint. Ansätze dazu finden sich bei Dramatikern, die in der Brecht-Tradition schreiben, bei Strittmatter in seinem Stück Katzgraben (1953) wie auch bei Sakowskis Steine im Weg (1962), wo jetzt nicht nur die Frauengestalt, sondern auch die Nebenfiguren differenzierter, das heißt, wirklichkeitsnäher dargestellt werden als bei Reichwald. Jedoch bleibt die Frau auch im Drama der sechziger Jahre Mitgestalter statt Gestalter sozialistischer Wirklichkeit. Erst in Volker Brauns Tinka (1973) zeigt sich eine Wende tradierter Figurendarstellungen, zeigt sich der Kampf der Frau um Selbstverwirklichung als beherrschendes Thema. Fred Reichwalds Maria Diehl ist dagegen nur noch von literarhistorischem Interesse - auch in der DDR -, denn es bietet gute Vergleichsmöglichkeiten zu dramatischen Versuchen, in denen sich eine Überwindung stereotyper Darstellungsweisen anbahnt.

Smith College

Anweisungen

[1] Lutz-W. Wolff, Hrsg., Frauen in der DDR: Zwanzig Erzählungen (München: Deutscher Taschenbuch Verlag, 1976), S. 251.

[2] Vgl. Wolfgang Emmerich, "Identität und Geschlechtertausch," Basis, 8 (1978), 130f.; und Michael Rohrwasser, Saubere Mädel, starke Genossen - proletarische Massenliteratur? (Frankfurt/M.: Verlag Roter Stern, 1975). Zur kritischen Wertung der Rohrwasser-Studie vgl. Wolfgang Emmerich, "Review Essay," New German Critique, No. 10 (Winter 1977), 179-189.

[3] Fred Reichwald, "Das Wagnis der Maria Diehl," Junge Kunst, 1, No. 3 (1958), 40-56. Seitenangaben im Text beziehen sich auf diese Ausgabe.

[4] Willi Bredel, "Petra Harms," in Lutz-W. Wolff, Hrsg., _Frauen_ _in_ _der_ _DDR_, a.a.O., S. 18-25.

[5] Emmerich, "Identität und Geschlechter-tausch," S. 132.

[6] Reichwald, S. 40.

[7] Werner Mittenzwei, _Gestaltung_ _und_ _Gestalten_ _im_ _modernen_ _Drama_ (Berlin-Ost: Aufbau-Verlag, 1969), S. 371.

[8] Manuskript des Henschelverlags, Berlin-Ost. Zitiert nach Werner Mittenzwei, Hrsg., _Theater_ _in_ _der_ _Zeitenwende_ (Berlin-Ost: Henschelverlag, 1972), II, 427.

[9] Zitiert in _Theater_ _in_ _der_ _Zeitenwende_, II, 65.

The Reception of Pablo Neruda's Works
in the German Democratic Republic[1]

Bonnie A. Beckett

The Chilean communist author and Nobel Prize
winner Pablo Neruda is one of the most widely
known, respected, and read poets in the German
Democratic Republic. Tracing the complex process
of the translation, dissemination, and evaluation
of Neruda's works in the GDR since its founding in
1949 reveals that certain works have been readily
available and critically acclaimed, while others
either remained untranslated for a long time or
were ignored entirely. Although historical, political, and personal circumstances undeniably influenced Neruda's reception in the GDR, the Kulturpolitik promulgated by the SED had an even more
decisive and clearly discernible effect.

For readers unfamiliar with Pablo Neruda's
life, political commitment, and writings, a very
brief sketch of his works will provide background
necessary for the analysis of the reception of his
works in the GDR. Neruda began his career writing
intimate, private poetry, turned in his thirties
to highly engaged poetry, and in his fifties resumed writing personal and private poetry while
continuing his political and public poetry. In
his early poems (c. 1920 to 1924), Neruda used
fairly traditional formal metrical schemes to offer melancholy descriptions of his solitude. The
most outstanding work from Neruda's early period
is Veinte poemas de amor y una canción desesperada
(Twenty Love Poems and a Cry of Desperation, 1924),
a short, unconventional volume of love poems
reflecting the writer's struggle to transform his

remembrances of two women into poetry.

Between 1925 and the mid-1930s Neruda broke away from traditional forms and began to write more stylistically innovative and somewhat surrealistic works, retaining and intensifying his earlier themes. The most significant of these works, Residencia en la tierra (Residence on Earth, 1935), depicts a world of fragmentary and deformed objects from which there is no escape. Man's sense of alienation from other people, from social institutions, objects, and matter itself pervades Residencia en la tierra, considered by many western critics to contain Neruda's greatest poems. These volumes reflect the acute loneliness which haunted Neruda as he served in a series of obscure diplomatic posts in the Far East, and his loathing for the bureaucratic nature of his job.

The Spanish Civil War and the deaths of close friends jarred Neruda, then on diplomatic assignment in Madrid, out of his isolation. His concept of poetry and the function of the poet shifted dramatically as he became politically committed. The poems of España en el corazón (Spain in the Heart, 1937), later incorporated into Tercera Residencia (Third Residence, 1947), deal with ordinary people, with injustice, and political issues. Neruda's highly personal and emotional reaction to the death of Federico García Lorca and to the Spanish Civil War helped blend his intimate personal poetry with new public themes, resulting in some of his finest poems. After the fall of Spain to Franco, Neruda fled to Paris and ultimately to Mexico City, where he served as the Consul General of Chile in Mexico, aided in the resettlement of political refugees, and joined German exiles in opposing Hitler's actions in Germany and Russia. A strident sense of political immediacy in his poems about Stalingrad, the Red Army, and Russia, collected in Tercera residencia, overshadows any sense of personal or cultural involvement, creating problematic incidental poems which fail to offer much beyond hollow political rhetoric.

Toward the end of _Tercera residencia_ Neruda becomes conscious of his historical and cultural roots in Latin America, and they become an important sustaining element which lends new substance to the immediate and political realities which he chronicles. A visit in 1943 to the ancient ruins of Machu Picchu, his joining the Chilean Communist party (1945) and running for senator, and his outspoken opposition to Chile's dictator Gabriel González Videla, which forced Neruda underground in 1948 and into exile in 1949, coalesced in poetic form in _Canto general_ (_General Song_, 1950). This massive Whitmanesque epic describes the history and geography of the Americas, fulfilling Neruda's role as a public poet, yet contains the highly personal story of his own life and artistic development as well. The broad historical perspective and autobiographical elements in _Canto general_ anticipate the two basic strains in Neruda's later poetry, the public and the private.

After _Canto general_ the two strains exist separately in Neruda's poetry. The new personal poetry is not a rejection of his political and public poetry, but its complement. The turning inward of the later poems arises not from a feeling of isolation or alienation from people, society, or the _materia_, but from a thirst for solitude, silence, and loving communion as respites from the responsibilities of the world. The poet seeks in solitude and in love the peace necessary for the renewal of his strength. Love between man and woman is the most basic form of communication for Neruda and does not contradict in any way the public poet's commitment to the people of the _pueblo_. Neruda refuses to reject the rigors and difficulties engendered by his engaged poetry, and consciously affirms his dual role as public and private poet. Neruda's long writing career ended in 1973 with his death in the confusion following the military coup in Chile lead by General Pinochet. The coup culminated in the death of the poet's life-long friend President Salvador Allende and brought to an end the social revolution which the _Unidad Popular_ had set in motion.

The study of the reception of Neruda's works in the GDR does not begin with the founding of a separate state in 1949, but with friendships and contacts formed by Neruda more than a decade earlier. Many of the future GDR translators, editors, and critics of Neruda's works made preliminary contact with him in Madrid or Paris during the Spanish Civil War or in Mexico City in the early 1940s. Both Mexico City and Santiago de Chile became gathering places for exiles who formed social and cultural groups, produced numerous exile journals, and even founded a publishing house.[2] Virtually all those Germans who later emerged as important intermediaries between Neruda and his GDR audience had been forced into exile by their difficulties under Hitler's regime, among them Anna Seghers, Ludwig Renn, Alexander Abusch, and Erich Arendt, the most prolific translator of Neruda's works into German.

Neruda's anti-fascist activities drew support and appreciation from a broadly-based group of international exiles, but, even during the 1940s, communist and non-aligned groups chose very different works for translation and publication in their respective exile journals. The few poems published in the Mexican exile periodicals Freies Deutschland and Alemania Libre dealt with the resistance efforts in Stalingrad. Not even the poems about the Spanish Civil War were considered politically current enough to be included in Freies Deutschland, whose editorial staff was dominated by Stalinist-oriented members of the Communist party. Exile periodicals not dominated by the Communist party, for example Deutsche Blätter, published by Catholic and conservative anti-Nazi forces in Santiago de Chile, printed a radically different selection of Neruda's poems, which included several of his early love poems. This split between the publishing practices of communist-dominated and non-aligned exile journals foreshadows decisive future trends in the GDR and western reception of Neruda's works.

Of those exiled Germans who returned to Germany with any awareness of Neruda's writings or personality, virtually all had Communist party affiliation, and most eventually settled in the Soviet occupied zone. In their efforts to find new literary models for German writers, Anna Seghers and others familiar with Neruda introduced his works to a wider German public.

In the fall of 1948 six of Neruda's public poems from España en el corazón, Tercera residencia, and Canto general, translated by Stephan Hermlin, appeared in Ost und West.[3] The effect of life, war, and death upon simple people links these poems thematically. The poems reject the inhumanity of war and stress the need for peace, freedom, and human rights. In broad terms, they reflect tolerance for humanistic, anti-fascist democratic works, and are less immediately political than the poems which had appeared in the Mexican exile periodical Freies Deutschland. Scattered Neruda poems were published in several journals over the next few years.

The first articles devoted entirely to Neruda and the first anthology of his poems, Beleidigtes Land, edited by Anna Seghers, appeared in 1949.[4] The anthology combined political poems written in response to the war with other works describing the South American continent. Because of the time lag of approximately two years between the editorial decision to publish and the actual appearance of Beleidigtes Land, this anthology must be understood as a product of the immediate postwar period when broadly humanistic, anti-fascist democratic ideals prevailed in literature.

In the early 1950s, single poems by Neruda and articles about him began to appear with some regularity in major GDR journals. The impact of the emerging Kulturpolitik and political developments on the reception of Neruda's works in the GDR between 1949 and 1959 can be seen in the selection of works published, the changes in critical standards by which his works were judged, and in the personal image of Neruda established in the press. Peter Huchel, the poet and liberal editor of _Sinn und Form_, printed a series of poems from _Canto general_ which reflected Neruda's desire to portray not merely concrete political figures and events, but to show these people and situations as related to the historical context of Latin America as a whole. In contrast, the selections printed between 1952 and 1956 in _Aufbau_ focused almost exclusively on works from _Las uvas y el viento_ (1954) which deal with immediate political conflicts and praise the guidance by Stalin and the Soviet Union. These poems about Russia and Berlin reinforced the GDR's own ideal image of itself and the SED view of the relationship between the GDR and Russia; they are, however, some of Neruda's weakest poems. Russian acceptance of Neruda, and the poet's travels to the Soviet Union and the GDR helped pave the way for further GDR translation and favorable evaluation of his works.

During the early 1950s Neruda's friends from exile wrote the only articles with even a rudimentary awareness of his development as a writer, of his literary techniques, and of his personal blending of politics with poetry.[5] Minor articles in the period following the adoption of socialist realism as the official literary doctrine tended to stress Neruda's role in the struggle for freedom in Madrid and Mexico. The words "Freiheit" and "Frieden" recur in reference to Neruda,[6] emphasizing an image created in part by his political engagement, but also by his having been awarded the International Peace Prize, and by the "Friedenslied," Brecht's loose adaptation of a poem from _Canto general_ set to music by Paul Dessau, which became a popular folk song in the GDR.

At the end of 1953 Neruda was awarded the Stalin Peace Prize, and the complete translation of _Der große Gesang_ (_Canto general_) was published.[7] The book sold poorly, probably at least in part as a result of the high price, the reading public's lack of interest in poetry, and the general ignorance of Latin American literature shared by critics and readers alike. Still, the

reviews of Der große Gesang by Anna Seghers and
Alexander Abusch helped make Neruda's name a by-
word in literary discourse, a model held up for
other writers to emulate. Although many of the
reviews which appeared in Neue deutsche Literatur,
Börsenblatt für den deutschen Buchhandel, and Die
Buchbesprechung were brief, they maintained a
fairly literary and not merely rhetorical level
during this period of thaw in GDR Kulturpolitik.
Critics accepted the social and socialist content
of Der große Gesang without losing sight of the
literary and national aspects of the epic. The
tone of Neruda criticism in Die Weltbühne, Sowjetliteratur, and Arbeit: Zeitschrift für Theorie und
Praxis der Gewerkschaften contrasted with the essentially literary approach of reviews in the journals mentioned previously. These more political
journals conveyed the party line assessment of
Neruda's individual volumes, rejecting his early
books as purely lyrical and abstract works dominated by surrealist influences and limiting individualism.[8]

Translation and publication of Neruda's works
continued during the remainder of the 1950s and
included a somewhat broader selection of his poetry. Arendt single-handedly translated virtually
all the Neruda poems published during these years,
and in 1956 he received the translator's prize of
the GDR for his Neruda volumes. The highly political Die Trauben und der Wind (Las uvas y el
viento) appeared in 1955 and Spanien im Herzen
(España en el corazón) one year later.[9] Inexpensive reprints of parts of Der große Gesang, his
odes, and the entirely unpolitical Zwanzig Liebesgedichte und ein Lied der Verzweiflung (Veinte
poemas de amor y una canción desesperada)were published.[10] Arendt had translated the slim volume
of love poems before beginning work on Der große
Gesang, but the love poems were not printed until
1958 when Neruda's career as a political writer
was clearly established. Translations of other
volumes of Neruda's private poetry, such as Residencia en la tierra I and II, Los versos del capi-
tán (1952), Estravagario (1958), and Cien sonetos

de _amor_ (1959) were conspicuously absent. The restrictive Kulturpolitik which followed the Hungarian uprising did not allow enough latitude for the publication of such non-political works with obscure and surrealistic imagery.

The influence of Kulturpolitik on the selection of poems for publication in journals was even more apparent. Poems about the Soviet Union from Die Trauben und der Wind, about Madrid from Spanien im Herzen, and about the communist Luis Aragon and the People's Republic of China from Navegaciones y regresos (1959) appeared between 1952 and 1958 in Aufbau and Neue deutsche Literatur.[11] No selections from the love poems or private poetry were reprinted in journals, and only two of his odes.

Works by Neruda published in the GDR after 1953 were automatically proclaimed great by critics. Once the works were canonized, little genuine analysis, interpretation or evaluation of them was made. Since Neruda was already approved as a literary model, critics wound up defending, excusing, or ignoring his lapses from the ideals of socialist realism. Neruda's poetry proved to be too diverse, however, to fit neatly within the confines of any literary doctrine, let alone those of socialist realism. Despite Neruda's stated intention of making the language and imagery of his public poetry transparent, GDR critics still found Der große Gesang and even some of the odes difficult to understand. The combination of poetic obscurity and widespread public appeal of such early works as Veinte poemas de amor y una canción desesperada mystified the GDR critics, whose articles both praised the clarity of Neruda's poems and expressed frustration at their obscurity. Selective publication practices were, therefore, frequently employed to present a Neruda canon more or less acceptable under the guidelines of Kulturpolitik. Residencia en la tierra I and II, Veinte poemas de amor y una canción desesperada, and Estravagario are concrete examples of works which Arendt and the publishers withheld for several years from publication, although they recognized the enduring greatness of these poems. The availability of good translations was not a factor in the delays, since the Arendt translations of each of these volumes had been completed several years prior to publication. Only in a few fortuitous instances did the dictates of Kulturpolitik concerning political correctness, engagement, and immediacy coincide with genuine quality in Neruda's poetry, as in the case of Der große Gesang. The result was a lopsided GDR image of his development as a poet and an individual, an image which persisted for nearly twenty years with little variation.

By the first Bitterfeld Conference in 1959 Neruda was revered along with other venerated models: Walt Whitman, Paul Eluard, Vladimir Majakowsky, and Nazim Hikmet. Neruda became a corresponding member of the prestigious Deutsche Akademie der Künste in Berlin, and critics proclaimed his volumes as masterpieces of socialist realism. Part of the reason for his continued favor under the new Bitterfeld Kulturpolitik may have been that his role as a public poet and his concept of "impure" poetry anticipated some of the goals of the Bitterfeld conferences. His rapport with working-class people and his focus on ordinary people, objects, and language became central themes in GDR praise for Neruda.

With the 1961 publication of the expensive edition of the complete Elementare Oden, the publishing house Volk und Welt ended its initial series of Neruda translations.[12] Aside from brief reviews of the odes in 1962, articles and reviews virtually disappeared until 1964, and individual poems by Neruda in newspapers and journals became more scarce. The reissuing of previously translated works by other publishing houses, such as the Reclam (Leipzig) paperback edition of Amerika, ich rufe deinen Namen nicht vergeblich an (canto IV of Canto general), dominated the years from 1961 to 1964.[13] Special, very limited editions of two of the odes relating to printing and typography were printed by vocational schools, but contributed little to the availability of Neruda's works to the general public or even to critics and scholars.[14]

Given the consistently warm acceptance of Neruda as a writer, what factors affected the six-year pause from 1961 to 1967, during which no new translations of works by him appeared? Although Erich Arendt had translated selected parts of such early works as Crepusculario (1923), Tentativa del hombre infinito (1925), Anillos (1926), and El hondero entusiasta (1923-24), they were not printed in the GDR. A complete version of Residencia en la tierra I-III, one of Neruda's most important works, existed in the late 1950s, but did not appear in the GDR until after his death in 1973. Melancholy tone, lack of political commitment, doubt, and surrealistic imagery prevented the publication of the work antedating his political conversion. An openly sensual quality probably hindered the reprinting of Zwanzig Liebesgedichte und ein Lied der Verzweiflung after the official GDR rejection in 1965 of sexuality and brutality in literature.

The situation was very different for the more political poems. Canto general and Las uvas y el viento had been translated and published with amazing speed in the late 1950s. Acceptable political content did not necessarily expedite translation and publication, however. For example, although the poems about Lenin from Navegaciones y regresos were printed in GDR journals in the 1950s, a complete version of this volume never appeared. A number of poems from the highly political Tercera residencia had not been published, and even new volumes of political poetry like Canción de gesta (1961), celebrating the Cuban revolution, remained unpublished during this six-year pause. Political content worked, at times, to prevent the publication of Neruda's works. Memorial de Isla Negra (1964), which was his attempt to come to grips with his own earlier enthusiasm for Stalinism, could not be published as long as discussion of

214

the mistakes of the Stalin era remained taboo.

The renewal of GDR interest in Neruda and his works manifested itself in a number of ways after 1967. Publication resumed with Extravaganzen Brevier (Estravagario),[15] and Neruda was accorded several major honors, among them an honorary doctorate from Karl Marx University in Leipzig. Major articles by Georg Maurer and Carlos Rincón became part of an important new GDR trend toward the understanding of Neruda's public poetry in terms of its development from the earlier pre-1936 private poems.[16] The 1969 announcement of Neruda's candidacy for the presidency of Chile on the Communist party ticket sparked a rash of enthusiastic biographical articles detailing his struggles for working-class people. When Allende became president of Chile in 1970 on a coalition ticket supported by the Communist party, GDR interest in the politics, culture, and literature of Chile soared. Books about Allende, Neruda, and Chile were published, among them Klaus Möckel's 1972 translation of Neruda's only play, Glanz und Tod des Joaquín Murieta (Fulgor y muerte de Joaquín Murieta, 1967).[17] By the early 1970s, GDR critics had begun to move toward a more comprehensive awareness of Neruda's poetic and personal development.

The renewed repressions in GDR Kulturpolitik in mid-1976 do not seem to have negatively affected the publication or reception of Neruda's works. In September, 1973, General Pinochet led a military coup which toppled the Allende government and caused the elderly, terminally-ill Neruda to be placed under house arrest. Neruda died less than two weeks after the coup, and those close to him attributed his death directly to the shock of Allende's death and to the heartbreak of watching Chile's progressive government replaced by a military dictatorship. Allende, Neruda, and others were mourned in the GDR as martyrs. Solidarity meetings, fund-raising drives, tributes, and scathing articles criticizing the new regime in Chile became commonplace in the GDR. Many articles were not specifically concerned with Neruda's poetry, but the influx of information about Chile and Neruda, the presence of a number of Chilean refugees, and the stressing of parallels with Germany forty years earlier under Hitler created a climate of awareness and sympathy which was highly favorable to the reception of Neruda's works.

Frequent tributes in memoriam made Neruda's name a household word in the GDR, newspapers and journals printed a steady stream of his poetry, and his poetry was read at solidarity evenings. Participants in such gatherings included many of Neruda's old friends; the names sounded like an honor roll of major GDR authors: Erich Arendt, Volker Braun, Franz Fühmann, Stephan Hermlin, Eduard Klein, Hermann Kant, Sarah Kirsch, Günter Kunert, Anna Seghers, Kurt Stern, Paul Wiens, and Christa Wolf. Translations of Neruda's poetry were revived and a number of his works were set to music. Authorities renamed schools for Neruda, and classes read his poetry, studied his life, and made displays about Neruda and Chile. Basic literature textbooks used in schools mentioned his exemplary life and included his poems. "Camarada Neruda, presente," a television special, devoted prime viewing time to his life and to readings from his poetry.[18] Commercialization of Neruda for the purpose of solidarity and fund raising even led to the production of an expensive commemorative coin, a Neruda stamp, and the creation of the Neruda Medaille, an honorary award given to the factory, individual, or business making the greatest contribution to the solidarity effort.

The circumstances surrounding Neruda's death affected not only public awareness of him as a poet, but also influenced decisively the availability and marketing of his works. Reclam Verlag published an expensive edition of Aufenthalt auf Erden (Residencia en la tierra I-III), a volume originally criticized for its obscurity, with original woodcuts by HAP Grieshaber and a preface by Carlos Rincón, which provided much insight into Neruda's early private poetry.[19] This volume became a rallying point for GDR sympathy for the oppressed people of Chile, and copies were sold at solidarity gatherings for as much as 800 M. each. Paradoxically, the very volume whose publication had been suppressed for over a decade became acceptable after the poet's death and quickly assumed the position of recognized importance and quality it had long held in western criticism. The political coup and Neruda's death prompted the planning and publication of a rapidly produced, inexpensive, consumer-oriented anthology of poems selected from all stages of Neruda's work. Gedichte: 1923-1973 included a token poem or two from many works virtually unknown in the GDR, yet the majority of the poems came from the more political public volumes already available.[20] Despite the limitations of this anthology, Gedichte: 1923-1973 resulted in the first presentation of a broad sampling of Neruda's poetry at an affordable price and at a time when public sympathy for him was at its peak in the GDR.

A new wave of Neruda publication and criticism began in the GDR in late 1973; it still continues. Der große Gesang and Elementare Oden were reissued and a translation of Neruda's autobiography, Ich bekenne, ich habe gelebt (Confieso que he vivido: Memorias, 1974), by the FRG translator Curt Meyer-Clason was published one year after its appearance in the FRG.[21] Memorial de Isla Negra and an extensive two-volume anthology of Neruda's works were slated for publication. The number of major critical essays and book-length studies written about Neruda's life and poetry is indicative of his place of honor in political and literary circles and of the general public interest in him.[22]

Starting in 1974 works by Neruda began to be presented on the stages of the GDR. A group of Chileans formed a theater in exile in the GDR, which, in conjunction with the Volkstheater Rostock, has given bilingual productions of plays and skits based on Neruda's poems. Five GDR theater companies of diverse size and professional maturity staged Neruda's play before highly enthusiastic audiences. The productions of Glanz und Tod des Joaquín Murieta even generated the only book written about the play, Erfahrungen mit 'Murieta': Ein Kolloquium zu fünf Inszenierungen.23 The political sympathy for Neruda clearly enhanced the popularity of this play, the stepchild of western Neruda criticism, but other factors contributed to the success as well: parallels with Brechtian epic theater; the advice and cooperation of exiled Chileans; and the sheer vitality of the productions themselves.

Although Neruda's works have been well received by western and GDR critics, the critical emphases have been markedly different, especially prior to the last decade. As has been demonstrated in this study, the focus of GDR critics has, until recently, been on Neruda's public poetry. Western criticism, on the other hand, has gravitated toward the early private poetry, while both groups have neglected Neruda's mature public and private poetry. A cursory examination of the reception of Neruda's works in the FRG shows that the publication practices, critical focus, and evaluation of his poetry there relate more closely to western trends than to the reception in the GDR.

Prior to 1960 Neruda was virtually unknown in the FRG. Initial Neruda volumes published by FRG firms relied on Erich Arendt's translations censored in the GDR. A luxury edition of Arendt's translation of Residencia en la tierra I and II became available in the FRG thirteen years before the appearance of the complete volume in the GDR, while the highly political Tercera residencia was published in the GDR, but remained unavailable in the FRG.24 During the 1960s, when GDR interest in Neruda was relatively dormant, FRG publishers and critics began to devote more attention to him. Several anthologies were published in the FRG, including one of the most extensive and representative anthologies of Neruda's works in any language. Beginning in 1965, FRG translators began to produce their own translations of Neruda's poetry, probably in response to the "boom" in Latin

American literature, their own interest in his poetry, and the unavailability of Arendt's translations after the "Lex Biermann." The most important FRG contributions were the translation of Neruda's autobiography and the first German translation and production of his only play. After Neruda received the Nobel Prize in 1971, a number of new, more affordable volumes were published in the FRG. Still, critics in the FRG have, on the whole, been less sympathetic to Neruda and his poetry than GDR critics. Hans Magnus Enzensberger and Hans-Jürgen Heise, among others, have been sharply critical of Neruda's political poetry as a decline in quality from his first works.25 More substantial contributions to Neruda scholarship have been made by Dieter Saalmann, who has discussed aspects of Rilke's influence on Neruda's works, and by Elisabeth Siefer, whose book examines formal elements in Canto general.26

The reception of Neruda's works in both the GDR and the FRG has been decisively and discernibly affected by politics. Until recently, the images of Neruda created by the differing publication practices in the GDR and the FRG, and more broadly in Marxist and western countries, have seemed to polarize him into two nearly separate poets. The public poetry published and praised in the GDR was ignored in the West, while the FRG concentrated on the early private poetry. Only Canto general seemed to be accepted by both western and Marxist critics, although their analyses stressed different aspects of this epic. Since Neruda's death, both groups of critics have begun to examine his more mature public and private works and try to come to grips with Neruda's poetry as a continuous process of developments which spans over fifty years. The potential now exists for attaining the perspective which is needed for understanding Neruda's stylistic evolution and his dual role as political and personal, public and private poet.

Illinois Wesleyan University

[1] The substance of this paper is drawn from my dissertation: Bonnie A. Beckett, "The Reception of Pablo Neruda's Works in the German Democratic Republic" (Diss. Indiana University, 1977). A revised and updated version is forthcoming as a book under the same title in the Germanic Studies in America series published by Peter Lang in Bern.

[2] See Marianne O. de Bopp, "Die Exilsituation in Mexiko," in Die deutsche Exilliteratur 1933-1945, ed. Manfred Durzak (Stuttgart: Reclam, 1973), pp. 177, 180; and Robert E. Cazden, German Exile Literature in America 1933-1950 (Chicago: American Library Association, 1970), pp. 74-75.

[3] See Pablo Neruda, "Gedichte," trans. Stephan Hermlin, Ost und West, 2, No. 12 (1948), 23-34.

[4] See Pablo Neruda, Beleidigtes Land, trans. Stephan Hermlin (E. Berlin: Volk und Welt, 1949).

[5] See for example I. Anissimow, "Dichter entfachen den Friedenswillen," Börsenblatt für den deutschen Buchhandel, 118, No. 19 (1951), 241-242; Erich Arendt, "Pablo Neruda, Dichter des Friedens," Die Weltbühne, NS 6, No. 23 (1951), 755-759; and Anna Seghers, "Pablo Neruda," Heute und Morgen, 3, No. 5 (1949), 311-312.

[6] See Christel Schnelle quoting from a comment by Anna Seghers in 1953, "Volk bin ich, unzählig Volk," Neues Deutschland, Dec. 15, 1971, p. 4.

[7] See Pablo Neruda, Der große Gesang, trans. Erich Arendt (E. Berlin: Volk und Welt, 1953).

[8] See Inna Tynjanowa, "Pablo Neruda's 'Allgemeiner Sang,'" trans. Maximilian Scheck, Sowjetliteratur, No. 11 (1953), 179-186.

[9] See Pablo Neruda, Die Trauben und der Wind, ed. and trans. Erich Arendt (E. Berlin: Volk und

Welt, 1955).

[10] See Pablo Neruda, Zwanzig Liebesgedichte und ein Lied der Verzweiflung, trans. Erich Arendt (Leipzig: Insel-Verlag, 1958).

[11] The Spanish edition of Navegaciones y regresos was not published until 1959, so that the poems on Aragon and China must have been available separately prior to that time.

[12] See Pablo Neruda, Elementare Oden I-III, trans. Erich Arendt (E. Berlin: Volk und Welt, 1961).

[13] See Pablo Neruda, Amerika, ich rufe deinen Namen nicht vergeblich an, trans. Erich Arendt (Leipzig: Reclam, 1956, 1964).

[14] See Pablo Neruda, Ode an die Druckerei, ed. Géza Engl (Leipzig: Hochschule für Grafik und Buchkunst, 1961), and Pablo Neruda, Ode an die Typografie, trans. Erich Arendt (Leipzig: Institut für Buchgestaltung "Leipzig" und die Ingenieurschule für Polygrafie "Otto Grotewohl," 1964).

[15] See Pablo Neruda, Extravaganzen Brevier, trans. Erich Arendt and Katja Hayek-Arendt (E. Berlin: Volk und Welt, 1967).

[16] See Georg Maurer, "Welt in der Lyrik (1967)," in Essay I (Halle: Mitteldeutscher Verlag, 1968), pp. 35-172; and Carlos Rincón, "Pablo Neruda: Der Dichter des 'Großen Gesanges'--65 Jahre," Horizont, 2, No. 28 (1969), 29.

[17] See Pablo Neruda, Glanz und Tod des Joaquín Murieta, trans. Klaus Möckel (E. Berlin: Volk und Welt, 1972, 1974).

[18] See Fritz Rudolf Fries, "Chilenische Gespräche (2)," Neue deutsche Literatur, 22, No. 11 (1974), 55.

[19] See Pablo Neruda, Aufenthalt auf Erden,

trans. Erich Arendt and Stephan Hermlin (Leipzig: Reclam, 1973).

[20] See Pablo Neruda, Gedichte: 1923-1973, ed. Carlos Rincón (Leipzig: Reclam, 1973, 1975).

[21] See Pablo Neruda, Ich bekenne, ich habe gelebt, trans. Curt Meyer-Clason (Darmstadt, Neuwied: Luchterhand, 1974; E. Berlin: Volk und Wissen, 1975).

[22] The major GDR works on Neruda include: Christel Schnelle's dissertation, "Zu Tradition und Revolution im Schaffen von Pablo Neruda," written for the Latin American Institute of the Universität Rostock in 1975 and forthcoming in the Neue Beiträge zur Literaturwissenschaft series at Rütten und Loening Verlag; Hans Otto Dill's essay, "Nerudas poetischer Kosmos," in Sieben Aufsätze zur lateinamerikanischen Literatur (E. Berlin, Weimar: Aufbau, 1975), pp. 196-294; and Erfahrungen mit 'Murieta': Ein Kolloquium zu fünf Inszenierungen, ed. Verband der Theaterschaffenden der DDR, special issue of Material zum Theater, 62 (1975).

[23] See Erfahrungen mit 'Murieta'.

[24] See Pablo Neruda, Aufenthalt auf Erden, trans. Erich Arendt and Stephan Hermlin (Hamburg: Claassen, 1960, 1964, 1972).

[25] See Hans Magnus Enzensberger, "Der Fall Pablo Neruda," in Einzelheiten (Frankfurt/M.: Suhrkamp, 1962), pp. 316-333; and Hans-Jürgen Heise, "Lyrischer Katarakt: Pablo Neruda," Neue Deutsche Hefte, 19, No. 1 (1972), 125-132.

[26] See Dieter Saalmann, "Die Konzeption des 'hombre invisible' bei Pablo Neruda und Rainer Maria Rilke," Romanistisches Jahrbuch, 24 (1973, appeared 1974), 381-399, and "Der Tod als Sinnbild ästhetischer Affinität zwischen Rainer Maria Rilke und Pablo Neruda," DVJS, 48, No. 2 (1974), 197-227; Elisabeth Siefer, Epische Stilelemente im Canto general von Pablo Neruda (Munich: Fink, 1970).

Literary Caricature
in the German Democratic Republic

Gail P. Hueting

"A picture is worth a thousand words"--this
saying applies to the graphic arts in general and
to caricature in particular. Caricature is an art
form that employs "exaggeration by means of deliberate simplification and often ludicrous distortion of parts or characteristics."[1] It refers to
a representation of a person, object, or event
that exaggerates a key, characteristic feature of
that thing in order to make a point about it or
reveal its essence. Caricature traditionally
takes the form of a black and white pen-and-ink
drawing, but it can also be a colored drawing or
a painting, or have photographs incorporated into
it.

Caricature has become a major means of political communication. There is probably no political culture today that does not make use of caricature; most newspapers in the United States and
Europe print cartoons on their editorial pages.
For Georg Piltz, a researcher in the GDR, who has
written a history of European caricature, the political aspect is the only important function of
caricature.[2] Another widespread use, distinct
from the political function, is for portraiture.
With the prevalence of photography, there is room
for portraits that are not strictly realistic.

Caricature flourished in Germany, as in the
rest of Europe, during the nineteenth century.
One of the most famous forerunners of the German
caricaturists of today was Wilhelm Busch (1832-

1908). His works, such as <u>Max</u> <u>und</u> <u>Moritz</u> and <u>Die</u> <u>fromme</u> <u>Helena</u>, are picture stories, in which the text is as important as the pictures. Another development was the weekly satirical magazines, which began to appear in the 1850s and became especially prominent after 1870. Piltz points out that there were effective socialist as well as bourgeois satirical magazines.[3] The most famous and long-lived was <u>Simplicissimus</u>, which was published from 1896 to 1967, with its most illustrious period before 1914. A number of illustrators worked regularly for <u>Simplicissimus</u>, the most prominent being Th. Th. Heine, who drew many of the covers as well as the satirical series "Simpl-Woche." Yet another influence on caricature in Germany was Heinrich Zille (1856-1929), the self-taught Berlin artist whose characteristic subjects were the poor children of Berlin. His drawings have elements of naturalism as well as of caricature; in any case, they exemplify humor and sympathy for the people.

Caricature is important in the German Democratic Republic, both for its didactic potential and as an art form. In some respects the graphic arts and illustration are among the most interesting branches of the visual arts in the GDR, and both include caricature. There is a separate section of caricaturists in the <u>Verband</u> <u>Bildender</u> <u>Künstler</u> <u>der</u> <u>DDR</u>, and a number of theoretical articles on caricature, especially political caricature, have appeared in the association's monthly journal, <u>Bildende</u> <u>Kunst</u>.[4] The daily newspapers publish political cartoons. One publishing house, Eulenspiegel Verlag für Satire und Humor, specializes in humorous literature and caricature; it publishes many books of cartoons, including a series entitled <u>Klassiker</u> <u>der</u> <u>Karikatur</u>. The humor magazine <u>Eulenspiegel</u>, like its predecessor in the immediate postwar period, <u>Ulenspiegel</u>, devotes much of its space to cartoons. Quite popular in the GDR, it employs many of the most prominent caricaturists in the country. According to the DDR Handbuch, <u>Eulenspiegel</u> is more similar to its Soviet counterpart, <u>Krokodil</u>, than to <u>Simplicissi-</u>

mus, Pardon (the humor magazine currently being published in the Federal Republic), or the English Punch.[5]

   In the theoretical discussions of caricature in the GDR, the lack of realism implied in a medium based on distortion is, perhaps surprisingly, not an issue. Caricature is accepted as firmly based on realism, as a kind of heightened realism. Much of the discussion deals instead with the satiric aspects of caricature and with the function of satire in general. A distinction is made between satire and humor, as expressed by Wolfgang Sellin, the director of Eulenspiegel Verlag:

> Satire soll verändern. Aber es wäre ein Ammenmärchen zu glauben, sie solle behutsam und freundlich sein, nicht wehtun. Der frühere Redakteur des Eulenspiegel, Peter Nelken, hat einmal gesagt: Satire muß töten. Satire im Sozialismus darf nicht töten, aber die muß scharf sein, bissig, schmerzlich . . . Humor dagegen ist etwas Freundliches, aufs Allgemein-menschliche Gerichtetes.[6]

   The caricatures that I have been particularly interested in are neither political, nor are they primarily satirical. They are literary--that is, portrait caricatures of GDR writers. Such caricatures are generally respectful in their attitude towards their subject, although they may poke a little gentle fun at "das Allgemein-menschliche" in the figure. I first discovered these portrait caricatures when I was doing research on literary publishing in the GDR. Some are reproduced in the comprehensive accounts of GDR literature: Die Literatur der Deutschen Demokratischen Republik by Konrad Franke and Die Geschichte der Literatur der Deutschen Demokratischen Republik. Aufbau-Verlag has published a number of anthologies illustrated with caricatures of authors. Zunftgenossen und Kunstgefährten, published for the fourth Writers' Congress in 1956, included poems by Paul Wiens

225

and caricatures by Elizabeth Shaw. 56 Autoren, published in 1965 on the occasion of the twentieth anniversary of Aufbau-Verlag (a second edition appeared in 1970), features a photograph and a caricature, printed facing each other for comparison, of the authors represented. Liebes- und andere Erklärungen, a collection of writers' reflections about each other, includes forty-two portrait caricatures drawn by Harald Kretzschmar.[7]

Now I want to discuss briefly several caricatures of well-known GDR authors. They were chosen first as portraits of prominent authors and second as examples of the work of the individual caricaturists who drew them.

The artist who has been most frequently involved with literary caricature is Harald Kretzschmar (born in 1931). His cartoons in Liebes- und andere Erklärungen have already been mentioned. Another amusing project of his was a series of light-hearted book jacket designs that he drew for Aufbau-Verlag; in these he managed to caricature both the author and the title of the book at the same time. They were published in Neue Texte, Aufbau's almanac, in 1968, but were never actually used for book jackets.[8] Kretzschmar has also worked for Eulenspiegel and drawn a large number of political cartoons. The fact that he has done more than one caricature of many writers seems to indicate that he likes them and especially enjoys drawing literary caricatures.

In the first picture included here, Günter de Bruyn, looking somewhat somber and hollow-cheeked, is sitting at work, writing on a piece of paper headed Roman (novel). At the same time a small third hand reaches out from his chest and writes on a smaller sheet on top of the first, entitled Parodie (parody).[9] This image points to de Bruyn's serious attitude toward all the writing he does and at the same time to the self-mocking tone that often occurs in his work.

Two caricatures by Kretzschmar of GDR play-

Harald Kretzschmar.   Günter de Bruyn

wrights follow. Claus Hammel, chunky and affable, is shown wearing a dark sweater and holding a cigar in his right hand. He holds a small box in front of him, evidently a miniature stage with two actors. Perhaps it represents Hammel's inner vision of what his new drama will look like on stage. Armin Stolper is shown in profile, wearing wire-rimmed glasses and smiling. He holds a small watering-can labeled Sowjetliteratur and looks at a flower in a pot labeled DDR-Dramatik.[10] The image of the writer tending and watering a plant occurs frequently in Kretzschmar's literary caricatures; it represents one aspect of the creative work of writers and of literary influence.

Other cartoons by Kretzschmar that I like but cannot reproduce here are his portraits of Günter Kunert and Günter Deicke. One of Kunert shows him in an artist's smock with a high collar and a dark bow at the neck. He has no hair on the top of his head, only a dark fringe around his ears and a moustache. In his left hand he holds a small open book like a painter's palette and in his right hand he has a paintbrush, with which he is "writing" in the book. The mixture of symbols associated with writers and artists represents Kunert's double talent.[11] Another caricature of Kunert is found among Kretzschmar's book jacket designs. The title of the book, Unschuld der Natur, is printed in small letters as a thin fringe on the top of his head, and his name (as author) becomes an eyebrow. His eyes are wide and round, his expression solemn. His moustache here is drawn with a few whispy lines on either side of his mouth. In front of him reclines a shapely female nude with long hair. Kunert, however, is gazing pensively past her.[12] Kretzschmar has drawn his portrait of Deicke in two versions with the same image: Deicke being lifted up into the air, chair and all, by a sweet, round little muse, who is planting a kiss on his forehead. Deicke, holding a pen in his right hand, is straight-faced in spite of all this. On the desk below is a stack of manuscript pages labeled Lektorat VdN, a reference to Deicke's work as an editor at the publish-

Harald Kretzschmar. Claus Hammel

Harald Kretzschmar.   Armin Stolper

ing house Verlag der Nation. In the later version of this caricature, which appeared in <u>Liebes- und andere Erklärungen</u>, Deicke and his muse are facing forward, rather than to the side; the chair hovers even higher, almost at the top of the page; the muse's inspiration, invisible in the earlier drawing, takes form as a landscape with pine trees; and the manuscript is spread out on the desk.[13]

Elizabeth Shaw (born in 1920 in Belfast) is a caricaturist and illustrator of children's books.[14] Her portrait caricatures have some of the whimsical elements of her illustrations for children. A representative one, from <u>Zunftgenossen</u> und <u>Kunstgefährten</u>, depicts Peter Huchel standing ankle-deep in a pond, leaning on a placid cow. Huchel holds a dandelion in his raised left hand; the cow munches on another dandelion. The two are being regarded by a disgruntled frog in the foreground and two puzzled children in the background. It is not clear why they have these expressions; maybe they are puzzled at the poet, who has invaded their world and stolen their pastime. Wiens' description accompanying the cartoon clarifies it somewhat. It reads:

> So wohl geformt wie gut gesinnt
> harrt er beim mondsichelhörnigen Rind,
> träumend in Luch auf karger Krume.
> Ja, Pustelblume![15]

A different kind of literary caricature is exemplified by a page drawn for <u>Eulenspiegel</u> in the mid-1950s by Harri Parschau, a regular contributor to the magazine. It is a series of eight rectangular panels in a format familiar since <u>Simplicissimus</u>. These cartoons are mildly satirical in their comments on cultural and literary institutions. They show eight GDR writers who were active in cultural affairs--Anna Seghers, Bert Brecht, Stephan Hermlin, Walther Victor, Willi Bredel, Johannes R. Becher, Kuba, and Jan Koplowitz--and suggest how they spend their time between Writers' Congresses. These comments are contained in the captions, and the pictures illus-

Elizabeth Shaw.   Peter Huchel

232

trate what is said. For example, Brecht gives young writers a chance to learn something from him (by letting them work with the Berliner Ensemble); Becher, as Minister of Culture, goes around replacing tattered slogans in streets and squares; and Bredel tries to get hold of yet another pipe to smoke. Some of the panels deal more with cultural policies, others with individuals' foibles. In either case, the pictures do not stand alone; they need the explanatory captions.[16]

Two other caricaturists are not represented by illustrations in this article but deserve to be mentioned. Günter Kunert (born in 1929), who is an artist as well as a writer and contributed both cartoons and poems to Ulenspiegel at the beginning of his career, has drawn caricatures of other writers and of himself. One of his self-portraits is interesting as a comparison with Kretzschmar's two Kunert caricatures. Kunert depicts himself with a very large nose (even larger than Kretzschmar shows it) but with hair all over his head (although his forehead is high). His moustache is just as whispy in his version as Kretzschmar draws it in his design for Unschuld der Natur.[17]

Herbert Sandberg (born in 1908) is the last caricaturist I want to mention. He has worked in many media but is primarily a graphic artist.[18] He was editor of Ulenspiegel between 1945 and 1949. His signature, which appears on all his work, is in itself a kind of caricature, a play on his name: the word "Sand" with a stroke from the initial "S" extending up over it in the form of a hill. Sandberg has drawn many caricatures; his best known literary caricatures are a series of drawings of Bertolt Brecht and his productions with the Berliner Ensemble. They were published in Mein Brecht-Skizzenbuch and are also on display at the Theater am Schiffbauerdamm. One of the most expressive-- and most famous--of Sandberg's Brecht caricatures is a lithograph entitled "Brechts Verhör."[19] It shows Brecht seated comfortably in a small chair with his legs crossed, his familiar cap on his knee, and a sheaf of papers in his pocket. He

Captions under the eight panels of Parschau's
"Wenn grade mal kein Schriftstellerkongress stattfindet" (vis-à-vis):

. . . dann nimmt Anna Seghers Privatstunden in
Literatur bei Dr. Wilhelm Girnus, der es genau
weiß.

. . . dann gibt Bert Brecht dem Dichternachwuchs
Gelegenheit, dem großen Dramatiker einige Kniffe
abzugucken.

. . . dann übt sich Stephan Hermlin anhand einer
Armband-Stoppuhr im Konferenzrundlauf.

Walther Victor arbeitet an einem fortschrittlichen ärztlichen Ratgeber "Wie werde ich schlank
in drei Tagen?"

. . . dann versucht Willi Bredel, auch die letzte
ihm noch nicht gehörende Tabakpfeife seiner Pfei-
fensammlung einzuverleiben.

. . . dann kultiviert Johannes R. Becher als
Kulturminister Straßen und Plätze der DDR, indem er verwaschene und zerschlissene Transparente
völlig eigenhändig entfernt.

. . . dann beschäftigt sich Kuba mit der Sorge um
sein neuestes Werk.

. . . dann erzählt Jan Koplowitz immer mal wieder
denselben Witz, auf den die Umstehenden wie oben
reagieren.

Harri Parschau

holds a large cigar in his raised right hand, and the index finger of the same hand points toward a small, rotund figure in a business suit, who appears to be haranguing him. Three similar small figures have already been flicked off with the cigar ashes and are suspended in mid-air in falling postures. Brecht is obviously getting the better of the discussion. This amusing drawing represents Brecht's appearance before the House Un-American Activities Committee in the United States Congress.

These caricatures of GDR authors reveal the character of the authors and of the society in which they live. The drawings are often livelier and more expressive than photographs--as can be seen in 56 Autoren, where the two portraits of each author are printed side-by-side. The prevalence and popularity of these literary caricatures indicate something about the attitude toward writers in the GDR. Writers are widely known and admired, but they are not above having a little fun directed at them. Another factor related to the success of these cartoons is the personal friendship and ties which bind together the relatively small, close circle of writers, artists, and intellectuals in the GDR. The caricatures can be drawn so masterfully in part because the writers and the artists drawing them know each other; and they are enthusiastically received by an audience that knows and respects both.

University of Illinois

Notes

The author thanks Harald Kretzschmar, Elizabeth Shaw, and Harri Parschau for permission to reproduce the cartoons in this article, and Verlag Volk und Wissen for arranging this permission.

[1] Webster's Third International Dictionary,

p. 399.

[2] Georg Piltz, Geschichte der europäischen Karikatur (E. Berlin: Dt. Verlag der Wissenschaften, 1976), p. 6.

[3] Piltz, pp. 208-209.

[4] For example, see two round-table discussions: "Probleme der Karikatur," Bildende Kunst, No. 3 (1966), 115-123, and No. 8 (1967), 395-403.

[5] "Karikatur," DDR Handbuch, 2nd ed. (Cologne: Wissenschaft und Politik, 1979), p. 581.

[6] "Wo seriöse Menschen mit Witz ihr Brot verdienen," Börsenblatt für den Deutschen Buchhandel, 146 (1979), 603.

[7] Konrad Franke, Die Literatur der Deutschen Demokratischen Republik, 2nd ed. (Munich: Kindler, 1974); Geschichte der Literatur der Deutschen Demokratischen Republik, Geschichte der deutschen Literatur, 11 (E. Berlin: Volk und Wissen, 1977); Paul Wiens and Elizabeth Shaw, Zunftgenossen und Kunstgefährten (E. Berlin: Aufbau, 1956); 56 Autoren (E. Berlin: Aufbau, 1965); Liebes- und andere Erklärungen: Schriftsteller über Schriftsteller (E. Berlin: Aufbau, 1972).

[8] Harald Kretzschmar, "Betr.: Kalte Umschläge," Neue Texte (E. Berlin: Aufbau, 1968), pp. 261-280.

[9] Harald Kretzschmar, "Günter de Bruyn," Liebes- und andere Erklärungen, p. 45.

[10] Harald Kretzschmar, "Claus Hammel" and "Armin Stolper," both in: Geschichte der Literatur der Deutschen Demokratischen Republik, p. 672.

[11] Harald Kretzschmar, "Günter Kunert," in: Franke, p. 233.

[12] Kretzschmar, "Betr.: Kalte Umschläge," p. 265.

13 The first version is in 56 Autoren, p. 166;
the second version, in Liebes- und andere Erklärungen, p. 58.

14 There are some biographical details on
Shaw in "Mit Illustrationen von Elizabeth Shaw,"
Bildende Kunst, No. 3 (1970), 160-163.

15 Wiens and Shaw, Zunftgenossen und Kunstgefährten, pp. 28-29; the cartoon is also reproduced in Geschichte der Literatur der Deutschen
Demokratischen Republik, p. 83.

16 Harri Parschau, "Wenn grade mal kein
Schriftstellerkongreß stattfindet," reproduced in
Geschichte der Literatur der Deutschen Demokrati-
schen Republik, p. 218.

17 Günter Kunert's self-portrait is to be
found in 56 Autoren, p. 239.

18 A survey of Sandberg's life and work:
Lothar Lang, Herbert Sandberg: Leben und Werk
(E. Berlin: Henschel, 1977).

19 Herbert Sandberg, Mein Brecht-Skizzenbuch
(E. Berlin: Aufbau, 1967); "Brechts Verhör" is
reproduced in Lang, p. 75.

Opera of the 1960s and 1970s in the GDR

Gordon Tracy

The GDR has become a major producer of opera. In the last two decades an impressive number of new operas have been premiered, to say nothing of a great number of operettas and musicals. There are 43 opera-stages in the GDR, the main centers being Berlin, with the Staatsoper and the Komische Oper, Leipzig, Dresden, and Weimar; Stralsund, Halberstadt, Neustrelitz, and Greifswald are also active. The late Paul Dessau, Siegfried Matthus, Gerhard Rosenfeld, and Udo Zimmermann, composers of some international stature, have turned their hand to opera, as have important composers like Ernst Hermann Meyer, dean of living GDR composers, Rainer Kunad, Fritz Geissler, and Günther Kochan.

Foremost among the directors of opera in the GDR are the late Walter Felsenstein, Joachim Herz, Harry Kupfer, and Ruth Berghaus. In his productions at the Komische Oper, Felsenstein put great stress on the "theater" in Musiktheater and rejected the elegant spectacle and the mere sensuous titillation, the concert in costume, of much traditional opera. Both Felsenstein and Herz have striven to realize the musical intention of the composer and the message of the librettist. Felsenstein spoke repeatedly of fidelity to the original work ("Werktreue") and pursued for himself and his musicians an exhaustive study of the works he produced; he did intensive textual criticism, restoring blurred or suppressed social implications to the librettos and re-translating them. Herz, Felsenstein's successor at the Komische Oper, also studies the librettos closely. He recently restored passages of social significance to the libretto of <u>Madame Butterfly</u> and prepared a new translation.

The operas most frequently performed in the GDR are still those of Mozart, Lortzing, Wagner, Puccini, Verdi, and Bizet. Also played, although less frequently, are the works of the progressive composers of the 1930s and 1940s (Wolf-Ferrari, Orff, Egk, Wagner-Régeny, Dessau) and those of Prokofiev, Shostakovich, Janacek, Schönberg, Berg, and Heinze. Newer GDR operas suffer from the domination of the rich operatic heritage, the <u>Erbe</u>, but interest in them is on the increase.

Brecht thought of learning and thought as pleasures. He felt that the distinction made between "entertaining" ("unterhaltsam") and "instructive" ("lehrreich") was an expression of bourgeois and undialectical thought.[1] The intention behind good art, Brecht felt, is not the glorious transfiguration ("Verklärung") of reality, but its clarification ("Erklärung").

GDR opera might be called operative opera as opposed to traditional opulent opera. It is designed--and Brecht's aesthetics are of course a decisive contributing factor--both to provide an experience of art and to evoke conscious intellectual activity, to impart political instruction. Opera is intended to be socially productive, i.e., to treat the aims and tasks of society and to help the spectator discover new qualities of life, perhaps even to embark on a new way of life. Performances of opera are to be both stimulating and enjoyable intellectual encounters.

In GDR opera one finds a new relationship between text and music. The music is intended to comment on the text and the action, in some cases to criticize, parody, or poke fun at them. In such situations, music and text are <u>verfremdet</u>, alienated, and in a contrapuntal relationship; a dramaturgic counterpoint results. This frequently happens in Dessau's <u>Puntila</u> and <u>Lanzelot</u>. Music is not an ornamental accessory but a vehicle of comment and clarification. Such music expresses socially important attitudes and is therefore "gestic" in the Brechtian sense.

Both Peter Hacks and the librettist-composer Rainer Kunad have written enthusiastically about opera. Hacks has called it "the most soulful of the dramatic genres."[2] For Kunad, opera is "the highest form of theater," for he considers it not a luxury, but the highest cultural necessity. He believes that its realism makes it a critical force which changes people and society and helps humanity progress.[3] Kunad says that older opera was characterized by a one-sided flow of the "Affekt." What makes GDR operas more potent, in his view, is that polydynamic, dialectical dramaturgical conceptions are at work.[4]

Alongside such enthusiasm for opera there is continuing criticism and rejection. Eckart Kröplin raises questions in an article in Theater der Zeit about the message of operas of the 1960s by Dessau, Goldmann, Kunad, Matthus, Rosenfeld, and Zimmermann in which the central problem is the great or creative personality in conflict with the social system. Kröplin's main concern is whether such figures have a positive or negative effect on the audiences, whether they encourage the spectator to integrate himself into the community or to isolate himself from it. Kröplin says that his land expects from art a happy consciousness of "perspective" (a long-range view of things), confirmation of what has been achieved with such great effort, and release from the pressures imposed on all workers in the socialist economy by the demands of production and of state-planning.[5] Ernst Schumacher also has serious doubts about the rational and social function and the aesthetic value of opera. He says that music is essentially irrational and finds fulfillment in irrational librettos. He angrily attacks a 1971 production of Verdi's La forza del destino at the Komische Oper, saying that Verdi's music is culinary and mystical ("kulinarisch-mystisch") and that it is "completely useless and damaging to bring this Christian and fatalistic opera to the socialist stage."[6]

One finds a good deal of material from the classics in the music of contemporary GDR opera. There are many quotations from Bach, some from Mozart and Schubert, in Dessau's _Einstein_. Dessau uses such material to parody or denounce, but also as a symbol of humane values; Bach's music suggests how civilization and culture are betrayed by the Nazis and, at the same time, stresses that humane cultural values will live on and prevail. Puntila's carryings-on in Dessau's _Puntila_ are parodied in passages in the style of Wagner and Richard Strauss.

Mozart, "the Shakespeare of the opera" (Peter Hacks), remains an important model, partly because of the continuing adherence to the number-principle of his operas. The number-principle, as opposed to through-composition, remains the basic structural principle and is consonant with Brecht's dictum "every scene for itself" ("jede Szene für sich") in his table of dramatic and epic theater.[7]

Modern styles and techniques are being increasingly used. The 12-tone row has assumed an important position, although it was earlier felt to be distinctly late-bourgeois and was used critically. Dessau's _Lukullus_ and other operas contain passages of electronic music. Kunad claims to have learned how to express the comical (for him, gaiety combined with feeling) in a 12-tone row or an aleatoric passage.[8] Matthus tries to mask traditional pitches and intervals by means of 1/4 and 3/4 tones in his _Omphale_; he also aims at a new type of rhythmic fusion by imposing one rhythm on another. Jazz, rock, and beat elements are woven into the fabric of some of Forest's operas.

In GDR operas, particularly the more "serious" ones, one finds a great variety of singing styles. Alongside traditional singing, one also

242

hears singing without words (vocalizing), recitative, parlando, speech-song (<u>Sprechgesang</u>), and transitions between song and speech. Hennenberg writes of the different uses of the voice in the work of Dessau: the normal singing voice, the voice singing in falsetto, the speaking voice, the voice speaking in falsetto, the voice speaking near a given pitch, and the shifting back and forth from speech near a given pitch to singing.9

A new popular or folk-tone (<u>Volkstümlichkeit</u>) can be found in much recent opera of the GDR. There are elements of folk-theater in Dessau's <u>Lukullus</u>, <u>Puntila</u>, and <u>Einstein</u>, but Dessau's <u>Volkstümlichkeit</u> remains somehwat intellectual and austere. A more genuine folk-tone, without sacrifice of musical substance and meaning, can be found in the work of Werzlau, even more in that of Hannell and Katzer.

I shall now attempt to characterize a few GDR operas of the 1960s and 1970s; first four operas of Paul Dessau, then a work by each of nine other composers, most of whom have also composed a good deal of orchestral, chamber, and choral music. I shall concentrate on the message of the operas and comment only briefly on what I consider the main features of the music. The operas selected for discussion all contain a serious social-political message, are thought-provoking and artistically advanced. They will be seen to be of three different types: (a) philosophically and artistically "heavy"; (b) lighter, more cheerful, but thoughtful; (c) very humorous, even hilarious. It is a question here of the degree to which the social-political statement is presented clearly and vigorously or is transformed and lies beneath the cheerful or comic surface of words and music. Among the themes of the operas of the first group are: war, revolution, love, racial prejudice, and conflict; operas of this kind are inclined to be difficult and demanding of performer and spectator. In the 1970s there was a turn towards lighter treatment of more general or historical,social, and political themes.

243

Paul Dessau was the first truly productive composer of opera in the GDR. I shall attempt to characterize briefly his first four operas: Die Verurteilung des Lukullus, Puntila, Lanzelot, and Einstein. Lukullus (1st performance 1951, revised since; libretto by Brecht) is intended as an "opera of peace" (Dessau) and an indictment of all imperialist conquerors. Lukullus is condemned, at his death, as a mass-murderer and destroyer who must be consigned to the void. Puntila (1st performance 1966, libretto by Peter Palitzsch and Manfred Wekwerth after the Volksstück of Brecht) is a study of Puntila, representative of the wealthy class of big land-owners, of his two conditions: drunkenness and sobriety or pseudo-humaneness and exploitativeness, and of his relationship with his chauffeur Matti, representative of the proletariat. In Lanzelot (1st performance 1969, libretto by Heiner Müller after the fairy-tale comedy Der Drache by Yevgeny Schwarz) the dragon represents fascism, modern capitalism, and imperialism, Lancelot the forces of freedom and justice, which prevail despite the dragon's seeming omnipotence. The dragon is associated with the demonic aspects of modern weaponry and technology; he throws every conceivable weapon into the struggle against Lancelot and in one scene he sits in a TV-room with screen, control-panels, and flashing lights, from which he surveys the idle, depraved life of a whole city. Lancelot, who, it is suggested, is descended from Heracles, experiences great hardships and agony before his final victory over the dragon. Einstein (1st performance 1973, libretto by Karl Mickel) treats the responsibility of the scientist to humanity and his time. Einstein, in the U.S., urges that the atom bomb be built so that German fascism can be quashed, but he sees a new fascism arise in the land to which he has entrusted his special knowledge. The first atom bomb dropped on Japan weighs heavily on his conscience and, despairing of the humanist value of his work, he burns, at the end of the opera, a new formula, the result of twenty years of work. Among the major figures is a clown (Hanswurst)who represents the people and expresses, in zany an-tics, their will to live.

The music of these four works moves through a considerable range of styles. In _Lukullus_ it is polytonal, with touches of electronic music and _musique concrète_. As in all four works of Dessau, the music is critical or parodistic much of the time. Loud brass and thundering drums express the pompously warlike stance of the title-figure and his men; dissonances and squeaky woodwinds poke fun at their martial posturings. The women of the people all sing alto; alto voices are intended to suggest honesty and strength, as are baritone voices. Soprano and tenor voices are meant to express self-assertiveness and insecurity. Lucullus is a heroic tenor, the queen a soprano; most of the coloratura passages are given to the queen, and her refined and delicate aria suggests a false and hollow elegance. _Puntila_ stands in the tradition of the _opera buffa_, and Dessau referred to it as a cheerful, funny work ("ein heiteres Werk"). The music is basically dodecaphonic, but the 12-tone music is associated in the main with Puntila and is thus used to express social criticism. The chauffeur Matti expresses himself for the most part in a dry _Sprechgesang_ or recitative, which is intended to suggest _not_ that he is inarticulate or unartistic but that he is strong, cool, and confident. In _Lanzelot_ the music is angular and saccadic. It criticizes by hyperbolic means--as in passages of deafeningly loud brass and orgies of noise from the percussion--or by wrily parodistic effect, as when the president's vocal part dives down two octaves when he sings of the "ascent" of the fish from the muddy pond to the silver platter. Elements of _musique concrète_ and electronic effects accompany the electronic technology and the technology of war. The simple leitmotival melodies sung by Lancelot are of two types, one lyrical and reflective, one dynamic and suggestive of action. _Einstein_ is a 12-tone work with touches of _musique concrète_. The quotations from Bach, Mozart, and Schubert which punctuate the work have, as mentioned above, both a bitterly parodistic function and one symbolic of the great humanist tradition

245

of Germany.

We shall now consider a small selection of
operas by the generations following Dessau, first,
three operas of the more complex and grander type:
Siegfried Matthus' Der letzte Schuß, Udo Zimmermann's Die zweite Entscheidung, and Ernst Hermann
Meyer's Reiter der Nacht.

Matthus' Der letzte Schuß (1st performance
1967, on the occasion of the 50th anniversary of
the October Revolution, libretto by Matthus and
Götz Friedrich after a novel by Boris Lavrenyov)
plays in 1919 and has to do with the tension between individual happiness and revolutionary conflict. A member of the Red Army, Marjutka, a
woman of great courage and integrity, shoots and
kills the man she loves, an officer of the White
Guard and her prisoner, to prevent his escape from
their island refuge on a boat of the White Army.
While on the island they experience the joy of
true love and the hostility born of ideological
differences. The music is polytonal, with some
12-tone segments. The chorus and orchestra are in
three groups, and their locations have dramaturgic
implications. An interesting feature of the libretto and score is the presence of inner voices
(Gedankenstimmen) which express not yet formulated
or understood thoughts and feelings of the main
characters. Whispering voices (Flüsterstimmen)
are also heard. The work is framed by two full
choruses: the first sings of the divisiveness of
war and revolution, the concluding one of the new
life born of fire and pain, the hope of love.

Udo Zimmermann's Die zweite Entscheidung (1st
performance 1970, libretto by Ingo Zimmermann),
the action of which takes place in an unnamed
large city in the GDR, has as its theme the responsibility and struggle of conscience of the
scientist. The title refers to the decision of
the biogeneticist Hausmann to deliver a paper on
startling new findings, a gene he has isolated, in
the hope that they will be used for the elimination of hereditary diseases and cancer. His first

246

decision had been to suppress the report for fear that his findings would be misused, with disastrous consequences for individual distinctiveness in the human race of the future. In three interludes, Hausmann splits himself into two egos and discusses the problem with himself. Both figures speak against the background of a hidden chamber choir; the "other" Hausmann, who urges that Hausmann deliver the paper and shoulder his responsibility to society and human life, is backed by an invisible speech-choir which chants, in an aleatoric and unrhythmic style, sentences which express the essence of his position.

Meyer's Reiter der Nacht (1st performance 1973, libretto by Günther Deicke after a novel by Peter Abrahams) is an attack on racial terrorism in South Africa. The riders of the night of the old legend, a man and a woman, rode through the land spreading beauty, gentleness, and love wherever their shadows fell; in the opera, a young African teacher and a white girl want to change the world with their love. The African wants to teach the black farm-workers and their children "that men are born free and equal," but the love between the two is seen by the South African regime and its adherents as a crime and the lovers are murdered by white farmers. This is a choric opera, and the strong will of the people is expressed in many choruses. Meyer weaves much South African folklore into his music, using older country songs and more recent songs of the urban proletariat.

Let us now consider three operas written, however serious their subject, in a lighter vein: Jean Kurt Forest's Die Blumen von Hiroshima, Fritz Geissler's Der Schatten, and Rainer Kunad's Litauische Claviere.

Forest's Die Blumen von Hiroshima (1st performance 1967, libretto a free adaption of the novel of the same name by the American Edita Morris) has to do with the physical and psychic results of the dropping of the atom bomb in August,

1945. Sam, a young American, is the guest of a
Japanese family. Fumio, the head of the house,
was seriously burned on the fateful day and is declining slowly but irreversibly. Sam and Ohatsu,
Fumio's sister-in-law, fall in love and when Fumio
dies Ohatsu runs away, fearing that she too has
been affected by the radiation. This is in many
ways a chamber opera and a revival of the Sing-
spiel, with ballet-scenes and orchestral inter-
mezzos. The quiet, reflective music is in the 12-
tone style, with touches of jazz to suggest American (imperialist?) intrusions into the Japanese
life of the time.

Geissler's third opera, Der Schatten (1st
performance 1975, libretto by Günter Lohse after
the fairy-tale comedy of the same name by Yevgeny
Schwarz) is subtitled a "phantastische Oper." It
treats a series of irreal events which have a concrete connection with social and psychic reality.
The theme of the work is man's struggle with his
shadow, which takes on an independent existence;
the shadow represents the negative side of the individual, that conscienceless part of the personality which manipulates other people in order to
acquire power and wealth. This shadow is defeated
by a superior power: that of the people. Geissler's music is strong and positive, often playful
and witty, but just as often an expression of tension and conflict, lament and pain. Geissler
makes occasional use of the 12-tone system and
other modern techniques.

Kunad's most unusual opera Litauische Claviere. Oper für Schauspieler (1st performance
1976, libretto by Gerhard Wolf after the novel of
the same name by Johannes Bobrowski) is set in the
Memel area in 1936. It has to do with the attempt
of a scholar and a musician to write an opera
about Donelaitis, a Lithuanian clergyman, poet,
and piano builder, against a background of racial-
nationalist tension and the imminent Nazi invasion of Lithuania. The multi-scenic dramatic action takes place on several levels at once; two
musical festival plays, one Lithuanian, one Ger-

248

man, and the Donelaitis opera are discussed and re-
hearsed during the action. This of course gives
the impression of plays within a play and produces
much dramaturgic counterpoint! All possible tonal
effects are used in the voice-parts, from speech
and unison melody to whispering rhythmic speech,
screams, glissandos, and folkloric effects. In
style, the music ranges from the diatonic to the
12-tone, with quotations in the style of other
composers, and aleatoric effects. Lithuanian folk
music is also woven into the score. The notion of
an "opera for actors" is of course contradictory,
but Kunad notes in the score that the performance
of the work rests on "the charm of non-professional
singing."

Finally, we shall consider three cheerful,
often uproarious, operas of recent years: Joachim
Werzlau's <u>Meister Röckle</u>, Robert Hannell's <u>Reise</u>
<u>mit Joujou</u>, and Georg Katzer's <u>Das Land Bum-Bum</u>
<u>oder Der lustige Musikant</u>.

Werzlau's <u>Meister Röckle</u> (1st performance
1976, libretto by Günther Deicke based on motifs
from a children's book by Ilse and Vilmos Korn and
a fairy tale that Karl Marx made up for his own
children), an opera for big and little people, is
a cheerful and optimistic work. Meister Röckle,
a puppeteer, keeper of a toy shop, and a very in-
ventive spirit, demonstrates in his puppet plays
that people can have a better life if they overcome their fear of the devil and of the propertied
class and factory owners who are in league with
him. Röckle is working on a telescope through
which one will be able to see the better times
ahead. He makes a pact with the devil, Flammfuß,
in order to gain access to the sun-stone, which
the devil has stolen and which will help Röckle
with the telescope and other inventions which will
improve the lot of his fellowmen. With the help
of the people he is then able to extricate himself from the power of the devil; the people laugh
at the gloomy predictions of Flammfuß, and their
laughter frees Röckle. The sprightly music is occasionally reminiscent of Shostakovich, but, on

the whole, Werzlau uses traditional major-minor
tonalities, firm tone-relationships, and a regular
rhythm. There are good dances in the work and two
choruses, one on earth, the other in hell. Röckle's song is catchy and widely known.

Hannell's tenth opera Reise mit Joujou (1st
performance 1976, libretto by Hannell and Klaus
Eidam after Ball-of-Fat and two other stories by
De Maupassant), "eine musikalische Komödie," is
a hilarious work which plays in Prussian-occupied
France of about 1872. The self-righteousness and
arrogance of the nobility, the clergy, and the ambitious middle class of the day are objects of de-
licious satirical attack. Joujou, the heroine and
representative of the class which was despised at
the time, is a kind, generous, witty, and truly
human figure. She makes the others look like
snobs and selfish boors and takes sweet revenge on
them at the end. Hannell makes much use of older
French music and dances in his score, including
musette-waltzes and other folkloric elements.

Katzer's Das Land Bum-Bum (1st performance
1978, libretto by Rainer Kirsch after a story by
Dobrovensky), another opera for children and
adults, is a frolicsome work which treats the adventures of Karl, the merry musician who knows all
the happy songs of the whole world, in Bum-Bum, a
distant land in which people nourish themselves by
music alone and which is ruled by the dictatorial
King Double B-Flat Minor II, who controls even the
music of the land. The King has decreed that C
Major is the official key and has banned all happy
music as harmful. The "good" characters however
prefer other keys, and the heroine is programmati-
cally called Twelve-tone (Zwölfklang). The itin-
erant Karl and some newly made friends among the
citizens of Bum-Bum are imprisoned because of the
merry songs they sing, but Karl and one supporter
escape. Karl finally mobilizes the people of Bum-
Bum and helps them to discredit the king's authoritarian rule and the "state secrets" on which it is
based. Karl returns to his home, but Twelve-tone
cannot accompany him, because the noise in Karl's

homeland would upset her stomach beyond endurance. The music, with its many happy songs, is lively and rhythmic throughout.

Analytical and critical thought have permeated all branches of the arts in the German Democratic Republic, including music, opera, and even the musical, which I cannot discuss here. As Brecht maintained, entertainment--even rollicking entertainment--and critical social thought can be most effectively combined.

University of Western Ontario

Notes

[1] Bertolt Brecht, "Zu Die Mutter," Gesammelte Werke (Frankfurt/M.: Suhrkamp, 1967), XVII, 1069.

[2] Peter Hacks, Oper (Berlin and Weimar: Aufbau-Verlag, 1975), p. 229.

[3] Rainer Kunad, "Realismusprobleme in der zeitgenössischen Oper," in Sammelbände zur Musikgeschichte, Band II (Berlin: Verlag Neue Musik, 1971), p. 77.

[4] Kunad, p. 77.

[5] Theater der Zeit, 34, No. 6 (1979), 28f.

[6] Ernst Schumacher, Schriften zur darstellenden Kunst (Berlin: Henschel, 1978), p. 231.

[7] Brecht, XVII, 1010.

[8] Kunad, p. 81.

[9] Fritz Hennenberg, Dessau-Brecht. Musikalische Arbeiten (Berlin: Henschel, 1963), p. 548.

Politics of the Invisible:
Slatan Dudow's Stronger than the Night

Margaret Morse

    Stronger than the Night (1954) has long been recognized as "one of the best East German films-- beautiful, quietly moving, and totally ungratuitous in its effects,"[1] as "unashamedly socialist-real- ist" but "socialist realism at its best."[2] The moving story of a resistance fighter who refuses to despair was filmed by Slatan Dudow from a script by Jeanne and Kurt Stern; it is the only film Dudow ever directed which he did not write. Dudow was attracted to the script by the "fascinating, ethi- cal-philosophical thought"[3] embodied in the charac- ter of the hero, Loening. Loening is a worker and communist party functionary who resists Hitler's power until his execution in 1945 in spite of the discouraging results of his organizing efforts and the separation from his family, imprisonment, and torture which they cost. Under constant police surveillance and put before the choice of losing his head or keeping his silence--the words "It means your head" accompanied by a rapid pull into a close-up is a constant refrain of the film-- Loening chooses to risk death. The effectiveness of Loening's willingness to sacrifice for his be- liefs comes, according to Hermann Herlinghaus, Du- dow's biographer, not from an orientation toward a future socialist Germany, which would be the more typical socialist realist way of motivating a character, but from the way Loening lives out his principles in spite of everything, "how he shows a way out of a hopeless situation through a clever, systematic struggle for the hearts and minds of human beings and is thereby of infinite ethical

253

superiority" (p. 38).

Reflection on the ethical-philosophical basis of Loening's heroism shows that it is different from that of socialist realism of the <u>Aufbau</u> period (1949-55), during which the film was made: rather than a sacrifice of self in terms of <u>postponement</u> of self-realization to a future "glowingly near," ultimately linked to a linear and determinist view of history, Loening's act is a refusal to sacrifice himself, i.e., the speaking, choice-making, loving subject that he already is, by being silent. He is an I who will never cease calling forth the you that his own subjectivity demands, even if he meets with silence. The full implications of Loening's autonomy are developed only much later in the work of Christa Wolf, where they win a basis for the critique of her own socialist society. Dudow does not have Wolf's reputation as a protest figure, nor does he deserve it, having eluded such labels despite his controversial career; but it is interesting to consider that Dudow's film career in the GDR shows a history of raising questions which are voiced by other cultural figures only much later. For instance, Dudow undertook work on <u>Stronger than the Night</u> only after a script of his own, treating a subject that Christa Wolf first raised in GDR literature in 1963 in <u>Divided Heaven</u>, was turned down by DEFA officials.[4]

Wolf's work in literature raises questions not only at the level of the subject matter; she also seeks out ways of enunciating the questions, innovating prose forms which are no longer in the category of the traditional novel. Dudow, on the other hand, does not have a reputation for formal innovation in his GDR career; he is even given credit for having established the socialist realist film, a form with all the familiar conventions of the Hollywood film--surprising, considering the fact that Dudow's first feature film, <u>Kuhle Wampe</u> (1932) made with Bertolt Brecht, is regarded as the model attempt to apply Brechtian ideas to film. However, closer examination of his work

254

shows that Dudow had not abandoned his efforts to transform traditional forms in ways which would call forth subjects from the passive spectators. It is this aspect of _Stronger than the Night_, i.e., the level of enunciation or the way in which the story of Loening is told in terms of camera-work and editing, with which this analysis is primarily concerned.

The story begins with Hitler's rise to power. Loening's campaign of speeches and leafletting eventually leads to being hunted by the police and the necessity of going into hiding. He and his comrades are rounded up and subjected to torture in a remarkable sequence which is intercut with the childbirth of his wife, Gerda. While Loening and his friend, Erich, spend about eight years in prison, Gerda works and raises their son. Erich, however, is betrayed by his wife, who can't bear loneliness or the financial insecurity of being on her own. She takes an ex-party member as her lover, a man who is an opportunist motivated primarily by fear. Erich and his wife have a weak relationship to begin with, divided by a traditional sexual division of labor (which Dudow takes every opportunity to combat in all his films). There is a second contrast couple to Loening and Gerda, a pair of petit-bourgeois neighbors, for whom Hitler at first means an end to unemployment; later they lose their two sons at Stalingrad. A Nazi policeman in charge of Loening and his rotund superior officer complete the range of supporting characters in a spectrum of acting styles reaching from the dignity and understatement of the Loenings through the awkwardness of the weaker couple and the ordinary obtuseness of the petit-bourgeois couple to the utter grotesqueness of the Nazis. The film ranges in mood from heroic stoicism to black humor. An instance of the former is when, in reaction to her husband's decision to resume his resistance activities after he is released from prison, a tear rolls down Gerda's otherwise calm expression and is brushed away. An example of Gerda's dry wit and Dudow's penchant for the grotesque (which found little outlet in his GDR

255

career) is a scene in which Gerda and the woman
neighbor huddle in the ruins of their bombed-out
apartment building. Gerda says among Dudow's
pasteboard ruins, "And you said nothing would happen if we would just stay out of politics."

The tiny resistance cell is eventually discovered, but not before Gerda and Loening exchange
roles, she undertaking a dangerous mission to Berlin from Hamburg, while he waits anxiously at home
with their son. The unfaithful wife also has a
chance to redeem herself by warning her estranged
husband that the identities of the resistance
workers have been discovered. She also exchanges
roles with her husband by being sent to prison as
he escapes. Their moment of mutuality is signi-
fied by a kiss. The kiss in this film is reserved
for such a moment of human perfection. Preceded
by years of physical separation or misunderstand-
ing and followed by instant separation, the kiss
is a moment of union which is more than physical,
reserved for those who are politically and private-
ly at the highest level of moral development. In
Dudow's films, love and politics are simply two
manifestations of the same attitude toward the
world. After Loening's arrest and execution, "the
film ends on a happy note: his wife and child read
his letter which encourages them not to mourn his
death, but to continue the struggle. The film's
final images show reconstruction in East Germany."[5]

Actually, the final montage sequence, along
with the opening montage, which form a frame
around the story of Loening, are a key to the project of transforming subjectivity embodied in the
form of the film itself and in the way it addresses
the spectator. Perhaps some knowledge of film theory is needed to appreciate what Dudow has done;
however, whether or not the spectator has the theoretical acumen to be aware of it, at an elemental
visual and kinetic level he or she will be set in
a different relation to the world. The camera
movement and editing at first embody the central
and omniscient position of the spectator of the
classical realist film. This position is trans-

formed in the final montage to that of a decenter-
ed and changing subject in a situation without
closure.

Dudow's visual and kinetic program of transformation, introduced and completed in the framing
montage, is developed throughout the film. Actually, even the opening credits introduce motifs in
graphic form which will later become important as
camera movements: the view through bars from below
later becomes a tilt up; the strong directional
slant of letters to the right becomes a pan or
track. Once the credits list the production crew,
the names of the cast in scale and composition, if
not order, indicate a fairly equal team, not stars
with which a centered subject will be invited to
identify. The name of the main actor, Wilhelm
Koch-Hooge, is truncated to "Wilh. Koch-Hooge" for
the benefit of overall composition and equality of
space with "Helga Göring," the name of the actress
who plays Gerda Loening. The slicing of Koch-
Hooge's name resembles another motif: the close-up
of Loening's head each time he is reminded that
his clandestine activities are a capital offense.
The close-up both slices off his head and creates
an icon with a frontal gaze, inviting maximum identification of the spectator with it.

In Freudian terms, the theme is castration,
and Loening is a paradoxical figure who both accepts death and loss as part of his entry into the
symbolic realm of the social subject and also
serves the imaginary of others as a charm against
loss. Loening's dual nature and the dual nature
of the film is reiterated at a thematic level by
the recurrence of images as icons (of Lenin, Lieb-
knecht, Beethoven, and Hitler) and of the word in
the form of letters. Those familiar with Marxist
aesthetic debates will find Dudow's position on
realism and formalism, on identificatory or transforming art symbolized in the juxtaposition of the
image and the word.

After the credits, a remarkable montage sequence, linked by a continuous pan or horizontal

257

movement of the camera on a stationary base, begins on the theme of "Germany." The continuous pan to the right is initiated with an extreme long-shot of an alpine setting (with appropriate music) and continues across Germany from South to North and from the Alps to Hamburg. The effect is to create an imaginary central and omniscient viewpoint from which the Fatherland, devoid of people, can be surveyed--in a series of post-card-type scenes, the locations of both legend and national socialist mythology. The viewpoint is, of course, impossible: a seemingly continuous pan is in reality several 180° pans linked by dissolves. What should be a spiral of circa 900° or a fluted trajectory of half circles is constructed by the viewer into a central view of a subject who can move closer and farther along a radius at will. But this impossible view is an ingenious expression of the imaginary subject position in the classical realist film, with its 180° rule (hiding the place of production and the mediation of the camera) and its implications of voyeurism and mastery. The montage challenges the claim of the panoramic shot to greater authenticity and the claim to the experience of space itself rather than "the picture of space in perspective presentation." Pans are normally unedited and link objects "in the same order as that in which they are aligned in reality." Thus pans are supposedly less deceptive and more real.[6] Dudow pans <u>and</u> edits, selecting and ordering shots in the way that the ideology he seeks to transform finds "natural."

A look at the montage sequence in detail reveals this series: the extreme long-shot dissolves to a long-shot of an alpine village, where a voice-over "Deutschland" is heard on the sound-track. The next shot after the dissolve is a pan across a snowy, forested plain, nearer yet and linked by a match on a tree form. Dissolve to a pan in extreme long-shot of the Rhine valley near the Lorelei, then dissolve to a shot of a beach washed by waves and finally to a medium long-shot over the roofs of Hamburg. The camera tilts down, and the story begins. However, the beach scene is actually an anomaly in the apparent continuous pan, for the camera is stationary for the entire shot. Yet the imaginary continuity of movement is maintained by the movement of the waves from right to left. (The effect is like sitting in a train stopped at a station and perceiving that one's train is pulling away when in reality the train in the window is moving in the contrary direction.) It is possible to not even notice the interruption of movement, especially since it is resumed in the next shot above the city. The anomalous shot becomes laden with meaning as the film progresses, both through an incident in the story--a beach idyll with Loening, his wife and child--and through the formal motif of counter-movement from right to left. Here it is nearly invisible, but the movement gathers political, temporal, and geographical motivations throughout the film.

The political significance of the right to left movement begins as the story opens, with two contrasting movements: a truck full of brownshirts makes its way across the screen in a curve which moves from top right to left and around to the right, ending on a medium shot of a Nazi banner. The heroine, Gerda Loening, walks past the banner and makes the opposite curve from left to right and after a cut reenters the top of the frame and moves from right to left, leaving the camera focused on the sign of the local communist party headquarters. The political conflict indicated in this contrast between movements right and left is additionally motivated by map directions and movement from the Soviet Union toward Germany later in the film.

The temporal meaning of the movement is more complex. The normal reading pattern in western culture is from left to right; in film, too, temporal and physical progression are often directional to the right, and the counter-movement, especially when sustained, is against the grain (and can even give the impression of going backwards in space _and_ time). Aside from this, screen direction and position are thought of as neutral, sim-

259

ply a way of separating protagonists and counterparts on the screen and in the mind of the audience. Alternation of the camera from one protagonist to the other installs rather a central viewpoint and ultimately an identification of the future and truth with the vanishing point at the center of the screen's illusory depths. (For example, the hero, having proved himself, walks off into the sunset and infinity.) What Dudow's film apparently seeks to do is to shift the "spatialization" of the temporal from the central vanishing point to the lateral movement left to right. Then, the movement from right to left, in addition to being in contrast and contradiction to "normal" temporal progression, becomes a movement from the future. When, for instance, in the vacation idyll (possibly because the Soviet Union is winning the war), Loening is washed up on the same beach setting as in the opening montage, he is both a harbinger of the future (like a messenger from a better world—and the Soviet Union) and an enjoyer of a rare moment when he is with his loved ones and the world fits together—human perfection. The same movement from the future can mean conflict and struggle when it occurs in less propitious political conjunctures; but, in the closing montage sequence, the movement of contradiction becomes productive.

The "centrality" of the subject position and the ideological implications of mastery of the subject over the world and primacy of one controlling viewpoint are "built into" film as a cultural form. From the Renaissance projection of a vanishing point and the one central spectator position created by the lens to the central position of the "invisible quest" created by alternation, film form builds a subject position which is at once passive and possessed of an illusory mastery—supporting a static, centered, and eminently individualist personality. Film theorists and practitioners have thought of various ways of undermining that centrality built into film, for example, by separating sound and image tracks. Dudow exploits what is a contradiction built into film between centrality and laterality. The shift to a future to the right has the advantage of making it open and transforming the subject into a mobile position submitted to constant change.

The final montage sequence is a transformation of the opening montage, by implication the "other side" of the 180° line of the former, the place of production in cinematic terms and of the GDR in geographic terms. The first transformation is of the pan into a tracking movement. (The camera, usually mounted on tracks or wheels, moves through space.) A worker turns a wheel, initiating a movement which is picked up by the camera in a track to the right, tilt up and dissolve. This pattern is repeated in a series of shots of people involved in the construction of a socialist society; the viewing subject is dynamic rather than voyeuristic. The series is finally resolved in a stationary shot of the same beach setting as before, where a couple faces right towards the motion of oncoming waves. The effect of mastery and stability of the opening montage is destroyed by a subject position which moves toward the off-screen space and the unexpected on the right. The dynamism of the movement is not fully explained by the tracking shots, however; the shot series also develops and transforms the motif of the counter-movement.

The first shot to the right over a construction scene ends with a tilt up to the top of a building in progress. The tilt, which punctuates the end of each tracking movement, both contrasts with the tilt down at the end of the first montage and reiterates the tilts up in the film during Loening's years in prison. The earlier tilts revealed nothing more than bars or a bird, but they were associated with an attitude of hope. These final montage tilts always reveal something and in that sense they bring both formal and ideological closure. In the context of the final montage these icons or images are a source of stability in an otherwise unsettling dynamism. In the second shot, the tracking camera follows a group of young women into the gates of Humboldt University and then tilts up to a Humboldt statue. In the next shot, the track right across a field of grain encounters a counter-movement of a tractor moving right to left and tilts up on the tractorist. The double- and counter-movement of the camera subject and the tractorist is one of contradiction, a harbinger of the future, which may challenge the subject, but which can, as in the case of the couple on the beach, be faced with confidence. The sequence ends with a turn of the camera to the right and toward the sea. The last image is of the horizon slicing the sea from the sky in the frame.

The transformation of the subject position in the two montage sequences does not undermine the spatialization of the temporal associated with socialist realism--it rotates the future toward an orientation on the contradictory and invisible off-screen right. The stabilizing and collectivizing goals of socialist realism are not abandoned--images and icons interplay with a dynamic subject position and open framing.

Even the construction of Loening as icon, the image of the worker-hero-resistance leader, while being quintessential socialist realism, has its moments of displacement and a dynamic effect on the viewer-subject. The hero Loening is first seen directly below an icon of Lenin at party headquarters. At several points in the film Loening's intense gaze at the camera is followed by a shot of a room, at times bulging with the crowd, at other times pathetically empty. Loening repeats this intense gaze before his execution, assuming the frontality and posture of a Byzantine saint. Such a position and direct gaze are an invitation to identify with a mirror image: they occur rarely in fictional film except as part of a shot-reverse-shot (frontal shot of A/frontal shot of B, sutured together by the spectator, who construes that A and B, though looking at him, are gazing at each other and that he is an invisible presence in their midst). In the shot-reverse-shot, the frontal gaze is recaptured by the diegesis or story--characters look at each other, not the audience--while

maintaining the subliminal invitation to identify.
Loening's last gaze, however, escapes the diegesis
because it is not followed by any recapturing re-
verse-shot: at first his gaze is glassy, looking
into the future, then it is directed sharply at
the camera. With a little shock of consciousness,
the spectator realizes, "He's looking at me." The
reverse field is that real space of the spectator
on the other side of the screen. However fictional ultimately, the direct address from an I to a
you escapes both the story space and the narcissis-
tic space of the mirror-screen. The shock regis-
ters a moment of awareness of the film as construction and intention.

Instances of such direct address, while not
common, are not unheard of. Eisenstein's Alexander Nevsky ends with a direct gaze at and exhorta-
tion of the crowd--in the cinema. The Russia of
legend fades and suddenly it's 1938. The difference between Dudow's icon and Eisenstein's is a
matter of degree: Nevsky's gaze at that point simply reinforces the allegorical currents of 1937-38,
which had been flowing underneath events throughout the film. The diegesis (or referential world
of the fiction) wasn't escaped so much as knotted
together, and judging from my students, it is possible to be unaware of Nevsky's change of regis-
ters at that point. Loening's gaze, however, seems
to inevitably bring that shock of recognition that
escapes the diegesis. Again the effect is to
shift away from centrality and to challenge the
safety of the voyeur behind the 180° line.

From the character Loening's point of view,
such a gaze addresses not a camera or a mirror but
emptiness. The gaze on emptiness is prepared in
earlier scenes in the film. The most telling in
this regard is the one in which Loening, Gerda,
and their comrade Erich, who has recently been released from prison, take frontal positions at the
window. Their gaze is directed at what in the diegesis is a Nazi parade in the streets below, but
is actually the area below the screen and in the
front of the spectator position within the projec-

tion room. In response to the discouraged and bitter comments of his comrade Erich, Loening points to off-screen left; the home of a comrade and a wash-filled window is revealed in the next shot. Loening admits that the resistance at that point consists of four anti-fascists--but that comrade next door "sees what one doesn't see, all those who don't march along."

> Erich: And he overlooks the thousands down there?

> Loening: No, he doesn't ignore them, otherwise he'd be a bad comrade. He even looks at them very carefully, because he knows that among them are many we must win over.

> Gerda: Win over? These Nazis?

> Loening: Yes, some of them. With whom are we going to build the Germany of tomorrow? Our Germany? With Germans, aren't we? Who says the Germans are doomed to remain political blockheads in all eternity?

Note the "slippage" in the dialogue from the invisible non-participants in fascism to the crowd below, the object of the three comrades' gaze. The invisible object of the three comrades' gaze remains off-screen. Thus, their gaze never lifted from the real space of projection room and the spectator. The uncomfortable identification of the audience with a Nazi past may have been all too true in 1954. But Loening never takes on the paralyzing aspect of the Stone Guest or super-ego: he is an ideal and intercessor. The subtle slippage of the film from concern with the resistance to those who went along with Hitler seems intended to relieve the guilt which acted as a significant barrier to the creation of subjects by fixing a hierarchy of innocent/guilty. The film addresses

264

indirectly the problem which is the topic of Christa Wolf's Kindheitsmuster (1976). Loening does not assume the unchanging and hence ever guilty (and ever dominant or submissive) German, but the subject-to-be-called-forth. In his mouth, the "Germany" of the opening montage voice-over gains different connotations.

That voice-over "Germany" occurs in at least two other places in the course of the narrative: during a scene of representative beatings and torture (generalized by use of actors not in the story) and as Gerda and her neighbor, a Nazi-sympathizer, huddle in the bombed-out ruins of their city. In Loening's mouth, however, the word becomes a focus of hope, persuasion, and sacrifice. Loening's reported last words and the last words of the film are "Long live Germany!" Words of closure, to be sure, but immediately relayed into the final montage sequences.

Other moments in the film offer little comfort in the way of closure: in one instance, while the tiny resistance group picnics and plans ("We're just scattered . . .") the camera pans towards the left and halts on an empty field, with a birdsong on the soundtrack. A dissolve indicates time has passed, and the camera slowly returns to the picnic. In two other instances in the film, this pullaway and dissolve device is motivated by discretion and narrative economy; here it leaves the spectator with an uncomfortable vision of emptiness; the film seems to comment on the lack at which the project of the resistance group is directed, not a visible, albeit scattered community, but rather an empty place. Loening's project cannot be fulfilled by some pre-existing subject of address--they must be created or called forth.

Other gaps in the film and gazes which by all rights should disclose nothing are filled--by reverse-shots of letters. So it is when Loening is a fugitive and Gerda is left alone. No one is there with whom she could exchange glances--until we see a subjective shot of a letter from Loening.

265

So it is too after Loening's execution, when his letter is read to an assembly of friends. The news of hope and encouragement is relayed on to one prison after another and finally ends in the "Long live Germany!" which opens the final montage.

But the film not only displays gaps, it also matches pieces which do not fit. The alternation between Gerda and Loening and his comrades early in the film is a special example. When Loening leaves a political gathering to join his pregnant wife, who is waiting for him at home, he is confronted by Nazis marching in a counter-direction. One Nazi fires a shot at Loening, but on a cut the bullet seems to reach a different destination as Gerda clutches her womb. As comrades are rounded up by police and beaten, Gerda's childbirth is intercut. The meaning of the alternation is ambiguous. It implies simultaneity of events; it suggests that through coincidence or premonition Gerda is aware of Loening's danger. It is also a kind of metaphor which reveals similarity in different fields of reference--here the tertium comparationis is pain, and the terms are childbirth and torture. There is something enigmatic and slightly outrageous in this comparison, in which Gerda's service is as great as those of the men tortured for their beliefs; the intercutting asserts an equality between the two sides of the division of labor. Finally, the intercutting contrasts life and death and their association with two different ideologies.

It is said of Dudow that the selection of a camera set-up could be the object of hours of lively discussion with the entire cast and crew until he was satisfied that it was right. Once he had made up his mind he was known as "Dudow--the Uncompromising."[7] Certainly a closer examination of his work in terms of set-ups, camera movements and editing, the level of enunciation, is rewarding and an example of "a clever and systematic struggle for the hearts and minds of human beings."

266

Vanderbilt University

Notes

[1] Georges Sadoul, _Dictionary of Films_ (Berkeley: Univ. of Calif. Press, 1972), p. 354.

[2] John Hess, "Stronger than the Night," _Audio Brandon Films 1978-79_ (catalog description), p. 388. The film, original title _Stärker als die Nacht_, (112 minutes, black and white) is available for rental from Audio Brandon. Hess has reservations about the film as an interpretation of history. "It does not critically examine the reasons for the failure of the German working class to stop Hitler, choosing instead to blame it all on the social democrats. By refusing to deal with the Comintern's and the German Communist Party's complicity in world socialism's greatest disaster, the filmmakers undermine the credibility of their work" (p. 388). It is true that the film does not even try to supply an objective historical account of the Hitler era; the hero's opinions of his party and the Soviet Union are completely uncritical. But at a deeper level the film addresses the problem of what to do about the gaps in the world--how to face the failures of the working class and the party.

[3] Hermann Herlinghaus, _Slatan Dudow_ (E. Berlin: Henschel, 1965), p. 38. Translations are my own.

[4] Herlinghaus, p. 37.

[5] Hess, p. 388.

[6] Béla Balázs, _Theory of the Film: Character and Growth of a New Art_ (New York: Dover, 1970), p. 139. Balázs does not make a distinction between the panoramic and the tracking shot. Dudow creates an important opposition in the course of the film,

much as the difference between right and left movements on screen becomes significant.

⁷ Herlinghaus, p. 44.

Teaching GDR Literature:
Premises and Problems

Gisela E. Bahr

The teacher of GDR literature is faced with
specific problems that do not come up when teaching West German, Austrian, or Swiss literature.
For, unlike the other German speaking countries,
the German Democratic Republic is still too little
recognized in this country and, therefore, quite
alien to the average American student. If our
students are aware of the existence of the "other
Germany" at all, they often know but one fact,
that it is a socialist country. They have precon-
ceived notions about socialism and the GDR that
are often far from reality.

In the fall 1979 issue of Die Unterrichtspraxis, Sara Lennox discussed the teaching of
Plenzdorf's Die neuen Leiden des jungen W. Although the article deals with the teaching of this
one literary work, her experience can easily be
generalized. Lennox notes that students often
notice only those aspects of a work that confirm
what she calls "their uninformed prejudices
against the GDR," and neglect the rest--primarily
because they are ignorant of the cultural and
historical presuppositions on which the work is
based.[1] The students' lack of background is a
problem we can overcome, but prejudice is much
harder to deal with. There will always be some
students who cannot be persuaded, even by the most
factual information, to let go of their long-held
biases.

In the case of Die neuen Leiden, Lennox found
that she had to acquaint her students with three

areas of thought essential to the understanding of the work: 1) the importance of the literary heritage for the present socialist society; 2) the importance of work in the lives of the GDR citizens; and 3) the prospect of self-realization through work under socialist conditions.[2]

My own position is a bit more radical. I do not believe in teaching GDR literature by itself; I doubt that it is possible to provide students with all the information they need in order to understand GDR literature by lecturing on the side about the GDR. Instead I have developed a course on the German Democratic Republic at the undergraduate level, consisting of three parts: 1) history; 2) social and cultural institutions; and 3) literature. In other words, only after the students have studied in detail the development of the GDR and its present institutions, and have acquired a framework of historical, social, and cultural references, do I read and discuss GDR literature with them. The literary works serve to illustrate and authenticate what they have investigated theoretically.

Using works of literature to this end, rather than considering them timeless artistic endeavors, is, to be sure, controversial among literary critics. However, no matter which method is used to study other literatures, I firmly believe that GDR literature ought to be read in the context of the society that produced it. More specifically, it seems to me that a country such as the GDR, in which literature has replaced the media in relevance and information value, can quite legitimately be studied through its literature. It is precisely because of the unusual importance of literature in the GDR that we should guard against misinterpretation and misinformation. Therefore I insist on extensive background studies for any student of GDR literature.[3]

Before sharing with you some of my experiences in discussing GDR literature with my students, I would like to back up a bit and expand on

270

my premises. For what applies to the study of literature equally applies to the study of culture and history of the GDR. There, too, the American student will come upon concepts that are quite alien to him/her. Probably the most important (and least comprehensible) is the concept of the state and its functions. Long before the inception of the GDR, the Germans' idea of what the state and the government were supposed to do was quite the opposite of what Americans typically want and expect in this regard. While Americans like to keep their government as far away from their lives as possible, the Germans--at least from the time Bismarck initiated national health insurance in the 1880s--have looked upon their government as the provider of certain services, and they have come to expect them as a right. As the term <u>Vater Staat</u> indicates, the state is seen by the Germans as a patriarchal figure that is supposed to take care of its "children." That the state, in turn, would demand obedience and service from its "children" was accepted as part of the parcel. We can trace this concept through the Second Empire, the Weimar Republic, and the Nazi regime. To varying degrees it continues in the two Germanies today, for example, in the extensive social and cultural services, such as national health insurance, public mail, public transportation, and subsidized arts. It can also be seen in the large component of civil servants in the work force of the Federal Republic and of party functionaries ir the GDR, as well as in certain attitudes of the people. One such example is the high voter turnout at elections in both Germanies, which according to political scientists is attributable more to the Germans' sense of civic duty than to their political interests.

For American students it is important, I think, not only to take note of this alien concept as a political and social fact but also to keep it in mind whenever they consider either of the two Germanies. As for studying the GDR, awareness of this overall German tradition should enable the students to assess more objectively what they find in that country, and not simply to ascribe it all to socialism.

In this context, let me give you an example of what the lack of such vital information can lead to. For her term paper, one of my students recently selected the GDR's health system. As always--this is a matter of principle with me--I gave her source material from both East and West Germany. It so happened that she knew nothing of the old German national health insurance because she had neither taken the preceding course on the Federal Republic nor did her GDR sources make any mention of it. She was led to believe that the state health system was entirely of the GDR's making. So she termed it "socialized medicine," and she reported all facts and figures as she found them in her GDR sources, without, however, offering her own comments or evaluation. Instead, she concluded her paper with the findings of an article in the West German magazine Der Spiegel,[4] according to which the GDR health system was beset by many problems, such as long waiting lines for patients, excessive paperwork, and "das deutliche Gefälle in der Versorgung [von Stadt und Land]."[5] It would have been a satisfactory paper, were it not for the fact that the student completely misread the Spiegel article. Except for the one mistake in translation, this was due to selective reading. Presumably, the student expected her own point of view--that "socialized medicine" can't work--to be reflected in this western publication. Actually, the Spiegel article was a comparative account of the health care in the GDR and the FRG (a clue that went unnoticed), with the GDR system coming out even and, in some areas, actually ahead of its West German counterpart. The report did list some problems, for example, long waiting lines, abuses, and less adequate care in the villages. But they were acknowledged to be gesamt-deutsch, that is, they exist in both Germanies. Altogether, this was a well-informed, balanced, comprehensive comparison, and not at all the critique that the student took it to be. The system as a whole was, of course, never challenged by the

<u>Spiegel</u> reporter--just as the term "socialized medicine" would be meaningless over there--because to all Germans, West or East, national health care is a natural part of life that they would not want to be without. This is the first thing an American student has to comprehend in this regard.

Let us now return to the field of literature and my experience in teaching it. One of the literary works I always include in the curriculum, preferably at the beginning of the literature part, is Stefan Heym's story "Ein sehr guter zweiter Mann."[6] It is the account of an engineer, the best in the country, who has been pushed into second place by another engineer, a non-entity in his profession, who succeeds by being good at public relations and pleasing the party. The students usually love the story. It is well written and, besides, it corresponds so well to their perception of the GDR as a repressive society. But when I raise the question whether or not something like this could happen in this country, most of them agree that it could. This is a good first step because once the students recognize some common human ground, the GDR is no longer quite as foreign as it was before. But then the question arises, why does Robert not fight back or quit instead of drowning his frustrations in alcohol? Here we come upon the same issue that Sara Lennox found necessary to explain to her students reading <u>Die neuen Leiden</u>: the importance of work and the possibility of self-realization through work. Professionalism is, of course, something our students understand, but they expect recognition for good professional work or, at least, the fight for recognition. The fact that a project could be more important than the individual carrying it out is difficult for young people who believe in individualism to comprehend. Therefore, most of them cannot identify at all with the deep commitment, both professional and political, that keeps Robert going.

The greatest problem, however, comes with the consideration of the author's criticism of the

GDR. Throughout the story, Robert is attacked by flies, and he kills them with great vehemence. This can easily be seen as compensation for his pent-up anger. But they are only flies, and one is reminded of Bertolt Brecht's short poem "Epitaph for M.," which reads:

Den Haien entrann ich	The sharks I dodged
Die Tiger erlegte ich	The tigers I slew
Aufgefressen wurde ich	What ate me up
Von den Wanzen.	Was the bedbugs.[7]

This allusion, together with the unequivocal affirmation of communism at the end of the story, should warn us against overestimating Heym's criticism. It is criticism of methods rather than of substance. Heym is attacking the mediocrity of the party functionaries, the flies and bedbugs, and their misuse of the ideology, rather than the ideology itself. Hence, in spite of the abuse he endures, his hero continues to serve his country for the sake of communism.

In my experience, this differentiation is the hardest point for students to accept. In fact, any positive depiction of communism, socialism, or the party in a work of literature will be disposed of as propaganda or an act of duty, rather than be understood as the honest conviction of a character or the author. With all our belief in pluralism and in the rights of people to differ in their political persuasion in this country, Americans are often unwilling to extend this right to Marxists.

Similarly, in Volker Braun's "Unvollendete Geschichte" the criticism of the party is picked up immediately, while the positive elements usually are not.[8] As you will remember, this is the story of the daughter of a high government official torn between her obedience to her father (who represents the state and the party to her) and her love for her boyfriend, whom she is ordered to let go because he is suspected of planning to leave the country. Until this is proven to be an unfounded suspicion the young lovers are the victims of the party functionaries' dogmatic rigor and disregard of human sensitivities, and they are completely alienated from society. While the American students can easily identify with these young people and their feelings, the daughter's dream and its positive message is usually overlooked. In it, the workers take up the case of the lovers, hold the functionaries accountable for their actions, and punish them accordingly. In other words, this dream spells out in a nutshell how things ought to be. It provides the utopian model against which the shortcomings of the present situation can be measured--and perhaps corrected. For, as long as the goal is clear, it should be possible to make the necessary changes. This dream, therefore, constitutes a positive element in this sobering story. With it the author provides hope not only for his heroine but for the reader as well.

Like Heym, Braun is criticizing the mistakes and abuses of the system, not the system itself. These authors are not deliberately "dissidents" as the students, and sometimes the press, would like them to be. It helps to remember that both stories were written for domestic consumption, in order to provide constructive criticism, and that they were published in the West only when publication in the GDR was denied.

The most rewarding and least problematic of all my literature selections in this course has always been Sarah Kirsch's story "Staffelschwimmen."[9] This is the account of a career woman, and although it is unmistakably a GDR career, the problems she is faced with are mainly the problems of any woman in a man's world, and in a high position. The story shows very clearly that, in spite of the advanced legal structure that the GDR has established to promote women's equality, the factual situation for women is lagging behind there as much as anywhere in the western world. This woman found that she had to choose between career and marriage. After her divorce and some success in her career, she could no longer find a compat-

ible male partner. She became a workoholic with
little private life except the care of her son.
On the job she had to cope with male chauvinism,
isolation, and gossip. In spite of this, she
reached a high position, but she knew very well
that certain other careers she might aspire to,
like the foreign service, would not be open to
her as long as she had no husband.

In discussing this story with American students, I have never encountered any problems.
There are no taboos, no sensitive areas, no prejudices. All aspects can be discussed freely.
From my experience it seems that there is more
common ground between the United States and the
GDR in the realm of women's rights and aspira-
tions than in the area of politics and ideology.
This should give us hope that the political taboos and biases can in time be eliminated, too.

Other works studied in the literature part
of this undergraduate course include: the short
stories "Blickwechsel" or "Juninachmittag" by
Christa Wolf, "Fahrt mit der S-Bahn" by Günter
Kunert, "Stallschreiberstraße 45" by Günter de
Bruyn, "Drei Tage unseres Lebens" by Erik Neutsch,
"Der Sohn der Scheuerfrau" by Karl Mickel; Heiner
Müller's play <u>Die Korrektur</u>; a selection of Wolf
Biermann's <u>Lieder</u>.[10]

Miami University

Notes

[1] Sara Lennox, "Teaching Plenzdorf's <u>Die
neuen Leiden des jungen W.</u>," <u>Die Unterrichts-
praxis</u>, 12, No. 2 (1979), 40.

[2] Lennox, pp. 40f.

[3] The basic text for the first part of this
course (and the one on the Federal Republic of

Germany) is Eckart Thurich and Hans Endlich,
Zweimal Deutschland. Lehrbuch für Politik und
Zeitgeschichte, 6th ed. (Frankfurt/M./Berlin/
Munich: Diesterweg, 1976).
For the second part of the course, the study of
the GDR's social and cultural institutions, each
student writes a paper based on a variety of
sources, for example, DDR Handbuch, ed. Bundesministerium für innerdeutsche Beziehungen (Cologne:
Wissenschaft und Politik, 1975), clippings from
West German newspapers and magazines, brochures
from the series "Aus erster Hand," published by
Panorama DDR (1054 Berlin, Wilhelm-Pieck-Straße
49), Statistisches Taschenbuch der Deutschen Demokratischen Republik (E. Berlin: Staatsverlag der
DDR, annually), clippings from East German newspapers and magazines. The papers are read and
discussed in class, and are supplemented by documentary and feature films from the GDR embassy,
and my lectures.

[4] "Mit dem Bewußtsein hapert es," Der Spiegel,
2 Dec. 1974.

[5] Wrongly translated by the student as "the
clear decline in supplies."

[6] Stefan Heym, Erzählungen (E. Berlin: Buch-
verlag Der Morgen, 1976).

[7] Translated by John Willett. Bertolt
Brecht, Poems 1913-1956, ed. John Willett, Ralph
Manheim, Erich Fried (New York: Methuen, 1976),
p. 405.

[8] First published in Sinn und Form, 27, No. 5
(1975), 941-979. West German edition: Frankfurt/
M.: Suhrkamp, 1977.

[9] Sarah Kirsch, Die Pantherfrau. Fünf unfri-
sierte Erzählungen aus dem Kassetten-Recorder.
Edition Neue Texte (E. Berlin/Weimar: Aufbau,
1973); Ebenhausen bei München: Langewiesche-
Brandt, 1975.

[10] These and other suitable stories can be found in the following anthologies: _Fahrt mit der S-Bahn. Erzähler der DDR_, ed. Lutz-W. Wolff, 4th ed. (Munich: Deutscher Taschenbuch Verlag, 1974); _19 Erzähler der DDR_, ed. Hans-Jürgen Schmitt, 4th ed. (Frankfurt/M.: Fischer, 1974); _Neue Erzähler der DDR_, eds. Doris and Hans-Jürgen Schmitt (Frankfurt/M.: Fischer, 1975); _Auskunft. Neue Prosa aus der DDR_, ed. Stefan Heym (Munich: C. Bertelsmann, 1974). Müller's play, in two versions and with commentary, in Heiner Müller, _Geschichten aus der Produktion 1_ (W. Berlin: Rotbuch, 1974). Biermann's _Lieder_ in Wolf Biermann, _Die Drahtharfe_, Quarthefte (W. Berlin: Wagenbach, 1965) and _Mit Marx- und Engelszungen_, Quarthefte (W. Berlin: Wagenbach, 1968).

Introducing GDR Literature and Culture at the Advanced Language Level

Gertraud Gutzmann
H. Jochen Hoffmann

We would like to describe a technique for introducing GDR literature and culture at the advanced language level (i.e., fifth semester), which we have developed jointly at Smith College over the last two years. Although the course treated both Germanies, we were particularly interested in sensitizing the students to aspects of GDR literature and culture. We hoped to stimulate interest in our advanced courses on GDR drama, GDR women writers, and the history and literature of the two Germanies, in which GDR literature and culture are studied more comprehensively.

Since we were primarily concerned with problems pertaining to the development of conversation and composition skills we developed an issue-oriented approach. We selected newspaper articles from the GDR and the FRG, fiction and other non-fiction materials which lent themselves both to the improvement of language skills and to the exploration of themes and topics common to the cultures of industrialized societies in general, regardless of their political orientation. The topics included education, employment, the work place, and the effect of these on the younger generation, the middle-aged, and the aged in the two Germanies and the United States.[1] We were interested in generating reflections on the similarities and differences between these three cultures in the age of technology. We assumed that the students could easily relate them to their own experiences.

No attempt was made at this time to interfere with the subjective nature of the students' responses; the instructor only interrupted to clarify questions of fact or language usage. Since the students' opinions were challenged by the reading selections, they felt encouraged to express opposing views, through which prejudices and instances of insufficient information could be identified. Our underlying assumption was that students who participated actively in the process of formulating and defending their own opinions and ideas would be better prepared for discussion in advanced literature courses and for study abroad. Our issue-oriented approach, in contrast to a "tourist-oriented" approach, provoked discussion among all students, and made it possible to focus on differences among American, FRG, and GDR cultures.

While reflecting on the changing roles of men and women in German-speaking countries, the students began to examine their own roles in society. Their observations in turn led to a theoretical discussion (to the extent that this was linguistically possible) of concepts such as work, leisure time, self-realization through work, art, and other activities. Where "brain-storming" did not produce sufficient clarification of concepts, individual students were asked to use reference works; and, once we started reading GDR literature, they were asked to check official definitions in the DDR Handbuch or the Wörterbuch zum sozialistischen Staat.[2] Some grasp of these concepts made the understanding of GDR literature easier.

Keeping in mind the themes discussed in the course thus far, we chose a number of short stories reflecting life in the GDR during diverse phases of its history. Anna Seghers' short story "Thomas" was selected because of the way it reflects Germany's new beginning after the war. Erwin Strittmatter's "Märtke" and Karl-Heinz Jakobs' "Das grüne Land" introduce questions regarding the reconstruction period, the building of socialism, and the importance of work in the lives of young

280

people.[3] In Maxie Wander's "Immer nur pünktlich zur Arbeit, das ist zu wenig" a young woman questions the socialist work ethic, while in Wolf Biermann's "Der kleine Herr Moritz" the artist and his critical function in the socialist state are highlighted.[4]

Our course culminated in the reading of Ulrich Plenzdorf's _Die neuen Leiden des jungen W._, which treats most of the themes we covered.[5] Since this was the last text in the course, the students were sufficiently prepared to recognize the themes in the work and were able to identify specific points of view expressed by individual characters. Students encountered little difficulty in moving from the general themes to their specific appearance in Plenzdorf's work. In discussing the GDR as an achievement-oriented society, in which everyone is supposed to work or study, for example, they soon focused on the concept of work as expressed by Edgar Wibeau, Charlie, the old Zaremba, and Addi. This inquiry in turn led to the question of self-realization of the individual: was it achieved through art, through work, or during leisure time? At such points additional texts and secondary sources were introduced, such as Marx' definition of labor or the debate about _Die neuen Leiden_ in _Sinn und Form_.[6]

The figure of Zaremba also prompted consideration of the topic of aging in society, and students contrasted Zaremba's life with the circumstances of other seventy-year-olds in diverse situations—at work, in retirement, or in nursing homes. In so doing, one of the aims of the course was fulfilled, specifically that of acquiring a critical awareness of social conditions in the other country as well as in one's own. Both the students' oral contributions and essays were allowed to remain subjective; that is, the instructor's primary concern was the development of language fluency rather than the teaching of political science or history. At times extreme biases were articulated. The students contended with these on their own to a significant extent, which resulted in a lively exchange. While no final resolution of differences of opinion seemed to be forthcoming, prejudices were overcome which might have precluded further study of GDR literature.

A brief discussion of the teaching of Plenzdorf's Die neuen Leiden will further illustrate our procedure in implementing the teaching objectives outlined above. On Mondays, a fifty-minute session, the students brought to class questions having to do with grammatical constructions, colloquial expressions, and concepts that obstructed full reading comprehension of the chapters assigned. Along with clarifying the text, we practiced conversational expressions vital to the undirected discussion at the end of the week, for example:

> "Ich verstehe nicht, was Edgar meint."
> "Das ist mir nicht ganz klar."
> "Das verstehe ich immer noch nicht."

All along, on the blackboard, the teacher kept track of concepts and expressions that were problematic for the students. The final activity of the first class of the week consisted of a question and answer exercise from the book. The questions were of a factual rather than interpretative nature. Students were asked to retell the plot or describe characters and situations.

On Tuesdays, a two-hour session, we spent the first hour with remedial work, reviewing syntactical structures and points of advanced grammar that caused problems for students in their weekly compositions and oral presentations. The content of the exercises designed for this part of the course work reflected our work with non-fiction and fiction texts. (See Appendix A.) We then proceeded to language practice, using a quiz-show format. Here a paraphrase of colloquial expressions, explained in the previous class session, was asked for, also identification of concepts and words previously collected. We concluded this exercise with selections from the text that require inter-

pretation, as opposed to simple identification.
(See Appendix B.)

The second part of the two-hour session served
as preparation for Wednesday's non-directed discussion. Having informally talked about those
passages in which Edgar Eibeau expresses his views
on work, art, and leisure time, we introduced
glossed handouts with thought-provoking excerpts
on the various aspects of work. (See Appendix C.)

For the discussion session during the final
class hour of the week, we asked for two volun-
teers to take a position--the theme in this case
was the significance of work in a person's life.
Both students referred to an American film, Norma
Rae, in their remarks. (See Appendix D.) As a
result of their choice, we not only discussed the
film, but also the value of film and fiction as
sources of information on social issues.

In order to assure participation in the debate, conversational expressions were reviewed on
Tuesday so that students could address themselves
to the various points of discussion, agreeing,
disagreeing, or taking a divergent tack. For instance, to express agreement, the following phrases
were practiced:

> "Das finde ich auch."
> "Da bin ich ganz deiner Meinung."
> "Da hast du recht."

Options to express disagreement included:

> "Da bin ich aber ganz anderer Meinung."
> "Das finde ich überhaupt nicht."
> "Ich sehe das ganz anders."
> "Hier kann ich leider nicht zustimmen."

To express a viewpoint the following phrases were
reviewed:

> "Ich bin der Meinung, daß . . ."
> "So wie ich das sehe, . . ." 7

Also helpful were expressions such as "das heißt," "damit will ich sagen," "ich meine," to further specify a given statement. Filler words such as "wie gesagt," "an und für sich," "im großen und ganzen,""ja, eigentlich," "das ist gewissermaßen," were also useful, allowing the students time to search for the right expression.

A spontaneous discussion resulted from most of the student presentations. What began as a discussion of the role that work plays in the life of the people of the GDR led ultimately to a consideration of the role of work in their own society. Grappling with such complex, cross-cultural issues facilitated the development and use of more sophisticated vocabulary, idioms, and syntactical structures. Students gained a better understanding of GDR literature and consistently progressed beyond the linguistic and conceptual level of previous fifth semester classes we have taught.

Smith College

Notes

[1] We used the text by Hilmar Kormann, _Kritisch betrachtet_ (Munich: Max Hueber, 1977) as required reading for the course; it is a most helpful book for an issue-oriented course. It treats topics similar to our themes and offers four to five short non-fiction selections from the Federal Republic, each offering a different point of view or critical opinion. One such section deals with the pros and cons of education in an achievement-oriented society as they were examined by teenagers, parents, educators, and a prominent athlete. The topic of work in the troubled western economy is also looked at from the vantage point of prospective vocational school students and members of the 1960s generation who had recently entered the working world.

[2] Peter Christian Ludz, ed., DDR Handbuch, 2nd ed. (Cologne: Wissenschaft und Politik, 1979); Wörterbuch zum sozialistischen Staat (E. Berlin: Dietz, 1974).

[3] All three stories are contained in the collection: Osten und Westen, ed. R. Grunwald (New York: Dutton, 1976).

[4] Maxie Wander, "Immer nur pünktlich zur Arbeit, das ist zu wenig," in her Guten Morgen, du Schöne (Berlin/Neuwied: Luchterhand, 1978), pp. 58-64; Wolf Biermann, "Das Märchen vom kleinen Herrn Moritz, der eine Glatze kriegte," in Junge Deutsche Prosa, ed. Irmgard Feix and Ernestine Schlant (New York: Holt, Rinehart, and Winston, 1974), pp. 50-58.

[5] Ulrich Plenzdorf, Die neuen Leiden des jungen W., ed. Richard A. Zipser (New York: John Wiley & Sons, 1978). This well-edited text is easy on the eyes of students who towards the end of the semester are near exhaustion. Because of the lay-out the time-consuming task of looking up words in the back of the book is greatly reduced, which allows us to give high priority to intensive speaking and writing practice. The remedial language work is closely coordinated with the readings at this point of the course.

[6] Karl Marx and Friedrich Engels, Die Deutsche Ideologie, Vol. III of Werke (E. Berlin: Dietz, 1974), p. 33; "Diskussion um Plenzdorf: Die neuen Leiden des jungen W.," Sinn und Form, 25, No. 1 (1973), 219-252.

[7] Here we follow Claire Kranische's article, "Getting the Ball Rolling--A Functional Approach to Teaching Conversation Skills," in Die Unterrichtspraxis, 12, No. 1 (1979), 3-13.

Wiederholungsübungen zum Passiv im Deutschen
(Textbezug: Schule und Ausbildung in der DDR)

Beispiel: Im Jahre 1949 gründete man die Deutsche
Demokratische Republik. (Aktiv)

Im Jahre 1949 wurde die Deutsche Demokratische Republik gegründet. (Passiv)

1. 1952 proklamierte man den Aufbau des Sozialismus.

2. 1955 führte man die polytechnische Erziehung
ein.

Übungen zu "da-Sätzen" im Deutschen
(Based on Plenzdorf's Die neuen Leiden)

Beispiel: sprechen von:

a) Edgar war immer in Bewegung.
Charlie spricht davon.

b) Charlie spricht davon, daß Edgar
immer in Bewegung war.

1. überzeugt sein von:

a) Addi hat keine eigene Meinung.
Edgar ist überzeugt davon.

b) _____

2. rechnen mit:

a) Er muß Selbstkritik üben.
Edgar rechnet damit.

b) _____

Appendix B

<u>Hausaufgabe</u> <u>für</u> <u>Dienstag</u>

1. Was verstehen Sie unter

    a. Brigade
    b. Altkommunist
    c. Ausweis und Aufenthaltsgenehmigung
    d. Selbstkritik

2. Sagen Sie mit eigenen Worten, was die folgenden umgangssprachlichen Wendungen bedeuten:

    a. Hut ab!
    b. Wovon hat er gelebt?
    c. Wir kannten uns von Kind auf.
    d. Mir ging ein Licht auf.

3. Was bedeuten im Textzusammenhang folgende Aussagen:

    a. Addi: "Edgar war ein wertvoller Mensch."
        (p. 141).

        "Der will auf unsere Kosten Geld verdienen" (p. 151).

    b. Im Hinblick auf Zaremba:

        "Das Glasauge hatte er sich im Spanienkrieg eingehandelt"(p. 145).

        "Er soll gleich nach Kriegsende für drei Wochen oberster Richter von Berlin gewesen sein" (p. 153).

        "Er soll ganz scharfe Urteile gefällt haben" (p. 153).

Appendix C

1. "Werther"-Zitate in den Neuen Leiden des
   jungen W. zur leistungsorientierten Gesellschaft:

   "Es ist ein einförmiges Ding um das Men-
   schengeschlecht. Die meisten verarbeiten
   den größten Teil der Zeit, um zu leben,
   und das bißchen, das ihnen von Freiheit
   übrigbleibt, ängstigt sie so, daß sie alle
   Mittel aufsuchen, um es loszuwerden" (p.
   163).

2. Auszug aus Karl Marx: Deutsche Ideologie
   über die Arbeitsteilung der modernen
   Industriegesellschaft im 19. Jahrhundert.
   (Karl Marx and Friedrich Engels, Werke,
   Vol. III, E. Berlin, 1974, p. 33)

3. Stichwort "Arbeit" im Kleinen politischen
   Wörterbuch (E. Berlin, 1974)

   "Arbeit ist zweckmässige bewußte Tätigkeit
   des Menschen, in der er mit Hilfe von Ar-
   beitsmitteln Arbeitsgegenstände verändert
   und sie seinen Zwecken nutzbar macht. Die
   Arbeit ist ein allen Gesellschaftsforma-
   tionen unerläßlicher Existenzbezug des
   Menschen."

Appendix D

Excerpt from a student position paper presented as an opener for undirected discussion of the concept of work.

Emily Fowler: "Dieser Film hat mir für viele Gründe besonders gefallen. Erstens, weil Sally Fields die Rolle der Norma Rae hervorragend spielt. Sie drückt ihre Gefühle so realistisch aus, daß man vergißt, daß sie nicht wirklich Norma Rae ist. Alle die Schauspieler in diesem Film sind ganz vorzüglich. Die Auswahl der Schauspieler in diesem Film für die verschiedenen Rollen, auch für die unbedeutenden Rollen, war ausgezeichnet, und trägt viel zu der wirklichkeitsgetreuen Darstellung des Stoffes bei. Zum Beispiel sehen wir die Arbeiter alle wie echte südliche Arbeiter. Die ermüdeten Gesichter der Arbeiter mit ihren Falten und Augen, die nur ihre Hoffnungslosigkeit zeigen, sagen mehr über den Zustand der Arbeiter als viele Worte. Und mit subtiler Kameraführung zeigt der Regisseur Martin Ritt die schlechten Arbeitsbedingungen in der Fabrik, wo die Arbeiter nicht als Menschen, sondern als Maschinen betrachtet werden. Er kontrastiert zum Beispiel eine Großaufnahme der Fabrik, in der die Menschen so klein unter den großen, geräuschvollen Maschinen aussehen, mit einer Nahaufnahme eines Arbeiters, die die Langweile und Eintönigkeit dieses Sackgassenberufes zeigt."

(Fall 1979)

289

A Bibliography for the Study of the GDR

Margy Gerber

The following bibliography is intended as an aid for students and colleagues beginning to work in the field of GDR studies. It does not pretend to be an exhaustive bibliography, nor does it attempt to evaluate the works listed. It includes Anglo-American, West German and GDR titles.

General Reference

DDR Handbuch. Ed. Peter C. Ludz. Bundesministerium für innerdeutsche Beziehungen. 2nd rev. ed. Cologne: Wissenschaft und Politik, 1979.

DDR. Tatsachen und Zahlen. Dresden: Zeit im Bild, published annually. Eng. ed.: GDR Facts and Figures. E. Berlin: Auslandspresseagentur.

Deutsche Demokratische Republik. Handbuch. Leipzig: VEB Verlag Enzyklopädie, 1979.

Deutschland. Bundesrepublik Deutschland - Deutsche Demokratische Republik. Daten und Fakten zum Nachschlagen. Gütersloh: Bertelsmann, 1975.

Kleines politisches Wörterbuch. 3rd rev. ed. E. Berlin: Dietz, 1978.

Kleines Wörterbuch der marxistisch-leninistischen Philosophie. Ed. Manfred Buhr, Alfred Kosing. 4th rev., enl. ed. E. Berlin: Dietz, 1979.

Kulturpolitisches Wörterbuch. 2nd rev. ed. E. Berlin: Dietz, 1978.

Namen und Daten wichtiger Personen der DDR. Ed. Günther Buch. 2nd rev. enl. ed. W. Berlin/

Bonn: Dietz, 1979.

Statistisches Taschenbuch der Deutschen Demokratischen Republik. E. Berlin: Staatsverlag der DDR, published annually.

Statistisches Jahrbuch der Deutschen Demokratischen Republik. E. Berlin: Staatsverlag der DDR, published annually.

Wörterbuch der marxistisch-leninistischen Soziologie. Ed. Georg Assmann, et al. E. Berlin: Dietz, 1977.

Wörterbuch zum sozialistischen Staat. E. Berlin: Dietz, 1974.

Documents

DDR-Gesetze. Textausgabe. Ed. Erika Lieser-Triebnigg, Dietrich Müller-Römer. Cologne: Wissenschaft und Politik, 1980.

Dokumente zur Außenpolitik der Deutschen Demokratischen Republik. Ed. Institut für Internationale Beziehungen der Akademie für Staats- und Rechtswissenschaft der DDR. E. Berlin: Staatsverlag der DDR, published annually.

Dokumente des geteilten Deutschland. Ed. Ingo von Münch. 2 vols. Stuttgart: Kröner, 1968/74.

Sozialismus in der DDR. Dokumente und Materialien. Ed. Rainer Rilling. 2 vols. Cologne: Pahl-Rugenstein, 1979.

Verfassung der Deutschen Demokratischen Republik. 2nd ed. E. Berlin: Staatsverlag der DDR, 1975.

General Treatment of the GDR

Behr, Wolfgang. Bundesrepublik Deutschland - Deutsche Demokratische Republik. Politik - Wirtschaft - Gesellschaft. Stuttgart: Kohlhammer, 1979.

Childs, David. East Germany. New York: Praeger, 1969.

Dornberg, John. <u>The Other Germany</u>. New York: Doubleday, 1968.

Erbe,Günter, G.-J. Glaeßner, et al. <u>Politik, Wirtschaft und Gesellschaft in der DDR. Studien-texte für die politische Bildung</u>. Opladen: Westdeutscher Verlag, 1979.

Gellert, Johannes F., and Hans-Joachim Kramm. <u>DDR: Land, Volk, Wirtschaft in Stichworten</u>. Vienna: Ferdinand Hirt, 1977.

Grätz, Frank. <u>Die DDR. Daten, Fakten, Analysen, Hinweise</u>. Munich: Heyne, 1979.

Hanhardt, Arthur M. <u>The German Democratic Repub-lic</u>. Baltimore: Johns Hopkins Press, 1968.

<u>100 Fragen - 100 Antworten: DDR</u>. Panorama DDR. E. Berlin: Auslandspresseagentur, 1978. Eng. ed.: <u>100 Questions - 100 Answers</u>.

<u>Introducing the GDR</u>. Panorama GDR. 5th ed. E. Berlin: Auslandspresseagentur, 1976.

Legters, Lyman H., ed. <u>The German Democratic Republic. A Developed Socialist Society</u>. Boul-der: Westview Press, 1978.

Ludz, Peter C. <u>Deutschlands doppelte Zukunft</u>. Munich: Hanser, 1974. Eng. ed.: <u>Two Germanies in One World</u>. Paris: Atlantic Institute for International Affairs, 1973.

----------. <u>The German Democratic Republic from the Sixties to the Seventies: A Sociopolitical Analysis</u>. Cambridge, Mass.: Harvard Press, 1970.

Pfeiler, Wolfgang. <u>DDR-Lehrbuch</u>. Bonn: Neue Verlagsgesellschaft Werge & Co., 1974.

Rausch, Heinz, and Theo Stammen. <u>DDR. Das poli-tische, wirtschaftliche und soziale System</u>. Munich: Beck, 1974.

Richert, Ernst. <u>Das zweite Deutschland. Ein Staat, der nicht sein darf</u>. Gütersloh: S. Mohn, 1964; Frankfurt/M.: Fischer, 1966.

Schneider, Eberhard. <u>Die DDR. Geschichte, Poli-tik, Wirtschaft, Gesellschaft</u>. Stuttgart: Bonn aktuell, 1975. Eng. ed.: <u>The GDR. The History</u>,

Politics, Economy and Society of East Germany. London: Hurst, 1978.

Schwarze, Hanns Werner. *DDR heute*. Cologne: Kiepenheuer & Witsch, 1970. Eng. ed.: *The GDR Today. Life in the "Other" Germany*. London: Oswald Wolff, 1973.

----------. *Die DDR ist keine Zone mehr*. Cologne: Kiepenheuer & Witsch, 1969.

Smith, Jean. *Germany Beyond the Wall*. Boston: Little & Brown, 1967.

Sontheimer, Kurt, and Wilhelm Bleek. *Die DDR. Politik - Gesellschaft - Wirtschaft*. 5th rev., enl. ed. Hamburg: Hoffmann & Campe, 1979. Eng. ed.: *The Government and Politics of East Germany*. New York: St. Martin's Press, 1976.

Starrels, John M., and Anita Mallinckrodt. *Politics in the GDR*. New York: Praeger, 1975.

Steele, Jonathan. *Inside East Germany. The State that Came in from the Cold*. New York: Urizen, 1977.

Thomas, Rüdiger. *Modell DDR. Die kalkulierte Emanzipation*. Munich: Hanser, 1972.

Geography

Geographic Manual. German Democratic Republic. Leipzig: Zeit im Bild, 1978.

Kohl, H., J. Marcinek and B. Nitz. *Geographie der DDR*. Studienbücherei Geographie für Lehrer, Vol. 7. Gotha: VEB H. Haack, 1978.

Mellor, Roy E. H. *Eastern Europe. A Geography of the Comecon Countries*. London: Macmillan, 1975.

----------. *The Two Germanies: A Modern Geography*. London: Harper & Row, 1978.

History

Badstübner, Rolf, and Siegfried Thomas. *Die*

Spaltung Deutschlands 1945-49. E. Berlin: Dietz, 1966.

----------, and Heinz Heitzer, eds. Die DDR in der Übergangsperiode. Studien zur Vorgeschichte und Geschichte der DDR 1945 bis 1961. E. Berlin: Akademie Verlag, 1979.

Baring, Arnulf. Der 17. Juni. Cologne: Kiepenheuer & Witsch, 1965. Eng. ed.: Uprising in East Germany: June 17, 1953. Ithaca: Cornell Univ. Press, 1972.

Buxhoeveden, Christina von. Geschichtswissenschaft und Politik in der DDR. Das Problem der Periodisierung. Cologne: Wissenschaft und Politik, 1980.

DDR. Werden und Wachsen. Zur Geschichte der Deutschen Demokratischen Republik. Akademie der Wissenschaften der DDR. E. Berlin: Dietz, 1975.

Deuerlein, Ernst, ed. DDR. 1945-1970. Geschichte und Bestandsaufnahme. 3rd rev. ed. Munich: Dt. Taschenbuch Verlag, 1971.

Doernberg, Stefan. Die Geburt eines neuen Deutschland 1945-49. Die antifaschistisch-demokratische Umwälzung und die Entstehung der DDR. 2nd ed. E. Berlin: Rütten & Loening, 1959.

----------. Kurze Geschichte der DDR. 4th rev. ed. E. Berlin: Dietz, 1969.

Heitzer, Heinz. DDR. Geschichtlicher Überblick. Schriftenreihe Geschichte. E. Berlin: Dietz, 1979.

Neef, Helmut. Entscheidende Tage im Oktober 1949. Die Gründung der Deutschen Demokratischen Republik. E. Berlin: Dietz, 1979.

Weber, Hermann. DDR. Grundriß der Geschichte 1945-1976. Hanover: Fackelträger, 1976.

----------. Von der SBZ zur DDR. 1945-1968. Hanover: Verlag für Literatur und Zeitgeschehen, 1968.

Biographies, Memoirs

Havemann, Robert. _Ein deutscher Kommunist. Rückblick und Perspektiven aus der Isolation_. Reinbek bei Hamburg: Rowohlt, 1978.

----------. _Fragen, Antworten, Fragen. Aus der Biographie eines deutschen Marxisten_. Munich: Piper, 1970.

Honecker, Erich. _Aus meinem Leben_. Oxford: Pergamon Press, 1980.

Kantorowicz, Alfred. _Deutsches Tagebuch_. 2 vols. Munich: Kindler, 1959/61. Shortened, revised paperback edition: Munich: Kindler, 1964.

Lippmann, Heinz. _Honecker. Porträt eines Nachfolgers_. Cologne: Wissenschaft und Politik, 1971. Eng. ed.: _Honecker and the New Politics of Europe_. New York: Macmillan, 1972.

Stern, Carola. _Ulbricht. Eine politische Biographie_. Cologne: Kiepenheuer & Witsch, 1963. Eng. ed.: _Ulbricht: A Political Biography_. New York: Praeger, 1965.

Government

Bothe, Michael. "The 1968 Constitution of East Germany," _American Journal of Comparative Law_, 18 (1969), 268-91.

Lapp, Peter Joachim. _Der Staatsrat im politischen System der DDR_. Opladen: Westdeutscher Verlag, 1972.

----------. _Die Volkskammer der DDR_. Opladen: Westdeutscher Verlag, 1975.

Müller-Römer, Dietrich, ed. _Die neue Verfassung der DDR_. Cologne: Wissenschaft und Politik, 1974.

Roggemann, Herwig, ed. _Die DDR-Verfassungen_. 2nd rev., enl. ed. W. Berlin: Berlin, 1976.

----------. _Die Gesetzgebung der DDR_. W. Berlin: Berlin, 1971.

----------. Die Staatsordnung der DDR. 2nd ed. W. Berlin: Berlin, 1973.

----------. Die Verfassung der DDR. Entstehen, Analysen, Vergleich, Text. Opladen: Leske, 1970.

SED

Institut für Marxismus-Leninismus beim ZK der SED. Geschichte der Sozialistischen Einheitspartei Deutschlands. Abriß. E. Berlin: Dietz, 1978. Western edition: Frankfurt/M.: Verlag Marxistische Blätter, 1978.

Ludz, Peter C. Parteielite im Wandel. Funktionsaufbau, Sozialstruktur und Ideologie der SED-Führung. Cologne: Westdeutscher Verlag, 1968. Eng. ed.: The Changing Party Elite in East Germany. Cambridge, Mass.: MIT Press, 1972.

McCauley, Martin. Marxism-Leninism in the German Democratic Republic. The Socialist Unity Party (SED). London: School of Slavonic and East European Studies, 1979; N.Y.: Barnes and Noble, 1979.

Neugebauer, Gero. Partei und Staatsapparat in der DDR. Aspekte der Instrumentalisierung des Staatsapparates durch die SED. Opladen: Westdeutscher Verlag, 1978.

Schneider, Eberhard. Die SED der 80er Jahre. Das neue Programm und Statut der Partei. Cologne: Berichte des Bundesinstituts für Ostwissenschaft und Internationale Studien, 1977.

----------, ed. SED: Programm und Statut von 1976. Opladen: Leske, 1977.

Staritz, Dietrich. Sozialismus in einem halben Land. Zur Programmatik und Politik der KPD/SED in der Phase der antifaschistisch-demokratischen Umwälzung in der DDR. W. Berlin: Wagenbach, 1976.

Weber, Hermann. Die sozialistische Einheitspartei Deutschlands 1946-1971. Hanover: Verlag für Literatur und Zeitgeschehen, 1971.

----------, Die SED nach Ulbricht. Hanover: Fackelträger, 1974.

----------, and Fred Oldenburg. 25 Jahre SED. Chronik einer Partei. Cologne: Wissenschaft und Politik, 1971.

Economy

Akademie für Gesellschaftswissenschaften beim ZK der SED, ed. Die Volkswirtschaft der DDR. E. Berlin: Verlag Die Wirtschaft, 1979.

----------, ed. Zur materiell-technischen Basis in der DDR. E. Berlin: Dietz, 1980.

Ambree, Kurt, Helmut Mann, and Günter Pöggel. Was ich vom Preis wissen muß. E. Berlin: Verlag Die Wirtschaft, 1978.

Bahro, Rudolf. Die Alternative. Zur Kritik des real existierenden Sozialismus. Frankfurt/M.: Europäische Verlagsanstalt, 1977.

Bartel, Horst. Die wirtschaftlichen Ausgangsbedingungen der DDR. Zur Wirtschaftsentwicklung auf dem Gebiet der DDR 1945-49/50. E. Berlin: Akademie Verlag, 1979.

Belwe, Katharina. Mitwirkung im Industriebetrieb der DDR. Planung - Einzelleitung - Beteiligung der Werktätigen an Entscheidungsprozessen des VEB. Opladen: Westdeutscher Verlag, 1979.

Biermann, Wolfgang. Demokratisierung in der DDR? Ökonomische Notwendigkeiten, Herrschaftsstrukturen, Rolle der Gewerkschaften 1961-1977. Cologne: Verlag Wissenschaft und Politik, 1978.

Bress, Ludwig, and Karl Paul Hensel. Wirtschaftssysteme des Sozialismus im Experiment - Plan oder Markt? Frankfurt/M.: Fischer, 1972.

Damus, Renate. Entscheidungsstrukturen und Funktionsprobleme in der DDR-Wirtschaft. Frankfurt/M.: Suhrkamp, 1973.

Deutsches Institut für Wirtschaftsforschung.

DDR-Wirtschaft. Eine Bestandsaufnahme. Frankfurt/M.: Fischer, 1971.

----------. Handbuch DDR-Wirtschaft. Reinbek b. Hamburg: Rowohlt, 1977.

Eckhard, Karl-Heinz. Die DDR im Systemvergleich. Didaktisches Sachbuch zum Verständnis von Plan- und Marktwirtschaft. Erläuterungen - Materialien - Arbeitsvorschläge. Reinbek b. Hamburg: Rowohlt, 1978.

Grundfragen der Wirtschaftspolitik in der DDR. Anschauungsmaterial. E. Berlin: Verlag Die Wirtschaft, 1980.

Hegemann, Margot. Kurze Geschichte der RWG. E. Berlin: Dt. Verlag der Wissenschaften, 1980.

Hilgenberg, Dorothea. Bedarfs- und Marktforschung in der DDR. Anspruch und Wirklichkeit. Cologne: Wissenschaft und Politik, 1979.

Immler, Hans. Agrarpolitik in der DDR. Cologne: Wissenschaft und Politik, 1971.

Leptin, Gert, and Manfred Melzer. Economic Reform in East German Industry. Trans. Roger A. Clarke. Oxford/New York: Oxford Univ. Press, 1978.

Lieber, Paul, and Udo Freier. Politische Ökonomie des Sozialismus in der DDR. Frankfurt/M.: Makol, 1972.

Merkel, Konrad, and Hans Immler, eds. DDR-Landwirtschaft in der Diskussion. Cologne: Wissenschaft und Politik, 1972.

Socialist Economy - aims and strategy. Facts and Figures from the GDR. Series First-hand information. Panorama DDR. E. Berlin: Auslandspresseagentur, 1977.

Die Volkswirtschaft der DDR. Landeskunde DDR für Ausländer. Leipzig: VEB Enzyklopädie, 1980.

Foreign Policy, German Question

Birnbaum, Karl E. East and West Germany: A

<u>Modus Vivendi</u>. Lexington, Mass.: Heath, 1973.

Bruns, Wilhelm. <u>Deutsch-deutsche Beziehungen</u>.
<u>Prämissen - Probleme - Perspektive</u>. Opladen:
Leske, 1979.

----------. <u>Die Uneinigen in den Vereinten Na</u>-
tionen. <u>Bundesrepublik Deutschland und DDR in</u>
<u>der UNO</u>. Cologne: Wissenschaft und Politik,
1980.

Croan, Melvin. <u>East Germany: The Soviet Connec</u>-
tion. Beverly Hills: Sage Publications, 1976.

Doernberg, Stefan, et al. <u>Außenpolitik der DDR</u>.
<u>Drei Jahrzehnte sozialistische deutsche Friedens</u>-
<u>politik</u>. E. Berlin: Staatsverlag der DDR, 1979.

Jacobsen, Hans-Adolf, ed. <u>Drei Jahrzehnte Außen</u>-
<u>politik der DDR. Bestimmungsfaktoren, Instru</u>-
<u>mente, Aktionsfelder</u>. Munich: Oldenbourg, 1979.

Kregel, Bernd. <u>Außenpolitik und Systemstabili</u>-
<u>sierung in der DDR</u>. Opladen: Leske, 1979.

Ludz, Peter C. <u>Die DDR zwischen Ost und West</u>
<u>1961-1976</u>. Munich: Beck, 1977.

Mallinckrodt, Anita M. <u>Die Selbstdarstellung</u>
<u>der beiden deutschen Staaten im Ausland. "Image</u>-
<u>Bildung" als Instrument der Außenpolitik</u>. Co-
logne: Wissenschaft und Politik, 1980.

Mattfeld, Antje. <u>Modelle einer Normalisierung</u>
<u>zwischen den beiden deutschen Staaten</u>. Düssel-
dorf: Droste, 1973.

McCauley, Martin. <u>East Germany. The Dilemmas of</u>
<u>Division</u>. London: Institute for the Study of
Conflict, 1980.

Merkl, Peter H. <u>German Foreign Policies West</u>
<u>and East</u>. Santa Barbara: American Bibliographi-
cal Center, 1974.

Moreton, Edwina N. <u>East Germany and the Warsaw</u>
<u>Alliance. The Politics of Detente</u>. Boulder:
Westview Press, 1978.

Radde, Jürgen. <u>Die außenpolitische Führungs</u>-
<u>elite der DDR. Veränderungen der sozialen Struk</u>-

tur außenpolitischer Führungsgruppen. Cologne: Wissenschaft und Politik, 1976.

Riege, Gerhard, and H.-J. Kulke. Nationalität: deutsch - Staatsbürgerschaft: DDR. E. Berlin: Staatsverlag der DDR, 1979.

Schwarz, H.P., and E. Meißner. Entspannungspolitik in Ost und West. Cologne: Wissenschaft und Politik, 1979.

Wettig, Gerhard. Die Sowjetunion, die DDR und die Deutschland-Frage 1965-1976. Stuttgart: Bonn Aktuell, 1976.

GDR Society and Social Questions

Auerbach, Th., M. Sallmann, et al. DDR - konkret. Geschichten und Berichte aus einem real existierenden Land. W. Berlin: Olle & Wolter, 1978.

Baylis, Thomas. The Technical Intelligentsia and the East German Elite. Legitimacy and Social Change in Mature Communism. Berkeley/London: Univ. of Calif. Press, 1974.

Bussiek, Hendrik. Notizen aus der DDR. Erlebnisse, Erfahrungen, Erkenntnisse in der unbekannten deutschen Republik. Frankfurt/M.: Fischer, 1979.

Grünberg, Hans. Die sozialistische Wandlung des Dorfes. E. Berlin: VEB Dt. Landwirtschaftsverlag, 1970.

Helwig, Gisela. Am Rande der Gesellschaft. Alte und Behinderte in beiden deutschen Staaten. Cologne: Wissenschaft und Politik, 1980.

How do people live in the GDR. Living standards and way of life under socialism. First-hand information. Panorama DDR. E. Berlin: Auslandspresseagentur, 1974.

Klix, Friedhart, et al. Psychologie in der DDR. Entwicklung - Aufgaben - Perspektiven. 2nd rev. ed. E. Berlin: Dt. Verlag der Wissenschaften, 1980.

Lemke, Christiane. *Persönlichkeit und Gesellschaft. Zur Theorie der Persönlichkeit in der DDR.* Opladen: Westdeutscher Verlag, 1980.

Ludz, Peter C. *Mechanismen der Herrschaftssicherung. Eine sprachpolitische Analyse gesellschaftlichen Wandels in der DDR.* Munich: Hanser, 1980.

----------, ed. *Soziologie und Marxismus in der Deutschen Demokratischen Republik.* Neuwied/Berlin: Luchterhand, 1972.

Manz, G., ed. *Lebensweise und Lebensniveau im Sozialismus.* E. Berlin: Die Wirtschaft, 1977.

----------, and G. Winkler. *Theorie und Praxis der Sozialpolitik in der DDR.* E. Berlin: Akademie Verlag, 1979.

Runge, Erika. *Reise nach Rostock, DDR.* Frankfurt/M.: Suhrkamp, 1971.

Sander, Günther. *Abweichendes Verhalten in der DDR. Kriminalitätstheorien in einer sozialistischen Gesellschaft.* Frankfurt/M.: Campus, 1979.

Schmickl, Emil. *Soziologie und Sozialismustheorie in der DDR.* Cologne: Wissenschaft und Politik, 1973.

Spahn, Peter. *Unterhaltung im Sozialismus. Traditionen - Ergebnisse - Tendenzen.* E. Berlin: Dietz, 1980.

Thomas, Rüdiger, ed. *Wissenschaft und Gesellschaft in der DDR.* Munich: Hanser, 1971.

Wie leben und arbeiten die Bauern in der DDR? Aus erster Hand. Panorama DDR. E. Berlin: Auslandspresseagentur, 1976.

Windmöller, Eva, and Thomas Höpker. *Leben in der DDR.* Hamburg: Gruner & Jahr, 1976. Paperback edition: Munich: W. Goldmann, 1980.

Legal System

Brunner, Georg. *Einführung in das Recht der DDR.* 2nd rev., enl. ed. Munich: Beck, 1979.

302

Finn, Gerhard. _Politischer Strafvollzug in der_
DDR. Cologne: Wissenschaft und Politik, 1980.

Fricke, Karl Wilhelm. _Politik und Justiz in der_
DDR. Zur Geschichte der politischen Verfolgung
1945-1968. Bericht und Dokumentation. Cologne:
Wissenschaft und Politik, 1979.

Lammich, Siegfried. "Das politische Strafrecht
in der DDR und den anderen sozialistischen Län-
dern. Ein Vergleich ausgewählter Formulierungen."
Deutschland Archiv, 13, No. 8 (1980), 843-854.

Schroeder, F. Ch. "Die neue Strafrechtsreform
der DDR." _Deutschland Archiv_, 12, No. 10
(1979), 1064-1078.

Church and Religion

Bloth, Peter, ed. _Christenlehre und Kathechume-_
nat in der DDR. Grundlage - Versuche - Modelle.
Gütersloh: Gütersloher Verlagshaus, 1975.

Fischer, Peter. _Kirchen und Christen in der_
DDR. W. Berlin: Gebr. Holzapfel, 1978.

Knauft, Wolfgang. _Katholische Kirche in der_
DDR. Gemeinden in der Bewährung 1945-1980.
Mainz: Matthias-Grünewald Verlag, 1980.

Koch, Hans-Gerhard. _Staat und Kirche in der_
DDR. Zur Entwicklung ihrer Beziehungen von 1945-
74. Darstellung, Quellen, Übersichten. Stuttgart: Quell, 1975.

Women and Family

Bronnen, Barbara, and Franz Henny. _Liebe, Ehe,_
Sexualität in der DDR. Interviews und Dokumente.
Munich: Piper, 1975.

Gast, Gabriele. _Die politische Rolle der Frau_
in der DDR. Düsseldorf: Bertelsmann, 1973.

Helwig, Gisela. _Frau '75. Bundesrepublik Deut-_
schland - DDR. Cologne: Wissenschaft und Politik, 1975.

Helwig, Gisela. Zwischen Familie und Beruf: Die Stellung der Frau in beiden deutschen Staaten. Cologne: Wissenschaft und Politik, 1974.

Kuhrig, Herta, and Wulfram Speigner, eds. Wie emanzipiert sind die Frauen in der DDR? Beruf, Bildung, Familie. Cologne: Pahl-Rugenstein, 1979.

Menschik, Jutta, and Evelyn Leopold. Gretchens rote Schwestern. Frauen in der DDR. Frankfurt/M.: Fischer, 1974.

Ministerium der Justiz, ed. Ehe und Familie. Eine Sammlung gesetzlicher Bestimmungen mit Anmerkungen und Sachregister. E. Berlin: Staatsverlag der DDR, 1979.

Plat, Wolfgang. Die Familie in der DDR. Frankfurt/M.: Fischer, 1972.

Rosenfeld, Klaus, and Eva Hein. Förderung und Schutz der Frau im Arbeitsrecht. E. Berlin: Staatsverlag der DDR, 1979.

Schnabl, Siegfried. Mann und Frau intim. E. Berlin: Volk und Gesundheit, 1978.

Staatliche Dokumente zur Förderung der Frau in der DDR. Gesetzesdokumentation. 2nd rev. ed. E. Berlin: Staatsverlag der DDR, 1975.

Wander, Maxie. Guten Morgen, du Schöne. Frauen in der DDR. Berlin/Neuwied: Luchterhand, 1978.

Women in the GDR: Facts and Figures. Dresden: Verlag Zeit im Bild, 1975.

Youth

Jaide, Walter, and Barbara Hille, eds. Jugend im doppelten Deutschland. Opladen: Westdeutscher Verlag, 1977.

Micksch, Jürgen. Jugend und Freizeit in der DDR. Opladen: Westdeutscher Verlag, 1972.

Pieper, Katrin, ed. Um 6 Uhr steh ich auf. Kinder aus der DDR erzählen. Reinbek b. Hamburg: Rowohlt, 1979.

Starke, Kurt. Jugend im Studium. Zur Persönlichkeitsentwicklung von Hochschulstudenten. E. Berlin: Dt. Verlag der Wissenschaften, 1979.

Youth. At work, at leisure and in politics.
First-hand information. Panorama DDR. E. Berlin: Auslandspresseagentur, 1977.

Zentralausschuß für Jugendweihe in der DDR.
Handbuch zur Jugendweihe. Eine Anleitung für
Mitglieder und Jugendstundenleiter. 2nd ed.
E. Berlin: Volk und Wissen, 1977.

Zur Erziehung junger sozialistischer Staatsbürger durch die Pioneerorganization "Ernst Thäl-
mann." 2nd ed. E. Berlin: Volk und Wissen,
1970.

Sports

Brux, Arnim. Sportlehrer und Sportunterricht in
der DDR. Eine empirische Untersuchung. W. Berlin: Verlag Bartels & Wernitz, 1980.

Fun - Health - Fitness. Physical culture and
sport in the GDR. First-hand information.
E. Berlin: Auslandspresseagentur, 1974.

Knecht, Willi. Fakten, Dokumente, Kommentare
zum Sport in der DDR. W. Berlin: Gebr. Holzapfel, 1978.

Riordan, James, ed. Sport under Communism.
Montreal: McGill-Queen's Univ. Press, 1978.

Education

Akademie der Pädagogischen Wissenschaften der
DDR. Das Bildungswesen der Deutschen Demokratischen Republik. E. Berlin: Volk und Wissen,
1979.

Bode, Dirk. Polytechnischer Unterricht in der
DDR. Frankfurt/M.: Campus, 1978.

Busch, Friedrich W. Familienerziehung in der
sozialistischen Pädagogik der DDR. Düsseldorf:
Schwann, 1972; Frankfurt/M.: Ullstein, 1980.

Glaessner, Gerd-Joachim, and Irmhild Rudolf. _Macht durch Wissen. Zum Zusammenhang von Bildungspolitik, Bildungssystem und Kaderqualifizierung in der DDR. Eine politisch-soziologische Untersuchung._ Opladen: Westdeutscher Verlag, 1978.

Hartwig, Jürgen, and Albert Wimmel. _Wehrerziehung und vormilitärische Ausbildung der Kinder und Jugendlichen in der DDR._ Stuttgart: Seewald, 1979.

Hearnden, Arthur. _Bildungspolitik in der BRD und DDR._ 2nd rev. ed. Düsseldorf: Schwann, 1978. Eng. ed.: _Education in the Germanies,_ Boulder: Westview Press, 1976.

Hegelheimer, Armin. _Berufsausbildung in Deutschland: System- und Reformvergleich der Berufsausbildung in der BRD und der DDR._ 4th ed. Frankfurt/M.: Europäische Verlagsanstalt, 1973.

Hettwer, Hubert. _Das Bildungswesen in der DDR. Strukturelle und inhaltliche Entwicklung seit 1945._ Cologne: Kiepenheuer & Witsch, 1976.

Klein, Helmut. _Bildung in der DDR. Grundlagen, Entwicklungen, Probleme._ Reinbek b. Hamburg: Rowohlt, 1974.

Mende, Klaus-Dieter. _Die polytechnische Erziehung im Schulwesen der DDR._ Bad Harzburg: Verlag für Wissenschaft, Wirtschaft und Technik, 1972.

Moore-Rinvolucri, Mina J. _Education in East Germany._ Hamden, Conn.: Archon, 1973.

Motzkau-Valeton, Wolfgang. _Literaturunterricht in der DDR._ Paderborn: Schöningh, 1979.

Schmid, Hans-Dieter. _Geschichtsunterricht in der DDR. Eine Einführung._ Stuttgart: Klett, 1979.

Schmitt, Karl. _Politische Erziehung in der DDR. Ziele, Methoden und Ergebnisse des politischen Unterrichts an den allgemeinbildenden Schulen der DDR._ Paderborn: Schöningh, 1980.

Schulz, Hans-Jürgen, et al. Das Hochschulwesen der DDR. Ein Überblick. E. Berlin: Dt. Verlag der Wissenschaften, 1980.

Vogt, Hartmut. Vorschulerziehung und Schulvorbereitung in der DDR. Grundlagen, Ziele, Inhalte, Realisationsformen. Cologne: Wissenschaft und Politik, 1972.

----------, et al. Schule und Betrieb in der DDR. Das Zusammenwirken von allgemeinbildender Schule und volkseigenem Betrieb bei der staatsbürgerlichen Erziehung und polytechnischen Bildung. Cologne: Wissenschaft und Politik, 1970.

Waterkamp, Dietmar. Lehrplanreform in der DDR. Die zehnklassige allgemeinbildende polytechnische Oberschule 1963-1972. Hanover: Schroedel, 1975.

Mass Media

Bergsdorf, Wolfgang. "Die Gleichschaltung wurde wiederhergestellt. Drei Jahrzehnte Medienpolitik der SED." Deutschland Archiv, 13, No. 8 (1980), 855-863.

Blaum, Verona. Journalistikwissenschaft in der DDR. Erlangen: Dt. Gesellschaft für Zeitgeschichtliche Fragen, 1979.

Friedrich-Ebert-Stiftung, ed. Pressefreiheit und Massenmedien in beiden deutschen Staaten. Bonn/Bad Godesberg: Neue Gesellschaft, 1973.

Goss, Anthony John. Deutschlandbilder im Fernsehen. Eine vergleichende Analyse politischer Informationssendungen in der Bundesrepublik Deutschland und der DDR. Cologne: Wissenschaft und Politik, 1980.

Holzweißig, Gunter. "Publikationen der DDR-Auslandspropaganda." Deutschland Archiv, 13, No. 1 (1980), 50-61.

Otto, Elmar Dieter. Nachrichten in der DDR. Eine empirische Untersuchung über "Neues Deutschland." Cologne: Wissenschaft und Politik, 1979.

Paulu, Burton. "German Democratic Republic."
In his Radio and Television Broadcasting in
Eastern Europe. Minneapolis: Univ. of Minne-
sota Press, 1974.

Picaper, Jean Paul. Kommunikation und Propaganda in der DDR. Stuttgart: Bonn Aktuell, 1976.

Richert, Ernst, et al. Agitation und Propaganda.
W. Berlin: Franz Vahlen, 1958.

Riedel, Heidi. Hörfunk und Fernsehen in der
DDR. Funktion, Struktur und Programm des Rund-
funks in der DDR. Cologne: Literarischer Verlag
Braun, 1977.

Cultural Policy

Gransow, Volker. Kulturpolitik in der DDR.
W. Berlin: Spiess, 1975.

Hanke, Helmut, Gerd Rossow, et al. Sozialistische Kulturrevolution. E. Berlin: Dietz, 1977.

Koch, Hans. Kulturpolitik in der Deutschen Demokratischen Republik. 2nd ed. E. Berlin: Dietz,
1976.

----------, and Helmut Hanke, eds. Die geistige
Kultur der sozialistischen Gesellschaft. E. Berlin: Dietz, 1976.

Nordmann, Ingeborg. Kulturrevolution bei Marx
und in der DDR. Über das Verhältnis von Theorie
und Praxis. W. Berlin: Spiess, 1980.

Richter, Rolf. Kultur im Bündnis. Die Bedeutung
der Sowjetunion für die Kulturpolitik der DDR.
E. Berlin: Dietz, 1979.

Rüss, Gisela, ed. Dokumente zur Kunst-, Litera-
tur- und Kulturpolitik der SED (1971-74). Stuttgart: Seewald, 1976.

Schubbe, Elimar, ed. Dokumente zur Kunst-, Li-
teratur- und Kulturpolitik der SED. Stuttgart:
Seewald, 1972.

Art, Architecture, Music, Film

Behr, Adalbert, Alfred Hoffmann, et al. Architektur in der DDR. E. Berlin: Henschel, 1979.

Gärtner, Hannelore, et al. Die Künste in der DDR: Aus ihrer Geschichte in drei Jahrzehnten. E. Berlin: Henschel, 1979.

Gassner, Hubertus, and Eckhart Gillen. Kultur und Kunst in der DDR seit 1970. Gießen: Anabas, 1977.

Hennenberg, Fritz. "Die Mittlere Generation: Versuch über sechs Komponisten der DDR." German Studies Review, 3, No. 2 (1980), 289-321.

Hennig, Gerd. "Mass Cultural Activity in the GDR." New German Critique, 1, No. 2 (1974), 38-58.

Hochschule für Film und Fernsehkunst der DDR. Film- und Fernsehkunst der DDR. Traditionen – Beispiele – Tendenzen. E. Berlin: Henschel, 1979.

Kersten, Heinz, Heiko R. Blum, et al. Film in der DDR. Munich: Hanser, 1977.

Krenz, Gerhard. Architektur zwischen gestern und morgen. Ein Vierteljahrhundert Architekturentwicklung in der DDR. Stuttgart: Dt. Verlagsanstalt, 1975.

Noack, Liesel, and Wolfgang Holzhäser. Bildnerisches Volksschaffen in der DDR. Leipzig: VEB E.A. Seemann, 1969.

Pohl, Edda, and Sieghard Pohl. Die ungehorsamen Maler der DDR - Anspruch und Wirklichkeit der SED-Kulturpolitik 1965-1979. W. Berlin: Europäische Ideen, 1979.

Prieberg, Fred K. Musik im anderen Deutschland. Cologne: Wissenschaft und Politik, 1968.

Schneider, Frank. Momentaufnahme: Notate zu Musik und Musikern der DDR. Leipzig: Ph. Reclam jun., 1979.

Stürzbecher, Ursula. Komponisten in der DDR.

17 Gespräche. Hildesheim: Gerstenberg, 1979.

Thomas, Karin. Die Malerei in der DDR 1949-1979. Cologne: DuMont Schauberg, 1980.

Literature

Diersch, Manfred, and Walfried Hartinger, eds. Literatur und Geschichtsbewußtsein. Entwicklungstendenzen der DDR-Literatur in den sechziger und siebziger Jahren. E. Berlin/Weimar: Aufbau, 1976.

Einhorn, Barbara. Der Roman in der DDR, 1949-1969. Die Gestaltung des Verhältnisses von Individuum und Gesellschaft. Eine Analyse der Erzählstruktur. Kronberg: Scriptor, 1978.

Flores, John. Poetry in East Germany. Adjustments, Visions and Provocations 1945-1970. New Haven: Yale Univ. Press, 1971.

Franke, Konrad. Die Literatur der Deutschen Demokratischen Republik. Munich: Kindler, 1971. Paperback edition: Kindler, 1980.

Geerdts, Hans Jürgen, ed. Literatur der DDR in Einzeldarstellungen. Stuttgart: Kröner, 1972.

----------, ed. Literatur der Deutschen Demokratischen Republik. Einzeldarstellungen, Bd. 2. E. Berlin: Volk und Wissen, 1979.

Gerlach, Ingeborg. Bitterfeld, Arbeiterliteratur und Literatur der Arbeitswelt in der DDR. Kronberg: Scriptor, 1974.

Hohendahl, Peter Uwe, and Patricia Herminghouse, eds. Literatur und Literaturtheorie in der DDR. Frankfurt/M.: Suhrkamp, 1976.

Huettich, H.G. Theater in the Planned Society. Contemporary Drama in the German Democratic Republic in its Historical, Political and Cultural Context. Chapel Hill: Univ. of No. Carolina Press, 1978.

Institut für Gesellschaftswissenschaften beim ZK der SED, ed. Zur Theorie des sozialistischen

Realismus. E. Berlin: Dietz, 1974.

Jarmatz, Klaus, ed. Kritik in der Zeit. Der Sozialismus - seine Literatur - ihre Entwicklung. Halle: Mitteldeutscher Verlag, 1969.

Kaufmann, Eva, and Hans Kaufmann. Erwartung und Angebot. Studien zum gegenwärtigen Verhältnis von Literatur und Gesellschaft in der DDR. E. Berlin: Akademie Verlag, 1976.

Klunker, Heinz. Zeitstücke. Zeitgenossen. Gegenwartstheater in der DDR. Hanover: Fackelträger, 1972.

Literatur der Deutschen Demokratischen Republik. Geschichte der deutschen Literatur, Bd. 11. E. Berlin: Volk und Wissen, 1976.

Löffler, Anneliese, ed. Auskünfte. Werkstattgespräche mit DDR-Autoren. E. Berlin/Weimar: Aufbau, 1974.

Münz-Koenen, Ingeborg, et al. Literarisches Leben in der DDR 1945-1960: Literaturkonzepte und Leseprogramme. E. Berlin: Akademie, 1979.

Nägele, Rainer. "Deutsche Demokratische Republik." In Geschichte der politischen Lyrik in Deutschland. Ed. Walter Hinderer. Stuttgart: Reclam, 1978.

Pracht, Erwin, et al. Einführung in den sozialistischen Realismus. E. Berlin: Dietz, 1975.

Raddatz, Fritz J. Traditionen und Tendenzen. Materialien zur Literatur der DDR. Frankfurt/M.: Suhrkamp, 1972.

Sachwörterbuch für den Literaturunterricht. E. Berlin: Volk und Wissen, 1975.

Schivelbusch, Wolfgang. Sozialistisches Drama nach Brecht. Neuwied/W. Berlin: Luchterhand, 1974.

Schlenstedt, Dieter. Wirkungsästhetische Analysen. Poetologie und Prosa in der neueren DDR-Literatur. E. Berlin: Akademie, 1980. Western edition: Die neuere DDR-Literatur und ihr Leser. Wirkungsästhetische Analysen. Munich: Damnitz, 1980.

Schmitt, Hans-Jürgen, ed. Einführung in die
Theorie, Geschichte und Funktion der DDR-Literatur. Stuttgart: Metzler, 1975.

Schriftsteller der DDR. Meyers Taschenlexikon.
Leipzig: VEB Bibliographisches Institut, 1974.

Theater in der Zeitenwende. Zur Geschichte des
Dramas und des Schauspieltheaters in der Deutschen Demokratischen Republik 1945-1968. E. Berlin: Henschel, 1972.

Walter, Joachim. Meinetwegen Schmetterlinge.
Gespräche mit Schriftstellern. E. Berlin: Verlag der Morgen, 1973.

Weggenossen. Fünfzehn Schriftsteller der DDR.
Leipzig: Ph. Reclam jun., 1975.

Anthologies

Auskunft. Neue Prosa aus der DDR. Ed. Stefan
Heym. Reinbek b. Hamburg: Rowohlt, 1974.

Auskunft 2. Ed. Stefan Heym. Frankfurt/M.:
Athenäum, 1978.

East German Poetry. Ed. Michael Hamburger.
New York: Dutton, 1973.

Erzähler aus der DDR. Ed. Konrad Franke and
Wolfgang R. Langenbucher. Tübingen/Basel:
Horst Erdmann, 1973.

Fahrt mit der S-Bahn. Erzähler der DDR. Ed.
Lutz-W. Wolff. Munich: dtv, 1971.

Frauen in der DDR. Zwanzig Erzählungen. Ed.
Lutz-W. Wolff. Munich: dtv, 1976.

Fünfzig Erzähler der DDR. Ed. Richard Christ
and Manfred Wolter. 2nd ed. E. Berlin/Weimar:
Aufbau, 1976.

Geschichten aus der DDR. Ed. Hans-Jürgen
Schmitt. Hamburg: Hoffmann & Campe, 1979.

Hörspiele aus der DDR. Ed. Stefan Bodo Würffel.
Frankfurt/M.: Fischer, 1980.

Lyrik der DDR. Ed. Uwe Berger and Günther
Deicke. 5th rev., enl. ed. E. Berlin/Weimar:
Aufbau, 1979.

Neue Erzähler der DDR. Ed. Doris Schmitt and
Hans-Jürgen Schmitt. Frankfurt/M.: Fischer,
1977.

Neunzehn Erzähler der DDR. Ed. Hans-Jürgen
Schmitt. Frankfurt/M.: Fischer, 1971.

Thinking It Over. 30 Stories from the German
Democratic Republic. Ed. Hubert Witt. E. Berlin: Seven Seas, 1977.

Journals

DDR Report. Bonn/Bad Godesberg: Verlag Neue
Gesellschaft. Monthly publication, brings
excerpts from GDR newspapers and journals.

DDR-Revue. Liga für Völkerfreundschaft der
DDR. Dresden: Verlag Zeit im Bild. Monthly
publication, appearing in various languages.

Deutschland Archiv. Zeitschrift für Fragen der
DDR und der Deutschlandpolitik. Cologne: Wissenschaft und Politik. Appears monthly.

GDR Monitor. Dundee, Scotland: University of
Dundee. Appears twice a year.

Prisma. A Quarterly Digest from the GDR. Panorama DDR. E. Berlin: Auslandspresseagentur.

Bibliographies

Collective at the University of Wisconsin at
Madison. "A Working Bibliography for the Study
of the GDR." New German Critique, 2 (Spring
1974), pp. 124-151.

Hardin, Russell. "Western Approaches to East
German History." New German Critique, 2 (Sp.
1974), pp. 114-123.

Hersch, Gisela. A Bibliography of German Studies, 1945-1971; Germany under Allied Occupation,

Federal Republic of Germany, German Democratic
Republic. Bloomington: Univ. of Indiana Press,
1972.

Ludz, Peter C., and Johannes Kuppe. "Literatur
zum politischen und gesellschaftlichen System
der DDR." Politische Vierteljahresschrift, 10,
Nrs. 2-3 (1969).

Merritt, Anna J., and Richard L. Merritt. Politics, Economics, and Society in the two Germanies, 1945-75. A Bibliography of English-language
Works. Urbana: Univ. of Illinois Press, 1978.